Listening **AVIATOR**  RUN 1

Sarah Taylor

Sarah Taylor attended St. Francis Xavier University in Nova Scotia, Canada, where she graduated with honors with a Bachelor of Arts in English Literature. She has been writing ESL materials and teaching English to students of all ages.

Listening AVIATOR RUN 1

Publisher Kyudo Chung
Editorial Director Juyon Choi
Editors Yoonyoung Hur, Jiyeon Min
Proofreader Brian Stuart, Michael A. Putlack
Designer Hwayoun Cho

First published in May 2009
By Darakwon, Inc.
Darakwon Bldg., 211, Munbal-ro, Paju-si,
Gyeonggi-do 10881 Republic of Korea
Tel: 82-2-736-2031 (Ext. 250)
Fax: 82-2-732-2037

Price ₩14,000
ISBN 978-89-5995-979-2 58740
     978-89-5995-994-5 58740 (set)

www.darakwon.co.kr

Components Main Book / Answer Book / 1 MP3 CD
18 17 16 15 14 13 12   23 24 25 26 27

Listening AVIATOR

Introduction:

Listening AVIATOR <RUN> is a three-book series for students of English as a second or foreign language. This series mainly targets students who are at a basic level or above in English listening proficiency. It focuses on helping them improve their listening ability and be prepared for various listening tests as well. Various interesting topics are presented with informative monologs and dialogs related to everyday life. Students can both grasp useful information about the topic and enjoy a feast of vivid English expressions.

Outline:

Each book in the **Listening AVIATOR <RUN>** series contains 12-page units covering a diverse range of topics common in everyday English. Each unit contains 14 listening passages with some specific mind maps for note-taking practice and multiple choice questions as well as vocabulary relevant to the topic.

Detailed Features:

Each unit in this book starts off with a fill-in-the-blank activity which introduces the key vocabulary and expressions essential to understand it. The listening passages which follow this introduction can be in either dialog or monolog form and are 60 to 120 words in length. Each of these passages is followed by one to three questions designed to see how well students can extract both general and detailed information as well as pick up on the tone, emotion, or purpose of the conversation or speech. After listening to a wide range of discussions about a certain subject and answering the provided questions, students will be able to detect more and more subtleties in spoken English and, as a result, gain confidence in their own listening abilities. An added feature of this book is the specific mind maps given in the Basic Drill section, which focuses on the improvement of students' note-taking skills.

How to Use **This Book**

Each unit follows the same set.

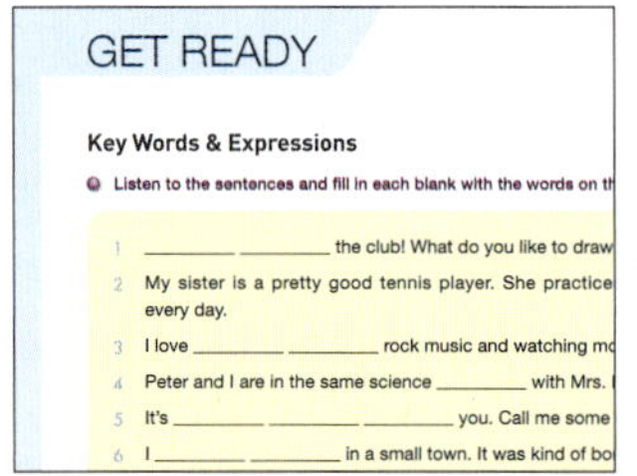

Get Ready

Key Expressions

Students listen to the sentences and fill in the missing key vocabulary words and expressions in each unit.

Questions & Responses

Students complete a question-and-answer matching activity which features key functions related to the topic.

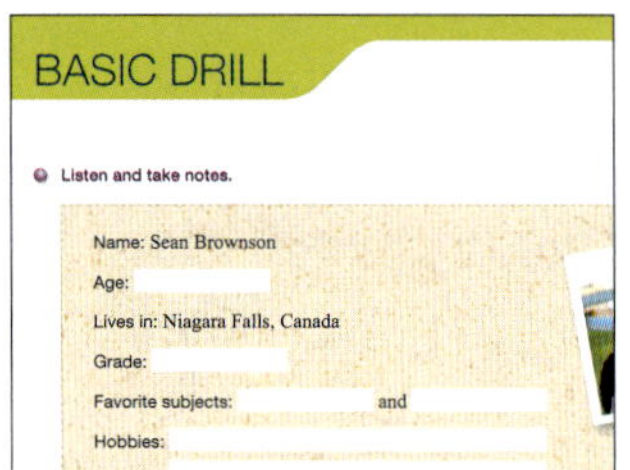

Basic Drills Step 1 & Step 2

Students are introduced to one of the most important listening skills in this section: note-taking skills. Each listening passage gives the mind map that is required to be completed by students while listening. Students listen to several monologs, take notes, answer the questions asking for the main idea or if the information is true or false based on the notes. Extra questions that demand details are also given. During this section, students can see how to screen for important information.

Exercise Step 1 & Step 2

Students listen to three passages in each section and answer a variety of questions which ask for general information, detailed information, implied information, and, in Step 2, a correct summary. The passages increase in difficulty as the unit progresses.

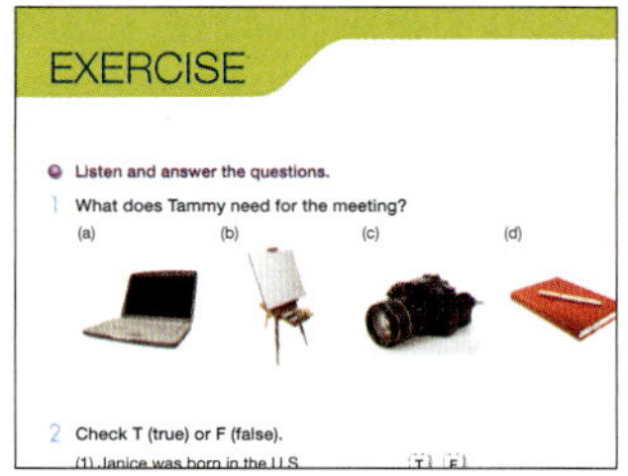

Practice Test

This section is a review of what students have learned in the unit. It consists of six passages and eight questions, including one task-based activity(Level up question). It is designed to test both the students' listening skills and their understanding of the topic they have been learning about.

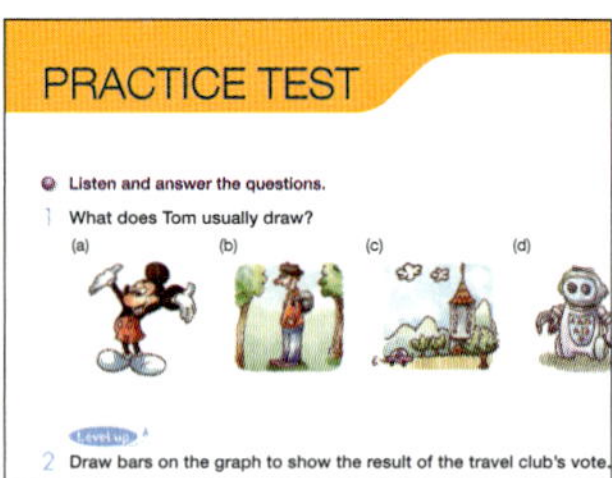

Dictation Step 1 & Step 2

Students will listen to the passages for the Exercise in Dictation 1 and the passages in the Practice Test in Dictation 2. Therefore, students will get a chance to review the key vocabulary words and expressions used in the passages.

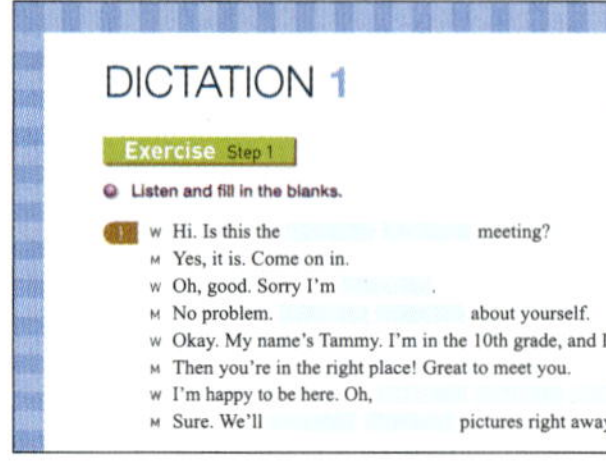

Contents

It's Great to Meet You

GET READY

Key Words & Expressions

Listen to the sentences and fill in each blank with the words on the list.

1 ____________ ____________ the club! What do you like to draw?

2 My sister is a pretty good tennis player. She practices ____________ ____________ every day.

3 I love ____________ ____________ rock music and watching movies.

4 Peter and I are in the same science ____________ with Mrs. Kelly.

5 It's ____________ ____________ ____________ you. Call me some time.

6 I ____________ ____________ in a small town. It was kind of boring.

7 Mrs. Jenkins ____________ ____________ the big house on the corner.

8 His favorite ____________ is music, but he's terrible at history.

9 Gloria ____________ outdoor sports. She's always hiking or swimming.

10 I ____________ ____________ for the newspaper club at my school.

| take photos | grew up | listening to | after school | welcome to |
| class | great to meet | subject | lives in | enjoys |

Questions & Responses

Match the questions with the responses.

1	Where do you live?	•	**a**	It's good. I'm enjoying it.
2	How old are you?	•	**b**	It's called Canyon High School.
3	What are your hobbies?	•	**c**	Music and math are my favorite classes.
4	What's your favorite class?	•	**d**	I'm seventeen.
5	What's the name of your school?	•	**e**	I live in Hamilton, Nevada.
6	How is school going?	•	**f**	I like hiking and listening to music.

Listen and check your answers.

Now practice with your friends.

● **Listen and take notes.**

● **Based on your notes, answer the question.**

Q What does the speaker mainly talk about?

(a) why high school is difficult

(b) his favorite classes

(c) his life in high school

(d) his hobbies and pastimes

■ **Listen again and fill in the blanks.**

Hi there. My __________ is Sean Brownson, and I'm 13 __________ old. I live in Niagara Falls, Canada, which is a pretty cool __________. I just started __________ nine at Laura Secord High School. So far, high school is difficult, but I like it. Gym and art are my favorite __________. My __________ are reading comic books and playing basketball. On the weekend, my friend Alex and I get together and __________ __________.

1-3

Listen and take notes.

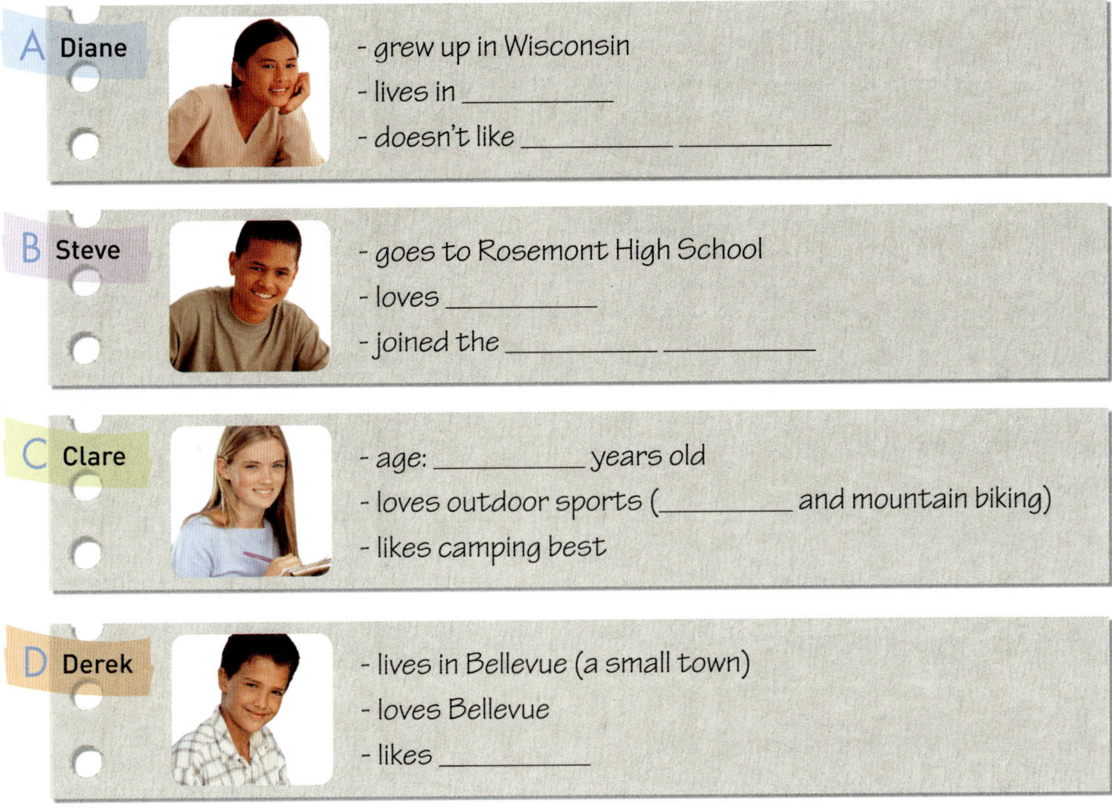

A Diane
- grew up in Wisconsin
- lives in ___________
- doesn't like ___________ ___________

B Steve
- goes to Rosemont High School
- loves ___________
- joined the ___________ ___________

C Clare
- age: ___________ years old
- loves outdoor sports (___________ and mountain biking)
- likes camping best

D Derek
- lives in Bellevue (a small town)
- loves Bellevue
- likes ___________

Based on your notes, answer the following questions.

1 What do the speakers mainly talk about?

(a) their school lives

(b) outdoor activities

(c) their likes and dislikes

(d) school clubs

2 Mark T (true) or F (false).

(1) Diane does not like cold weather. ______

(2) Steve is a member of the drama club. ______

(3) Derek swims in the river near his house. ______

■ **Listen again and check your answers.**

Plus⁺ Question

Q1. What is Clare's favorite thing to do?

(a) skiing
(b) camping
(c) playing sports
(d) going to the beach

Q2. Derek thinks his town is ___________.

(a) boring
(b) too small
(c) too quiet
(d) beautiful

● Listen and answer the questions.

1 What does Tammy need for the meeting?

(a) (b) (c) (d)

2 Check T (true) or F (false).

(1) Janice was born in the U.S. T F

(2) Janice liked science. T F

(3) Janice is a teacher. T F

(4) Janice acted in movies as a child. T F

3~4

3 What are the speakers' online names?

(a) darkboy12 and gamegirl1991

(b) darkboy1919 and gamegirl12

(c) darkgirl12 and gameworld1991

(d) darkboy12 and darkgirl1919

4 What do Troy and Jane both love?

(a) surfing the Internet

(b) online gaming

(c) reading magazines

(d) online chatting

Note taking

1

2

3~4
Their common interests
are ______________
______________ .

1-5

● **Listen and answer the questions.**

1 What is the relationship between the speakers?

(a) neighbors

(b) co-workers

(c) boyfriend and girfriend

(d) mother and son

(e) teacher and student

2 Which of the following is NOT true?

(a) The speaker and Andrew are cousins.

(b) The speaker and Andrew are sixteen.

(c) Andrew lives in London.

(d) Andrew is good at skateboarding.

(e) The speaker and Andrew play soccer.

3~5

3 What does Julie mainly talk about?

(a) her hometown   (b) wildlife safaris

(c) life in Alaska   (d) being pen pals

(e) traveling

4 What can you guess about Julie?

(a) She never goes on safaris.

(b) She likes to travel.

(c) She has never visited Alaska.

(d) She doesn't really like Cape Town.

(e) She wants to move to Alaska.

5 Which is the best summary?

(a) Julie writes a letter to her new pen pal Sandra, who lives in Alaska.

(b) Julie writes a letter to her friend Sandra, who is interested in visiting Cape Town.

Note taking

1
The speakers live in the
______________ apartment
building.

2
____
____
____

3~5
____
____
____
____

DICTATION 1

Exercise Step 1

● **Listen and fill in the blanks.**

1

W Hi. Is this the ________________ meeting?

M Yes, it is. Come on in.

W Oh, good. Sorry I'm ________ .

M No problem. ________________ about yourself.

W Okay. My name's Tammy. I'm in the 10th grade, and I love ________________ .

M Then you're in the right place! Great to meet you.

W I'm happy to be here. Oh, ________________ my camera to meetings?

M Sure. We'll ________________ pictures right away.

2

M Thanks, Janice, for ________________ interview you.

W It's my pleasure.

M Tell us about your life before you were a famous actress.

W Oh, wow, well... I had a ________________ . I grew up in small-town Australia. I moved to New York when I was 14.

M What were your ________ subjects in school?

W I was really ________________ math and science. I was terrible at history.

M Did you enjoy acting as a child?

W Yes, I did. My friends and I ________________ for our neighbors. It was great fun.

3~4

W Can I sit here?

M Sure, ________________ .

W What are you reading?

M It's a gaming magazine.

W Cool. I ________________ . My favorite game is *Dark Worlds*.

M Really? Me too! My handle is *darkboy12*.

W Nice. Online, I'm *gamegirl1991*.

M ________ . So, what's your real name?

W It's Jane. You?

M Troy. ________________ at this school?

W Yeah, I just moved here from Cleveland.

Exercise Step 2

● **Listen and fill in the blanks.**

1

W Oh, hello. You moved in yesterday, ________________? I'm Cindy.

M Yes, that's right. I'm Daniel.

W Nice to meet you, Daniel. ________________ the apartment building. I'm ________________ in number 602.

M I moved to number 502. Nice to meet you, too.

W So, are you from Wellington?

M Yes, I ________________ here.

W No way! Where?

M Down on Drake Road.

W What? On Drake Road? I ________________ in the big house on the corner!

M Are you serious? Wow! What a small world!

2

M Hey, guys! We have a ________________ this week. This is my cousin Andrew. He's 16, just like me. We don't see ________________ often because he lives in New Zealand. He's visiting London ________________, so I thought he could play soccer with us today. What do you think? He's a great soccer player, so don't worry. Oh, you should see him on a skateboard! He's so cool! Well, enough talking. Let's get this game started!

3~5

W Hi, Sandra! ________________ your letter. It's great to be your ________________. My name's Julie. I'm 12 years old, and I'm in the 9th grade. I live in Cape Town, which is a very pretty city in South Africa. A lot of people come to Cape Town to ________________ and to go on safari. You can see some pretty cool animals here! I'd love to hear more about your home. ________________ in Alaska? Write back soon! Your new friend, Julie.

PRACTICE TEST

● **Listen and answer the questions.**

1 **What does Tom usually draw?**

(a) (b) (c) (d) (e)

2 **Draw bars on the graph to show the result of the travel club's vote.**

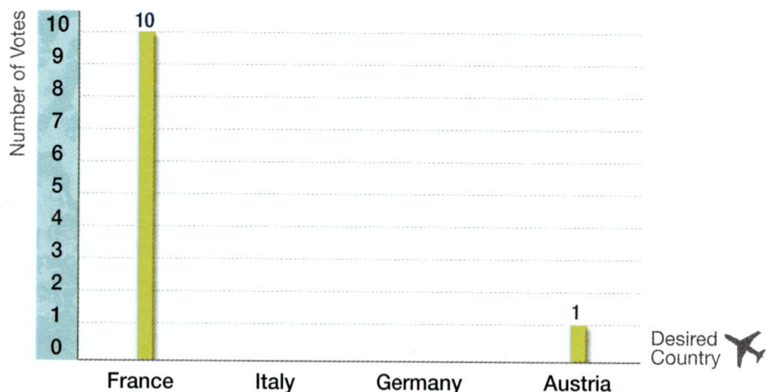

3~4

3 **Where are Lucy and James?**

(a) in the library
(b) in the gym
(c) in the classroom
(d) in the cafeteria
(e) on the playground

4 **What is the students' attitude toward school?**

(a) They're excited about it.
(b) They think it's okay.
(c) They love it.
(d) They don't like it.
(e) They don't like their teachers.

5 **What is Bradley doing?**

(a) He's speaking with a teacher.

(b) He's having a job interview.

(c) He's talking on the phone.

(d) He's talking to a friend.

(e) He's buying a newspaper.

6 **What do you think Peter Fulling said to Jenny at the end?**

(a) You can have my dog.

(b) You're not the right person for my dog.

(c) When do you finish school?

(d) It was nice talking to you.

(e) Can I call you back?

7 **Which expression best describes the situation?**

(a) All's well that ends well.

(b) It's a small world.

(c) He's a wolf in sheep's clothing.

(d) Let sleeping dogs lie.

(e) Out of sight, out of mind.

8 **Who is Mr. Watts?**

(a) Jack's friend

(b) the host of the party

(c) Linda's old classmate

(d) a teacher

(e) Alex's father

DICTATION 2

● **Listen and fill in the blanks.**

1 M I'm Tom. I'm 16 years old, and I'm from Ottawa, the _____________ of Canada. I love to draw pictures in my free time. I usually _____________ pictures of characters from _____________ movies. For example, I can draw a lot of Disney _____________. I take a special drawing class _____________ _____________. Maybe you'll see my drawings in some animated movies some day.

2 W Hi, I'm Alison. This is my first time at the _____________ club.
   M Welcome. I'm Tony.
   W Glad to meet you. So, Tony, what does the travel club do?
   M Every year we go on a _____________ trip.
   W Oh, wow! That's great. Where are we going this year?
   M Well, we _____________ _____________ _____________ last week. 10 people want to go to France, 7 people want to go to Italy, 3 people want to go to Germany, and 1 person wants to go to Austria.
   W Looks like we're _____________ _____________ _____________. Great!

3~4 W Can I sit here?
   M Sure, why not?
   W Thanks. When does this class start?
   M Um, I think in five minutes.
   W Ugh, I _____________ the first day of school.
   M Me too. By the way, I'm James.
   W I'm Lucy. How are your classes _____________ _____________?
   M Not good _____________ _____________. Gym is okay, but everything else is _____________.
   W Sorry to hear that. My classes aren't _____________ _____________, _____________.
   M Oh, no. The teacher's coming.

5 M Thank you for _____________ _____________. Let me tell you about myself. My name's Bradley Thomas, and I'm in the _____________ grade at Glendale Elementary School. I _____________ _____________ my bike, and I think that will help me in this job. I finish school at 2:30, so I have   free time to deliver newspapers. Also, I   in this neighborhood, so I know the houses well. I think I'm the perfect person for this job.

6

W Hello? Oh, hi. Is this Peter Fulling? Hi, I'm Jenny Stewart. I   in the newspaper about your dog   . I understand that you want a good home for your dog. I'm 14 years old, and I'm in high school. I   school every day at 3:00, so I have   to walk the dog. I just love dogs. I know I can give your dog a good home. [...] Sure, call me any time after 3:00. Have a good day! Bye!

7~8

W Hi. Great party, huh?

M Yeah, I'm   .

W That's good. I'm Linda.

M Hi, Linda. I'm Jack.

W Very nice to meet you, Jack.

M Nice to meet you, too. So,   have you known the host, Alex?

W He's an old   of mine.

M Is that right? I went to school with Alex, too!

W Really? That's so   . Wait a minute. Did you have math with Mr. Watts?

M Yeah, good old Mr. Watts! Are you Linda Robins?

W Yes! Jack Powers? This is so weird!   !

I Go to the Gym Every Day

GET READY

Key Words & Expressions

● Listen to the sentences and fill in each blank with the words on the list.

1   I usually get up when my alarm clock __________ __________.

2   These days, many kids __________ busy lives.

3   Chuck isn't a __________ __________. He's always late for class.

4   Many people __________ in the morning before work.

5   Many kids go to bed too late and don't __________ __________ __________.

6   I don't have time to walk the dog! I have __________ to do.

7   They sit at the same table at lunch __________ __________.

8   I have to take my brother to daycare __________ __________ __________ to school.

9   I'm __________ __________ my busy schedule. I just need a vacation.

10 You missed the bus again? Try __________ __________ earlier.

goes off	tired of	lead	on my way	every day
morning person	homework	get enough sleep	exercise	getting up

Questions & Responses

● Match the questions with the responses.

1	What time do you get up?	●	**a**	I usually have cereal and fruit.
2	What do you do first?	●	**b**	I always have breakfast first.
3	What do you have for breakfast?	●	**c**	I ride my bike when the weather's nice.
4	Do you shower at night or in the morning?	●	**d**	I try to get up by 7:30 a.m.
5	When is your first class?	●	**e**	Classes start at 8:30.
6	How do you get to school?	●	**f**	In the morning. It wakes me up.

● Listen and check your answers.

● Now practice with your friends.

2-2

● **Listen and take notes.**

● **Based on your notes, answer the question.**

Q **Which of the following is true about the speaker?**

(a) He always eats cereal for breakfast.

(b) He arrives at school before nine.

(c) He walks all the way to school.

(d) He showers after he eats.

■ **Listen again and fill in the blanks.**

I ________ ________ at about 7:00 a.m. in the morning. ________ ________, my mom yells upstairs to make sure I'm awake. Then, I ________ ________ ________ and go downstairs for breakfast, which is ________ eggs and toast with juice. I usually have to rush out the door at 8:00 to ________ ________ ________. Luckily, it stops right in front of my house. Once I'm at school, I ________ ________ with my friends until class starts at 9:00.

2-3

● **Listen and take notes.**

A Cindy
- very busy
- gets up at 5:00 a.m.
- goes to ____________ ____________ before school

B Cameron
- can't wake up ____________ ____________ ____________
- is often late for school

C Bev
- very busy
- gets ____________ in the evening
- goes to bed at ____________ p.m.
- studies, showers, and watches TV before bed

D Chris
- plays many sports
- Mon, Wed: ____________
- Tues, Fri: ____________
- Thurs: coaches a kids' soccer team

● **Based on your notes, answer the following questions.**

1 **What do the speakers mainly talk about?**

(a) sports　　　　　　　　　(b) their daily schedules
(c) getting up in the morning　(d) their lives at school

2 **Mark T (true) or F (false).**

(1) Cindy has hockey practice after school. ______
(2) Chris plays football and basketball. ______
(3) Cameron is sometimes late for school. ______

■ **Listen again and check your answers.**

Plus⁺ Question

Q1. What is Cameron's problem?
(a) He can't sleep.
(b) He is too busy.
(c) He doesn't have an alarm clock.
(d) He can't wake up in the morning.

Q2. What does Bev NOT do before she goes to bed?
(a) study
(b) watch TV
(c) shower
(d) listen to the music

Listen and answer the questions.

1 **Where are the speakers?**

(a)    (b)    (c)    (d) 

2 **Which of the following is NOT true about the speaker?**

(a) She has three kids.

(b) She gets up at 6:00 a.m.

(c) She eats breakfast with her kids.

(d) She leaves the house at 8:15 a.m.

3~4

3 **Which of the following is NOT true?**

(a) Tina walks her brother to school.

(b) Mr. Harris is Tina's teacher.

(c) Tina's brother goes to school on Woodlawn Road.

(d) Mr. Harris teaches Tina's brother.

4 **Why does Tina often miss the bus?**

(a) She sleeps in too late.

(b) She walks too slowly.

(c) She has to take her brother to school.

(d) The number 12 bus comes too early.

Note taking

1

2

3~4
Tina is often late for school.
- misses the __________ so often
- has to walk her __________ to his __________

2-5

● **Listen and answer the questions.**

1 Put the pictures in the correct order.

(a) (b) (c) (d) (e)

(c) → __________ → __________ → __________ → __________

2 Check T (true) or F (false).

(1) Brandy exercises for two hours a day. T F

(2) Brandy gets up early every morning. T F

(3) Brandy is a pop singer. T F

(4) Brandy is in a movie called *Double Time*. T F

(5) Brandy works until 9:00 p.m. T F

3~5

3 What kind of school does the boy go to?

(a) a science school

(b) an art school

(c) a restaurant management school

(d) a cooking school

(e) a music school

4 What do you think the boy is interested in besides cooking?

(a) history (b) traveling

(c) fashion (d) writing

(e) art

5 Which is the best summary?

(a) The boy goes to a special school for kids who want to be chefs.

(b) The boy wants to run a restaurant in another country some day.

Note taking

1
Night guard
- starts work at __________
- finishes at __________
- takes a __________
- sleeps until __________
- makes __________

2
____
____
____
____

3~5
____
____
____
____

DICTATION 1

● **Listen and fill in the blanks.**

1
M Hey, Lauren!   ?
W Hey, Dan! What are you doing here?
M I come to this   every day after work around 6:00.
W Oh, really? I'm usually here in the morning… most days by around 7:00.
M Ah, that's why we   each other here before.
W Yeah, I guess so.
M I wish I could exercise   like you, but I'm just not a morning person. I also start work at 8:00 a.m.
W Gotcha. I start at 9:30, so I have   time.

2
W Some days, I'm so busy that I forget to   ! I have three kids, so I have to get up at 6:00 a.m. every morning to get them ready for school. While they're   , I make them breakfast and   their lunches. We usually get out the door by 8:15. I never have time to eat breakfast. I   at school, and then I go to work. I usually pick up a coffee and a muffin on the way there.

3~4
W Excuse me, Mr. Harris. Sorry I'm late.
M Tina, you're   ?
W Yes, I'm sorry. I missed the bus again this morning.
M Why do you miss it   ?
W Well, I have to walk my little brother to his school in the morning. Sometimes he's a little slow.
M Where's his school?
W It's on Woodlawn Road.
M The number 12 bus   Woodlawn Road. Try that one tomorrow.
W I will. Thanks, Mr. Harris.

Exercise Step 2

● **Listen and fill in the blanks.**

1 M I don't have a ________________________. You see, I'm a night guard at a bank. I start work at 11:00 p.m. and finish at 7:00 a.m. I have to ________ all night. At first, it was hard, but now I don't mind it. After work, I go straight home and ________________. Then, I sleep until about 3:00 p.m. Then, I get up, make dinner, and relax for a few more hours until work starts again.

2 W Welcome to *Celebrity Snapshot*! Today, we're ________________ into the life of Brandy Williams, a rising actress. ________________ to be Brandy? Well, it's actually not that easy. Every morning, she gets up at 6:30 a.m. After a quick breakfast, she ________ for 1 hour and then does yoga for another hour. After that, she ________________ the set of her TV drama, *Double Time*. Most days, she works until 9:00 p.m. And you thought being a celebrity was easy?

3~5 M I have a slightly different day than most kids. I go to a ________ school in the morning, but at 1:00, I take a bus to another school. It's a school for kids studying to be chefs. I take ________________ cooking classes. My favorite class is called World Foods. Anyway, I study at that school until 7:00 in the evening. I have a longer day than other kids, but I love ________________. I can't wait to work in a restaurant overseas some day.

PRACTICE TEST

● **Listen and answer the questions.**

1 **Which of the following is true?**

(a) It's July now.

(b) The speaker likes studying.

(c) Summer vacation starts in August.

(d) The speaker is looking forward to summer vacation.

(e) Her schedule is not boring now.

2 **Fill in the pie chart.**

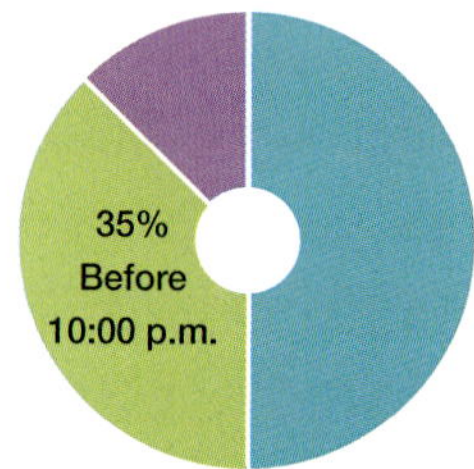

3 **Where are the speakers?**

(a) a fast-food restaurant

(b) a science lab

(c) a public library

(d) a classroom

(e) a school cafeteria

4 **What can you guess about the speakers?**

(a) They like the food at school.

(b) They don't have any friends.

(c) They eat out for lunch.

(d) They eat lunch at the same table every day.

(e) They have a science test on Thursdays.

5 **Which of the following is NOT true?**

(a) Daniel can watch TV at lunchtime.

(b) Daniel has to do homework.

(c) Daniel studies at home.

(d) Daniel has tests.

(e) Daniel thinks he works harder than his friends.

6 **How does the boy feel at the end of the conversation?**

(a) satisfied

(b) frustrated

(c) pleased

(d) proud

(e) excited

7~8

7 **What is probably the man's job?**

(a) gardener

(b) office worker

(c) farmer

(d) vet

(e) beekeeper

8 **Which expression best suits the man's schedule?**

(a) Kill two birds with one stone.

(b) Slow and steady wins the race.

(c) Time flies when you're having fun.

(d) The early bird catches the worm.

(e) Beauty is only skin deep.

DICTATION 2

● **Listen and fill in the blanks.**

1 w Dear Diary. It's June already. That means it's almost summer vacation. I'm really ________ ________ that. My schedule is ________ ________ now: I get up, go to school, do my homework... I'm so ________ ________ studying. It'll be great to sleep late every morning and ________ ________ ________ to the beach. Well, ________ ________ go to bed now. Another week starts tomorrow!

2 m This week, on *Your Health*, we will look at the busy lives of our children. These days, kids ________ ________ than ever with school, after-school activities, and sometimes extra classes. Because of this, they are not ________ ________ ________. We surveyed 100 kids aged 13~15 and ________ ________ that 50% go to bed after 10:00 p.m. and 15% go to bed after 11:00 p.m. That means that many kids are not getting the sleep they need.

3~4 m Hey, let's ________ ________ ________.

w Sure. What are they serving today?

m Um, what day is it? Thursday? Then it's spaghetti and meatball day.

w Right… Ugh, it's so gross.

m Let's go sit down.

w Hey! Someone's in ________ ________!

m Don't they know that's our table?

w Oh, well. Let's sit ________ ________.

m What class do you have after lunch?

w It's Thursday, so… science. I don't like Thursdays.

m ________ ________. Ugh, this spaghetti is disgusting. Want to ________ ________ after school?

w Sure, good call.

5 M I don't go to school. Actually, I am what you call "   ." My mom teaches me. My friends all say, "Oh, Daniel, you're so lucky!" but I think I   than they do. I study all the regular subjects, and I get lots of homework. I   TV during the day, even at lunchtime. I even   , just like at a school.

---

6 M Hey, Mom.
W You're late, Luke. Your dinner's   .
M Yeah, I had to stay after class.
W And I see your room is a big mess.
M I'm   my room!
W Busy? With what?
M I go to school early every day for volleyball practice. Then I come home, eat dinner, do my homework, and watch TV. I   !
W Well, find some time! You have to clean your room every day. Or…
M Or what?
W Or you're   !

7~8 W I'm   on careers. Can I ask you some questions?
M Sure, go ahead.
W Okay. About what time do you   in the morning?
M At about 4:30 a.m. I   and start work by 5:15.
W Why so early?
M I have to   when the sun comes up. I   and let them out. Then, I go to work in the fields.
W What time do you finish?
M   6:00 in the evening.
W That's a long day!
M Well, it comes with the job.

She's Quiet but Nice

GET READY

Key Words & Expressions

● Listen to the sentences and fill in each blank with the words on the list.

1 My brother and I are very different, so we don't __________ __________.

2 __________ are happy people who see the good side of everything.

3 Serena is the __________ in my class. She sometimes makes other kids do her homework.

4 You should choose a job that suits your __________.

5 If you're an __________ person, you'll learn languages easiest by speaking in groups.

6 We're looking for a __________ team player to join our company.

7 Some personality tests are good for helping you see your __________ __________ and bad points.

8 Money can't buy happiness. Money can make people cold and __________.

9 Don't judge people until you __________ __________ __________ them.

10 __________ do jobs well but sometimes get too stressed about minor things.

selfish	perfectionists	hardworking	bully	optimists
get along	get to know	personality	outgoing	good points

Questions & Responses

● Match the questions with the responses.

1	Who's your best friend?	●	**a**	We've known each for 6 years.
2	How long have you been friends?	●	**b**	Because he's always there for me.
3	What's he like?	●	**c**	His name is Ben Grenier.
4	How did you meet?	●	**d**	No, never. We always get along.
5	Do you ever fight or argue?	●	**e**	We met at our *taegwondo* club.
6	Why is he your best friend?	●	**f**	He's quiet sometimes, but he likes to joke around, too.

● Listen and check your answers.

● Now practice with your friends.

BASIC DRILL

Listen and take notes.

Friend's name:	
Friends since:	
Friend's personality:	

Based on your notes, answer the question.

Q How did Laura meet her best friend?

(a) They started doing an activity together.

(b) The teacher introduced her to Laura.

(c) They lived next door to each other.

(d) They played on the same sports team.

■ **Listen again and fill in the blanks.**

My name's Laura Doyle. My __________ __________'s name is also Laura, but her last name is Trent. Isn't that cool? We've been friends since second grade. I was __________ __________ alone when she asked to join me. Even though we have the same name, we're pretty __________. I'm __________ and __________, but she's __________. I call her a chatterbox sometimes, but she knows I'm joking. We __________ __________ so well.

3-3

Listen and take notes.

A Tony
- similar to the speaker
- so close that they're like ___________

B Rick
- a ___________ guy
- gets into trouble by being class ___________

C Alan
- gets good ___________
- baseball team ___________
- swimmimg instructor

D Jesse
- the speaker hates him
- tries to ___________ other people
- the speaker thinks he's a ___________

Based on your notes, answer the following questions.

1 **What does the speaker mainly talk about?**

   (a) his best friends
   (b) people around him
   (c) his heroes
   (d) his personality

2 **Mark T (true) or F (false).**

   (1) The speaker and Tony are brothers.   ______
   (2) Alan coaches a baseball team.   ______
   (3) Jesse is a nice kid.   ______

■ **Listen again and check your answers.**

Plus⁺ Question

Q1. Why does Rick get into trouble at school?

(a) He dresses like a clown.
(b) He jokes around too much.
(c) He insults other people.
(d) He pushes the other kids around.

EXERCISE

3-4

● **Listen and answer the questions.**

1 Which person is an optimist, and which one is a pessimist? Label the pictures.

(1)

(2)

_______________________   _______________________

2 Which of the following is NOT true?

(a) Carl and Alex don't get along.

(b) Carl greeted Alex at the park.

(c) Alex doesn't have many friends.

(d) Carl wanted to fight Alex.

3~4

3 Overall, Emma is _______________________.

(a) a good student

(b) a class clown

(c) an outgoing girl

(d) a bully

4 What is Emma's problem?

(a) She doesn't like her English class.

(b) She's too noisy in class.

(c) She doesn't have many friends.

(d) She doesn't speak often in class.

Note taking

1
- Optimists always see the _________ side of things.
- Pessimists are usually very _________.

2
____
____
____
____

3~4
- Emma _________ _________ and woks hard.
- She doesn't raise her hand often in class.

3-5

● **Listen and answer the questions.**

1 **Who is most likely the man's audience?**

(a) introverted people   (b) people learning a new language

(c) extroverted people   (d) teachers

(e) scientists

2 **Check T (true) or F (false).**

(1) The speaker has a brother and a sister.   T   F

(2) Jeff behaves well.   T   F

(3) Julie is relaxed and quiet.   T   F

(4) The speaker sometimes takes care of Jeff and Julie.   T   F

(5) The speaker and Julie are somewhere alike.   T   F

3~5

3 **As a child, Jim Carrey was _________ but _________.**

(a) successful / poor   (b) rich / funny

(c) poor / generous   (d) poor / talented

(e) talented / popular

4 **What kind of person does the speaker admire most?**

(a) someone who is funny

(b) someone who doesn't give up

(c) someone who earns a lot of money

(d) someone who is smart

(e) someone who helps others

5 **Which is the best summary?**

(a) The speaker's dream is to be a comedian like Jim Carrey because he is poor, like Jim Carrey was as a child.

(b) The speaker's hero is Jim Carrey, a Canadian movie star who started out poor but became very successful.

Note taking

1

2

3~5
- Jim Carrey had a
  _________ life.
- He finally achieved his
  dream.

DICTATION 1

● **Listen and fill in the blanks.**

1 W Some people are ____________, and some people are pessimists. Optimists always see the good side of things. They enjoy life. For them, "the glass is ____________ ____________." Pessimists, on the other hand, are usually very ____________. They often complain about minor things. For ____________, "the glass is half empty." Pessimists have to be careful. New studies show that pessimists have more health problems and do not live as long as optimists. Remember, ____________ ____________ ____________ ____________ can affect your body.

---

2 M Let's go ____________ ____________ ____________.
W Why? What's wrong, Carl?
M I just saw Alex. I'd rather not run into him.
W You guys ____________ ____________ ____________?
M Nope.
W What happened?
M I have no idea. I was at the park the other day, and I saw him there. So I said, "Hey, Alex. What's up?" Then he ____________ ____________.
W What did he do?
M He ____________ ____________ ____________ ____________ and tried to start a fight. I just walked away.
W Whoa.
M Yeah, weird, huh? I think he's ____________ ____________ ____________.
W I think you're right. He doesn't have many friends.

3~4 W Hi, I'm Mrs. Hill.
M Oh, yes. Emma's mother, ____________?
W Yes, that's right.
M Nice to meet you. Well, you'll be happy to hear that Emma is ____________ ____________ in my class.
W Oh, that's good.
M Yes, she ____________ ____________ and works hard. She is well-liked by her classmates.
W She enjoys your English class a lot.
M Good. The only problem is she's ____________ ____________ ____________.
W Oh, I see.

M　Yes, she's ＿＿＿＿＿＿＿, and she doesn't raise her hand often. I hope she can ＿＿＿＿ on this because she's a smart girl.

W　I'll talk to her about that. Thank you.

● **Listen and fill in the blanks.**

1　M　When learning a new language, it's important to remember that ＿＿＿＿＿＿＿＿＿＿ how you learn. ＿＿＿＿＿, or quiet people tend to like to study by themselves. They need more time to think before they speak. ＿＿＿＿＿, or outgoing people learn better by talking in groups. There is no "correct" way to learn a language. So ＿＿＿＿＿＿＿＿ if you prefer to study quietly alone or to talk out loud in groups. Find out what works best for you and ＿＿＿＿.

2　W　Sometimes my little brother and sister drive me crazy. Since I'm the oldest, I'm always stuck ＿＿＿＿＿＿＿＿＿ them when my parents aren't home. My brother, Jeff, is all right. He usually ＿＿＿＿. But my sister, Julie, is pretty wild. While my brother and I are pretty ＿＿＿＿＿＿＿, she's the total ＿＿＿＿. She's so loud, and she never listens to me. She sometimes ＿＿＿＿ my brother ＿＿＿＿, too. I don't know how we're so different, but we are.

3~5　M　My hero is Jim Carrey. He's a Canadian movie star who ＿＿＿＿＿＿＿＿＿＿ but made it big. When he was a kid, his parents were very poor. They sometimes had no home, so they lived in their car. But Jim had ＿＿＿＿＿＿＿. When he wasn't working, he did his ＿＿＿＿ in nightclubs. People loved him. Now, he's a ＿＿＿＿ and a millionaire. He's my hero because he never ＿＿＿＿＿＿＿, so he achieved his dream.

PRACTICE TEST

1 What sort of place is trying to find a new employee?

(a)   (b)   (c)   (d)   (e)

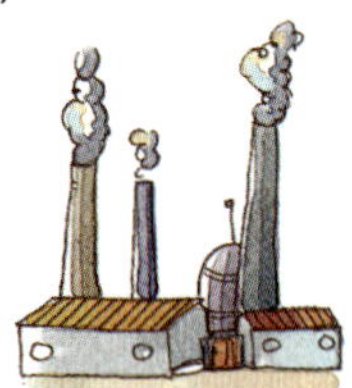    

Level up

2 Fill in the chart with Mr. Peterson's good points and bad points.

Good points	Bad points

3~4

3 What is Katie's bad point?

(a) She's too outgoing.

(b) She's unhelpful.

(c) She's unorganized.

(d) She can't solve problems.

(e) She talks too much.

4 Katie should be a teacher because _______________.

(a) she's unorganized

(b) it's her dream

(c) her mom wants her to

(d) she likes social studies

(e) she likes to help people

5 **What do you think is a good slogan for the movie, *The Family Man*?**
   (a) Money makes the world go round.
   (b) Money is the root of all evil.
   (c) Money creates enemies.
   (d) Money can't buy happiness.
   (e) Money can change your life.

6 **What expression best describes the boy's advice?**
   (a) Don't judge a book by its cover.
   (b) That's the way the cookie crumbles.
   (c) In one ear and out the other.
   (d) That's just what the doctor ordered.
   (e) Her bark is worse than her bite.

7~8

7 **What does Kelly's mom do?**
   (a) She flies airplanes.
   (b) She fixes airplanes.
   (c) She teaches science.
   (d) She's a mathematician.
   (e) She's an engineer.

8 **Which of the following is NOT true?**
   (a) Kelly takes after her mom.
   (b) Kelly likes math.
   (c) Kelly's dad writes history books.
   (d) Kelly's mom designs planes.
   (e) Kelly looks like her dad.

DICTATION 2

● **Listen and fill in the blanks.**

1 M We're ________________ ________________ to work at our store, Suits 'R' Us. These positions require people who are not ________________ ________________ to others. So we're looking for people who are ________________ and ________________. You also have to ________________ ________________ in men's fashion since part of your job will be helping men find the right suits. If you're a people person and are ready for a ________________, contact us at 555-3945.

2 W Okay, Mr. Peterson, tell me about yourself.

M Sure. Well, I'm very hardworking. I'm a perfectionist, so when I do something, I ________________ ________________ ________________. I'm also a ________________ ________________. I work well with others. You could say I'm a ________________ ________________.

W Good. That's what we're looking for. Now, what about your ________________ ________________?

M My bad points?

W Yes, what are you not good at?

M Hmm, well… I'm sometimes ________________ ________________.

W Explain.

M Well, like I said, I'm a ________________, so I sometimes ________________ ________________ trying to get things perfect.

W Good answer.

3~4 W How was school today, Katie?

W Good. Social studies was cool. We took a ________________ ________________.

M Oh, yeah? What did you find out about yourself?

W Mostly stuff I already knew. I'm outgoing, and I like helping people, I'm good at solving problems... stuff like that. I'm ________________ ________________ though.

M I see.

W Yeah, so at the end, the test tells you what kinds of jobs you'd be good at. I guess I'd make a good teacher or ________________ ________________.

M I agree with the test. You'd make an excellent teacher.

5 W I really enjoyed the movie *The Family Man*. It's about a rich man, Jack Campbell, who is very ________ and unhappy. He wakes up one morning to find that he has a ________. He has a wife, kids, a ________, and not a lot of money. Over time, he slowly ________ a more loving and ________ person as well as a good dad. This movie really shows how even very cold and selfish people can become better, happier people.

---

6 W So what do you think of that new kid? What's her name?
M Um… Lisa, I think.
W Yeah, Lisa.
M I don't know. She seems okay.
W Really? She ________.
M Yeah, well, maybe she's just shy. Or maybe she ________ ________ because she's at a new school.
W Yeah, you could be right. I don't really know her yet.
M Why don't you ________?
W Maybe I'll sit with her at lunch and see ________.
M I think she'd like that. Let me know how it goes.

7~8 M Kelly, who do you ________, your mom or your dad?
W Hmm, I think I look more like my dad, but my personality is more like my mom's.
M How so?
W Well, I'm really good at math and science, like my mom. She's an ________.
M Oh, I didn't know that.
W Yeah, she ________ airplanes.
M Cool!
W Yeah. But my dad is different. ________ history. He loves watching those ________ on TV. He also likes to paint.
M Yeah, you sound more like your mom.
W ________.

I Like Trying New Foods

GET READY

Key Words & Expressions

Listen to the sentences and fill in each blank with the words on the list.

1   I'm not a ___________ eater, but I don't like spicy foods.

2   ___________ ___________ ___________ something to drink while you're waiting?

3   Brad can cook many types of foods. His ___________ is Thai food.

4   Can you pick up some bread and milk for me at the ___________ ___________?

5   The waffles at the new café are ___________.

6   Every Sunday, I woke up to the smell of freshly ___________ apple pie.

7   Greek and Italian people have a lot of olive oil in their ___________.

8   The buffet looks incredible, and I'm ___________. Let's eat.

9   You can get ___________ for ethnic foods at the international supermarket.

10 I'm not a fan of Chinese food because I don't really like ___________ foods.

fried	baked	diets	would you like	picky
amazing	specialty	grocery store	ingredients	starving

Questions & Responses

● **Match the questions with the responses.**

1. What's your favorite type of food?
2. Are there any foods you don't like?
3. What's your favorite dish?
4. Do you eat a lot of junk food?
5. Can you cook?
6. Do you like trying new foods?

a. No. It's not healthy at all.
b. I love French food.
c. Of course. Trying new foods is great.
d. I can cook a little, but nothing complicated.
e. My favorite dish is *foie gras*.
f. Well, I don't like spicy foods.

● **Listen and check your answers.**

● **Now practice with your friends.**

BASIC DRILL

● **Listen and take notes.**

● **Based on your notes, answer the question.**

Q Which of the following is true?

(a) The man is a very picky eater.

(b) The man does not care for Thai food.

(c) The man really likes hamburgers.

(d) The man likes eating new foods.

■ **Listen again and fill in the blanks.**

I'm never afraid to __________ new foods. In fact, I find it exciting. I like hot and cold foods and __________, sour, and even __________ foods. Thai food is my favorite __________ of food, and Pad Thai noodles is my favorite __________. I don't like __________ __________ like hamburgers and French fries. It's __________. I think home-cooked food is much better.

4-3

● **Listen and take notes.**

A June
- likes ___________ food
- tried sushi a year ago

B Dwayne
- likes Indian food like ___________ ___________
- wants to learn to cook Indian food

C Emma
- likes Italian food like ___________ and ___________

D Jason
- likes ___________ ___________ like bacon double cheeseburgers
- eats it about ___________ ___________ a week

● **Based on your notes, answer the following questions.**

1 **What do the speakers mainly talk about?**

   (a) their cooking skills
   (b) the types of food they like
   (c) junk food and health
   (d) eating out

2 **Mark T (true) or F (false).**

   (1) June makes her own sushi. ______
   (2) Emma's favorite dish is spaghetti. ______
   (3) Jason wants to stop eating junk food. ______

■ **Listen again and check your answers.**

Plus⁺ Question

Q1. When did June try Japanese food?

(a) last year
(b) last week
(c) as a child
(d) on a trip to Japan

Q2. How often does Jason eat junk food?

(a) every day
(b) hardly ever
(c) three times a week
(d) never

EXERCISE

● **Listen and answer the questions.**

1 **Write the woman's shopping list.**

shopping list

2 **Which of the following is NOT true?**

(a) The dessert smells good.

(b) She's making a gingerbread house.

(c) She's baking cookies.

(d) She's using an old cookbook.

3 **Laura talks mostly about** __________________.

(a) European culture

(b) café food

(c) wine

(d) cheese

4 **What did Laura have with dinner?**

(a) cheese

(b) bread

(c) wine

(d) coffee

Note taking

1
The woman goes to the grocery store.

2

3~4
Laura traveled Europe.
She loved __________.

4-5

● **Listen and answer the questions.**

1 **Write the correct time period for each pie graph.**

(1) 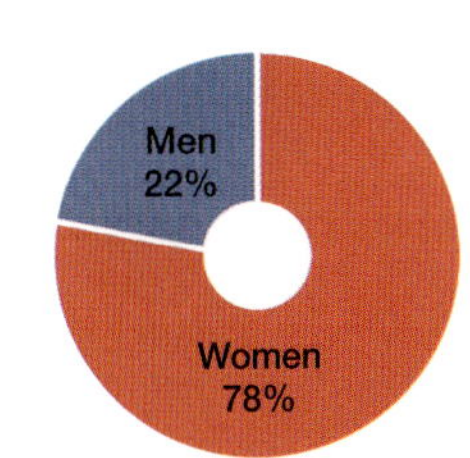

(2) 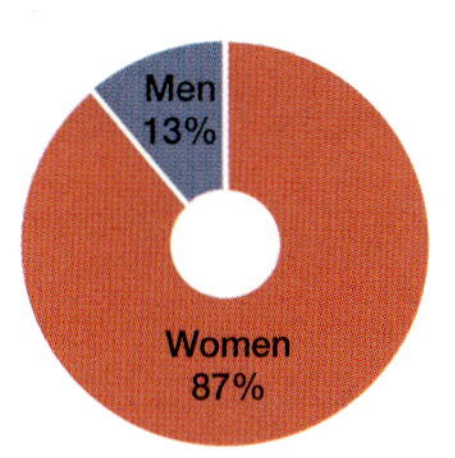

2 **Check T (true) or F (false).**

(1) The speaker made bread daily.   T   F

(2) The speaker had a big breakfast every day.   T   F

(3) The speaker ate sausages for lunch.   T   F

(4) The speaker doesn't remember much about the farm.   T   F

(5) The speaker was hungry at lunchtime.   T   F

3~5

3 **Where is the talk likely from?**

(a) the news   (b) the newspaper

(c) a novel   (d) an Internet blog

(e) a TV program

4 **What will the speaker probably recommend?**

(a) going to Greece

(b) eating more salads and meat

(c) going on a diet

(d) eating more olive oil

(e) eating more oily foods

5 **Which is the best summary?**

(a) Greek people live a long time because they eat a lot of olive oil.

(b) Greek people make the best olive oil and use it on everything.

Note taking

1

2

3~5

Greek people __________

longer because of their

__________.

DICTATION 1

Exercise Step 1

● **Listen and fill in the blanks.**

1
M Hey, where are you going?
W Oh, I'm just ________________ the corner store.
M Really? Can you stop by the grocery store? I need ________________ to make dinner.
W Sure, what do you need?
M Um, pick up two steaks, some potatoes, carrots, broccoli, and ________________ bread.
W What about ________ ?
M Well, I'll let you choose.
W Sure. I'll ________________ some ice cream then.

2
M Mom, something smells good. ________________ ?
W Oh, it's a ________________ an old cookbook.
M It ________ like cinnamon.
W Actually, it's gingerbread.
M Oh, you're making gingerbread cookies?
W No, I'm making a ________ house.
M Cool! Can I help you?
W Sure, Greg. When the gingerbread is finished baking, you can help me put the house together and ________________ with icing and candy.
M Oh, I can't wait!

3~4
M Hey, Laura! So ________________ to Europe?
W Oh, it was amazing.
M Really? What was your ________________ ?
W Well, I'd have to say the food. I just loved the cafés!
M Oh, really? What did you eat?
W You mean, what didn't we eat? Ha ha... We ate ________________ fruit, bread, cheese – lovely cheeses – and coffee. We also had some lovely dinners with wine. It was so delicious!
M Well, I have to admit I'm a little ________ !

Exercise Step 2

● **Listen and fill in the blanks.**

1 M Traditionally, women are the ones who ________________ in the kitchen. In the past, men rarely cooked ____________ to make a quick sandwich. But times are changing. Men are spending more time in the kitchen these days. ____________ that 22% of American men cook dinner in their homes. While 22% may not sound like a lot, it's a ____________ all-time high. In 1990, only 13% of men cooked.

2 W I ____________ those days on the farm like they were yesterday. I woke up every morning to the smell of ____________ ____________ ____________. In those days, my mother made bread daily. Every morning, we had a big breakfast of eggs, potatoes, sausages, toast, and fresh orange juice. I was always ____________ ____________ by lunchtime. I couldn't wait to get to the table for meat, vegetables, and hot biscuits. Those smells ____________ ____________ a lot of memories.

3~5 M Today on *Food Secrets*, we look at the power of olives. Scientists decided to ____________ why Greek people typically ____________ ____________ than other people. They looked at an ____________ Greek person's diet and found that it contains a lot of olive oil. Olive oil has some special powers: It lowers ____________ ____________ and reduces the ____________ ____________ ____________ ____________. The Greeks put olive oil on everything, from salads to breads to meat. This has ____________ ____________ good health for the Greeks.

PRACTICE TEST

1 **Where are the speakers?**

(a) at Bruce's home   (b) at a restaurant

(c) on a picnic   (d) on a plane

(e) in Susan's home

2 **Write down the customer's order.**

Shakin' Chicken Menu	
3-piece chicken combo	$5.00
5-piece chicken combo	$7.00
family chicken combo	$12.00
potato salad	$3.50
macaroni salad	$3.50
juice	$2.00
soda	$1.50
ice cream	$4.00
French fries	$2.50

Shakin' Chicken Order Sheet

Address: _______________________

Items: _______________________

____

____

____

____

____

____

Total: $_______

3~4

3 **What kind of meal is being served?**

(a) multi-course

(b) buffet

(c) three course

(d) English breakfast

(e) brunch

4 **How do the speakers feel?**

(a) disappointed

(b) angry

(c) serious

(d) emotional

(e) excited

5 **What did the speaker NOT put on the pizza?**

    (a) olives

    (b) cheese

    (c) mushrooms

    (d) green peppers

    (e) pepperoni

6 **What is the talk mainly about?**

    (a) world cultures

    (b) health and travel

    (c) famous restaurants around the world

    (d) trying new foods while traveling

    (e) new types of food

7~8

7 **Where does Sharon buy her spices?**

    (a) in India

    (b) at the international food store

    (c) over the Internet

    (d) at the grocery store

    (e) from an Indian neighbor

8 **What will the man probably say next?**

    (a) It's delicious.

    (b) I've been to India before.

    (c) Yes, you can.

    (d) Sorry, I'm busy tomorrow.

    (e) Sure, sounds yummy.

DICTATION 2

Practice Test

● **Listen and fill in the blanks.**

1
M Susan, please ______________ ______________ .
W Thanks. What a great place, Bruce!
M Thank you. Please ______________ ______________ ______________ while I finish up dinner.
W It smells great.
M Good. I hope you like ______________ ______________ .
W It's one of my favorites.
M Can I ______________ ______________ ______________ to drink while you're waiting?
W Sure, do you have any ______________ wine?
M Coming right up.

2
M Hello? Is this Shakin' Chicken? Yes, I'd like to order a 5-piece chicken combo, an order of French fries, a potato salad, ______________ ______________ ______________ soda, and... do you have desserts? [...] That sounds good. ______________ ______________ ______________ of chocolate ice cream. [...] Yes, that's everything. Oh, and I have a ______________ ______________ French fries. [...] Sure, I live at 52 Douglas St. Oh, ______________ will that be? 30 minutes? Super. Thank you. Bye.

3~4
W What a beautiful place for a wedding!
W No kidding!
M And did you see the ______________ ?
W No, not yet. How does it look?
M It's very nice. Salads, soups, beef, fish, and cake of course.
W Sounds lovely. Good thing I'm pretty hungry.
M You ______________ ______________ ______________ . There's even a chocolate fountain!
W Are you serious?
M ______________ ______________ .
W Well, let's go and say hello to the ______________ ______________ ______________ so we can start eating. ______________ ______________ .
M Excellent idea.

5 M Last night I cooked dinner for my family. I made pizza. Pizza's a pretty ________________ to make if you're not the best cook. You can put ________________ on it, so I think making pizza is much better than ________________.
Last night, I put on green peppers, onions, olives, pepperoni, and lots of cheese. Everyone loved it. Next time, I'd like to try making seafood pizza.

6 W When you travel, be prepared to try many ________________ food. For example, in France, you can eat ________________ and frog legs. In China, you can eat shark's fin soup. In Peru, it's common to eat guinea pigs. In many parts of Asia, bugs ________________ a good and ________________. Of course, you don't have to try everything on the menu, but food is a great way to ________ other cultures.

7~8 M What's your favorite type of food, Sharon?
W I'm ________________ Indian food.
M Oh yeah?
W Yes, I took a ________________ while traveling in India, and I really enjoyed it.
M Do you cook it at home?
W Yes, quite often.
M Isn't it difficult to find the right ________ here in Canada?
W Nope. There's a big international food store downtown that ________ all the spices.
M Cool! I had no idea.
W Well, how about ________________ some time for some curry and naan bread?

5 High School Is Tough Sometimes

GET READY

Key Words & Expressions

● Listen to the sentences and fill in each blank with the words on the list.

1. We're going on a history ___________ ___________ this Thursday.

2. I thought the test was a ___________ ___________ ___________ because I studied a lot.

3. I'd like to ask Karla to go to the ___________ ___________ with me.

4. The ___________ usually hang out in big groups outside the gym door or near their lockers.

5. Sean does peer ___________ in his spare time.

6. The ___________ committee is always looking for new photographers to take pictures at school events.

7. Most students in Malaysia have to wear ___________ ___________.

8. Nick got ___________ ___________ ___________ class yesterday for handing in a copied essay.

9. I'm a ___________ of the drama club at my school.

10. You can choose your classes and join a whole ___________ ___________ clubs.

tutoring	yearbook	kicked out of	school uniforms	jocks
member	school dance	field trip	bunch of	piece of cake

Questions & Responses

● Match the questions with the responses.

1	Are you in middle school?	•	**a**	Yes, I joined the drama club.
2	What grade are you in?	•	**b**	It's not bad so far.
3	Hey, aren't you in my economics class?	•	**c**	No, I'm in high school.
4	Did you join any clubs?	•	**d**	Yes, I do. It's gray pants and a blue cardigan.
5	How's school going for you so far?	•	**e**	I'm in the 10th grade.
6	Do you wear a uniform?	•	**f**	Yes, I think so. You sit in the second row, right?

● Listen and check your answers.

● Now practice with your friends.

● **Listen and take notes.**

Grade: nine

Class she takes: ____________

Clubs: ____________

● **Based on your notes, answer the question.**

Q **Which of the following is true?**

(a) The speaker is in the tenth grade.

(b) The speaker has just graduated from high school.

(c) The speaker decided not to join the band.

(d) The speaker is looking forward to high school.

■ **Listen again and fill in the blanks.**

I just started ____________ ____________ this year. Yep, grade nine! Although it's kind of tough being the ____________ at school again, I really like high school. I like that I got to choose some of my ____________, and there are many types of classes. For example, I'm ____________ business now. There are also a lot more ____________ to join than in ____________ ____________. I joined the ____________ committee and the junior band. I think the next four years are going to fly by.

● **Listen and take notes.**

A Ryan

- Activity 1: student government
- grade 11 ____________

- Activity 2: ____________ team
- won championship last year

- Activity 3: peer tutor
- tutors ____________ and ____________ to students who
  need help

- Activity 4: drama club
- does lighting and ____________ for school plays

● **Based on your notes, answer the following questions.**

1 **What does Ryan mainly talk about?**

(a) the sports he plays

(b) the school activities he does

(c) his love for his school

(d) the basketball championship

2 **Mark T (true) or F (false).**

(1) Ryan likes his school. ______

(2) Ryan helps students with their classes. ______

(3) Ryan is an actor. ______

■ **Listen again and check your answers.**

Plus⁺ Question

Q1. Where were last year's basketball finals played?

(a) Winchester

(b) Ryan's high school

(c) Los Angeles

(d) Oklahoma

Q2. What does Ryan do with peer tutoring?

(a) He does the lighting and music.

(b) He coaches basketball.

(c) He teaches English and math.

(d) He helps students with English and science.

EXERCISE

5-4

● **Listen and answer the questions.**

1 **Where do the jocks hang out?**

(a)  (b) 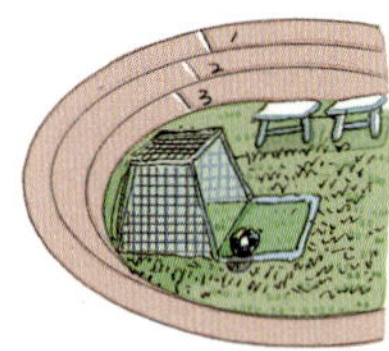 (c)  (d) 

2 **Which of the following is NOT true?**

(a) NYU is Marcel's top choice.

(b) Marcel is researching colleges.

(c) Marcel is in high school.

(d) Marcel wants to go to Harvard.

3~4

3 **Paul's mom feels _______________.**

(a) relaxed

(b) angry

(c) satisfied

(d) proud

4 **Why does Paul need to study?**

(a) His grades are lower than Kenny's.

(b) His dad tells him to.

(c) He has to help Kenny.

(d) He has exams next week.

Note taking

1
Jocks are the guys who only do __________ and always hang out near the __________.

2

3~4

● **Listen and answer the questions.**

1 **What are the senior members' jobs?**

Name	Job
Nicole	
Krista	
Charles	
Lee	

2 **Check T (true) or F (false).**

(1) Mrs. Cook is an English teacher. T F

(2) Mrs. Cook is a strict teacher. T F

(3) English 201 students read Shakespeare. T F

(4) Mrs. Cook allows cell phones in her classroom. T F

(5) English 201 is a large class. T F

3~5

3 **What kind of talk is this?**

(a) a first-day-of-school speech

(b) a graduation speech

(c) a student government meeting speech

(d) a travel club meeting speech

(e) a welcoming speech for a new teacher

4 **What will the speaker probably say next?**

(a) See you next year. (b) Pick up your yearbook at the door.

(c) Have a nice trip. (d) Nice to meet you all.

(e) Good luck and congratulations.

5 **Which is the best summary?**

(a) The man gives a speech to express his appreciation for the retirement gift.

(b) The man gives a speech to celebrate the graduation ceremony.

Note taking

1
____
____
____
____

2
____
____
____
____

3~5
The ___________ and
___________ we had
here at Elmwood High
School will help us
as we begin our next
journey.

DICTATION 1

● **Listen and fill in the blanks.**

1

M Hey, how's it going?

W Not bad. You?

M Can't ___________. Let's eat.

W Sure.

M Where should we sit?

W How about over there?

M Are you ___________? That's where ___________.

W Jocks?

M Yeah, the guys who only do sports and always ___________ near the ___________.

W Oh, I see. Yeah, I wouldn't ___________ with them. They're so loud.

M You've got that right. And don't forget that they're ___________, too.

2

W Hey, Marcel. What are all these papers?

M Oh, it's information from colleges ___________.

W Already? You have not even finished high school.

M I know, but I want to ___________ so that I make the right choice.

W So, what's your top choice?

M Well, in a ___________, I'd like to go to Harvard.

W Yeah, but you'll need a plan B ___________.

M Right. I'm thinking about NYU. It's a good school and is ___________ ___________ from home.

W For sure. And don't you have ___________ in New York?

M Yes, I've got some ___________ there. Maybe I'll go and ___________.

3~4

W Paul, where are you going?

M I'm just going to hang out at Kenny's place.

W ___________ exams next week?

M Yeah, I do.

W Well, shouldn't you be studying ___________ hanging out at Kenny's?

M Don't worry, Mom. I'm going to study this weekend.

W I don't think that's good enough. Your grades   . You call Kenny and tell him you're not going there.

M But Mom!

W Don't give me any "   "! You can   with Kenny when your exams are over.

M Fine…

Exercise Step 2

● **Listen and fill in the blanks.**

1 W Hi, everyone, and welcome to our first   meeting. I'm Nicole, the head of the committee. Thank you all   . I'd like to   our senior members. This is Krista, our head photographer. This is Charles, our   . And this is Lee, our designer. We have lots of work for you to do. We'll need lots of photographers and reporters for school events. If anyone   for a certain event, please let me know.

2 W Hello, everyone. Welcome to English 201.   ! My name is Mrs. Cook, and I'm a new teacher at this school. I hope we have a   together. I'm a pretty easygoing teacher, but I do have a few rules. First of all,   or gadgets in the classroom. Two, please   each other. Three, let's   . We're going to read some great stuff, like Shakespeare and Conrad, so   !

3~5 M Dear fellow students. Here we are   this chapter of our lives. Remember our first day here, when the hallways seemed so   ? We've certainly come a long way. We're older and hopefully wiser. Although we do not know what lies   , the experiences and friendships we had here at Elmwood High School will help us as we begin our   .   the memories we made here.

PRACTICE TEST

1 **What is the talk mainly about?**

(a) school uniforms in America

(b) fashion shows

(c) British schools

(d) American vs. British schools

(e) school traditions

Level up

2 **Check the classes that the speaker chose.**

☐ English	☐ math
☐ French	☐ art
☐ Spanish	☐ music
☐ science	☐ drama
☐ history	☐ business
☐ geography	☐ creative writing

3~4

3 **What event are Jules and Amy talking about?**

(a) a school meeting

(b) a sports day

(c) a party

(d) a wedding

(e) a school dance

4 **How does Jules feel at the end?**

(a) bored

(b) surprised

(c) excited

(d) angry

(e) disappointed

5 **Jan tells Will NOT to** _______________________.

   (a) hand in his paper late

   (b) bother her

   (c) fail the class

   (d) talk to the teacher

   (e) cheat

6 **What are the highlights on Tuesday?**

   (a) the Hall of Fame and the band festival

   (b) the Hall of Fame and the amusement park

   (c) the rock and roll concert and the amusement park

   (d) the band festival and the amusement park

   (e) free time and the Hall of Fame

7~8

7 **When does Jane and Justin's conversation take place?**

   (a) before their science exam

   (b) after their science exam

   (c) during science class

   (d) during their science exam

   (e) at lunchtime

8 **What is Justin's advice to Jane?**

   (a) Stop beating around the bush.

   (b) Birds of a feather flock together.

   (c) Don't count your chickens before they hatch.

   (d) Practice what you preach.

   (e) Cross your fingers.

DICTATION 2

Practice Test

● **Listen and fill in the blanks.**

1　w　School uniforms are a hot topic in many American towns. While some countries, like Britain, for example, have always had their students wear uniforms, America _________ _________ this tradition. Some schools do, but some don't. People who are _________ say that uniforms help students _________ _________ _________ since they are not _________ _________ a "fashion show" at school. People who are against uniforms say they are too expensive and _________. It looks like this debate will continue for some time.

2　m　Today I had to go to school _________ _________ and choose my 7 classes. Some classes are _________, which means I have to take them. I have to take English, science, math, and a social science. I chose history as my social science. That left me three classes to choose. It was tough _________ _________ _________. I wanted to take both music and drama, but I was only _________ _________ choose one art. I _________ _________ choosing French, music, and business. I hope I made the right choices!

3~4　w　Hey, Jules. The big dance is _________ _________, huh?
　　　　m　Yeah, I suppose so, Amy. Who are you going with?
　　　　w　Well, I was thinking of _________ _________, but I'm nervous.
　　　　m　Nervous? Why?
　　　　w　Well, I don't know if this guy really likes me.
　　　　m　But you _________ _________ _________ _________. Just ask him.
　　　　w　You think I should?
　　　　m　Sure! Why not?
　　　　w　All right. Jules, will you go to the dance with me?
　　　　m　What?
　　　　w　Will you go to the dance with me?
　　　　m　Uh… Um… I didn't know _________ _________ _________!
　　　　w　Well, what do you say?
　　　　m　Oh, all right!

5

M Hey, Jan!

W Hey, Will. What's up?

M I've got to ask you for a   .

W Sure, what is it?

M I didn't do my history essay, and it's   today. You have a different teacher…   one of your essays?

W No way!

M Why not? No one will find out!

W You want to bet? If my teacher finds out, I'll   the class.

M Well then, what do I do?

W Just go and see your teacher and ask to   .

M Do you think so?

W Yeah. He might   some points, but at least you won't be cheating!

6

M Okay, everyone. Here's a breakdown of our senior   to Cleveland. We'll be leaving on Monday, March 10. We'll   Cleveland at around 2:00. We will   to the band festival, where we'll perform at 4:30. After that, you'll have some free time in the evening. The next day, Tuesday, we'll be visiting the Rock and Roll Hall of Fame and Cedar Point   . We'll head home Wednesday morning. Please   the   and have a parent sign it by next Friday. Hope everyone can come.

7~8

M Hey, Jane. Wow, I'm glad   ! How do you think you did on that science exam?

W It was   . I aced it.

M Really? How can you be so sure?

W I just found it really easy.

M What about the plant cell diagram question? That was pretty   .

W Nah,   . Justin, science is easy for me.

M Hmm. Well, I hope you're right and that you   . But don't get too excited because you never know.

Action Movies Rule

GET READY

Key Words & Expressions

● Listen to the sentences and fill in each blank with the words on the list.

1 I love a movie with lots of suspense and a good __________.

2 My brother is a remote control __________. He never lets me watch anything.

3 I love eating buttery popcorn at the __________.

4 My boyfriend only likes __________ __________, but I can't stand them.

5 Tom Cruise's new action movie is being __________ this Saturday. Let's go!

6 Animal __________ work just as hard as human actors.

7 __________ __________ are super popular in America.

8 Christy __________ in the musical at her school.

9 Action movies are the best because they keep you __________ __________ __________ __________ your seat.

10 Oh, that movie is __________ __________. We'll have to see another one.

| plot | on the edge of | starred | released | theater |
| hog | reality shows | sold out | horror movies | actors |

Questions & Responses

● Match the questions with the responses.

1   What type of movie do you like best?   •
a   I think Jodie Foster is the best actress.

2   What's your favorite movie?   •
b   I can't resist nachos and cheese.

3   How often do you go to the theater?   •
c   I can't stand romantic comedies.

4   Who's your favorite actor?   •
d   I love science fiction movies.

5   What type of movie do you avoid?   •
e   *The War of the Worlds* wins hands down.

6   What do you snack on when you watch movies?   •
f   I go about once a month.

● Listen and check your answers.

● Now practice with your friends.

BASIC DRILL

6-2

● **Listen and take notes.**

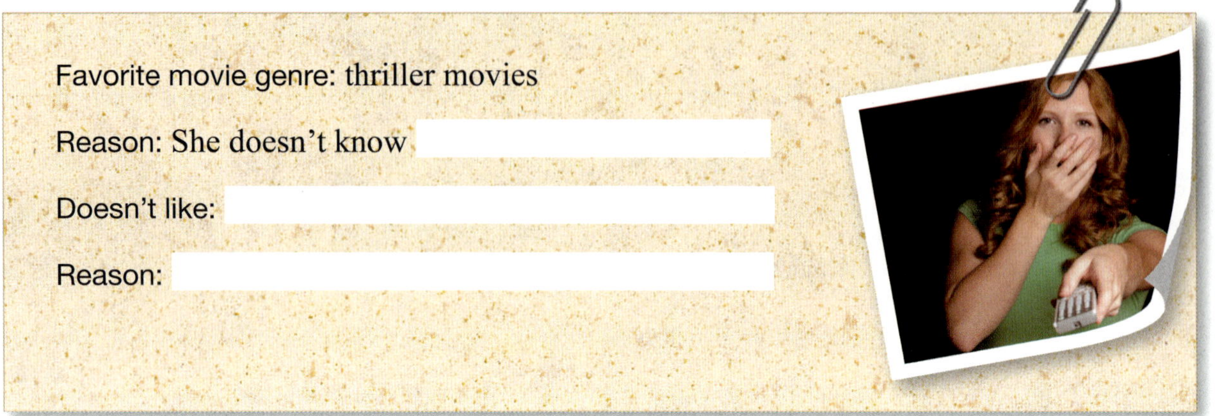

Favorite movie genre: thriller movies

Reason: She doesn't know ________________

Doesn't like: ________________

Reason: ________________

● **Based on your notes, answer the question.**

Q **What is the talk mainly about?**

(a) why thrillers are better than dramas

(b) why the speaker likes thrillers

(c) why the speaker dislikes horror movies

(d) what the speaker eats when watching movies

■ **Listen again and fill in the blanks.**

I've always been a big fan of __________ movies. There's nothing better than sitting down to a thriller with a big bowl of __________ while the lights are off. I think murder __________ thrillers are the best, but I'll watch anything full of __________ and __________. The best movies are the ones where you don't know what will happen at the end. That's why I don't like __________ movies. They're too __________.

6-3

● **Listen and take notes.**

A Patricia
- likes ___________ movies
- loves *Gone with the Wind*

B Trevor
- likes ___________ movies
- likes Arnold Schwarzenegger
- enjoys ___________ ___________ scenes

C Olivia
- likes dramas that ___________ ___________ ___________
  about ___________
- enjoyed *Forrest Gump*

D Victor
- likes ___________
- loved *Grease* and saw it on ___________

● **Based on your notes, answer the following questions.**

1 **What do the speakers mainly talk about?**

(a) their favorite movies
(b) their favorite types of movies
(c) classic movies
(d) going to the movies

2 **Mark T (true) or F (false).**

(1) Patricia's family likes watching *Gone with the Wind*. ______
(2) Trevor enjoys car chases in movies. ______
(3) Victor saw *Grease* on Broadway. ______

■ **Listen again and check your answers.**

Plus⁺ Question

Q1. Why did Victor see *Grease* on Broadway?

(a) because his music class went to see it
(b) because he loves music
(c) because he lives near Broadway
(d) because he liked the movie

EXERCISE

Listen and answer the questions.

1 **What movie will they probably see? Write the information on the ticket.**

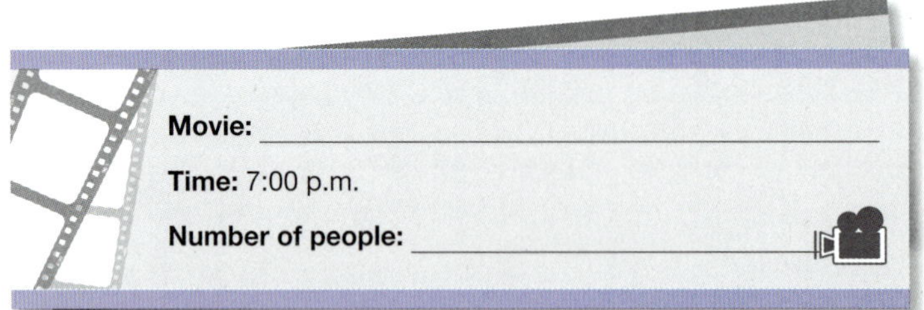

2 **Check T (true) or F (false).**

(1) John is having a party.   T F

(2) Tammy doesn't like awards shows.   T F

(3) Guests have to wear nice clothes to the party.   T F

(4) John wants Tammy to come to the party.   T F

3~4

3 **How does the man feel?**

(a) sad

(b) scared

(c) tired

(d) frustrated

4 **How does the man annoy the woman?**

(a) He watches TV in her bedroom.

(b) He watches dumb shows.

(c) He channel surfs.

(d) He watches dramas.

Note taking

1

There are ________

choices.: *Robot Island*,

________, ________

and *Henry VIII*

2

____

____

____

3~4

____

____

____

6-5

● **Listen and answer the questions.**

1 **How does the man feel?**

(a) confused   (b) scared

(c) bored   (d) relieved

(e) excited

2 **Check T (true) or F (false).**

(1) The speaker enjoyed the movie.   T   F

(2) New York is beautiful in the fall.   T   F

(3) The movie has good actors.   T   F

(4) The movie was exciting.   T   F

(5) The speaker recommends seeing the movie.   T   F

3~5

3 **What is the talk about?**

(a) the reality show *Survivor*

(b) the truth behind reality shows

(c) the creators of reality shows

(d) American reality show viewers

(e) the many types of reality shows

4 **According to the talk, who enjoys reality shows?**

(a) survivors   (b) worldwide viewers

(c) contestants   (d) producers

(e) action fans

5 **Which is the best summary?**

(a) Since 2000, TV viewers have loved reality shows even though much of the shows aren't real.

(b) Truthfully, TV viewers don't like reality shows because much of the shows aren't real.

Note taking

1

2

Title: ______________

- has an __________ cast of actors

- plot: ______________

- setting: ______________

3~5

DICTATION 1

● **Listen and fill in the blanks.**

1

M Okay, ________________ ________________. There are four movies playing at the theater. Which one do you want to see?

W What are the choices?

M Well, there's *Robot Island*, *Time for Love*, *Ghost Girl*, and *Henry VIII*.

W Hmm. How about *Ghost Girl*? I heard that's good.

M Oh, no, sorry… That one's ________________ ________________.

W Sold out? I don't know then. What would you like to see?

M Well, I like ________________ ________________, but I know you hate it. So, how about a ________________?

W Sure. Let's ________________ ________________ ________________.

2

M Hey, Tammy. Are you going to Ron's Academy Awards party?

W He invited me, but I don't know ________________ ________________ ________________.

M Why not?

W I'm ________________ ________________ ________________ awards shows, John. Plus, I don't have anything to wear.

M What do you mean?

W Didn't you read the ________________?

M No, not yet.

W Everyone ________________ ________________ ________________ their best clothes.

M Oh, I didn't know that. But, oh well, it'll be fun. Please come.

W Oh, all right.

3~4

M ________________ ________________ ________________.

W No.

M Then give me the remote control.

W Why should I? All you do is ________________ ________________. You never watch anything.

M Well, that's better than watching this silly drama!

W It's not ________________. I watch it every Monday night.

M Go watch it in your bedroom.

W I like this TV better.

M You're such a TV hog.

W You're ________________ ________________ ________________.

M I get the remote control after this   .

W Fine.

Exercise Step 2

● **Listen and fill in the blanks.**

1 M Angela… What are you doing here? I thought you were dead.

W Everyone   , Evan. Even myself.

M But where have you been all this time?

W It doesn't matter. I'm here, and that's   .

M But… but… everything is different now.

W Is it? There's still you and me.

M No, there isn't! You're   !

W I'm not, Evan. I'm right here   you.

M No. I   . What will I tell Lisa?

W Lisa? You…

M Angela, wait…

---

2 M After all the excitement   to the   of *New York Minute*, I thought I was in for a great movie. But, sadly, I was   .
This movie has an incredible cast of actors, but none of them gave their best performance in this movie. The plot was   and boring. The only good thing about it was the   of New York in the fall. If you're thinking of seeing this in theaters, don't. Just   .

3~5 W Since the year 2000, both American and international TV   have been watching reality shows. *Survivor* was the first   reality show, and since then, reality shows of all types   . But how real are they? In truth, the makers of these shows often tell the   and how to act. It's a mystery how much action on a reality show is real. But one thing is real: TV viewers can't   .

PRACTICE TEST

● **Listen and answer the questions.**

1 **What type of TV program is it?**

   (a) a talk show

   (b) a reality show

   (c) a movie

   (d) a soap opera

   (e) an awards show

Level up

2 **Fill in the graph.**

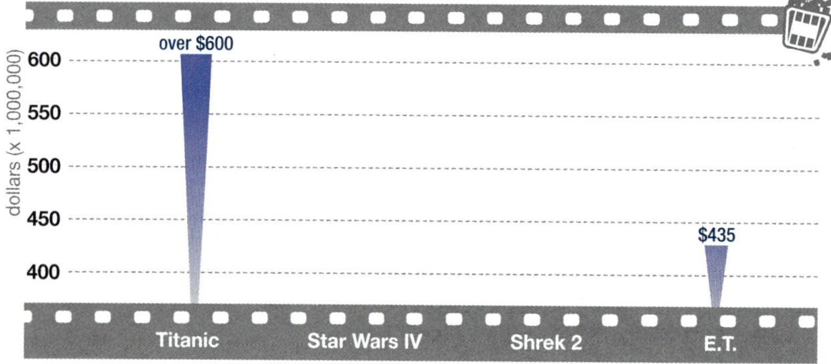

3~4

3 **What does June watch on TV?**

   (a) reality shows

   (b) nothing

   (c) the news and documentaries

   (d) game shows

   (e) the news and reality shows

4 **What is Tim's problem?**

   (a) His TV is broken.

   (b) He watches TV too much.

   (c) He never watches TV.

   (d) He's addicted to online games.

   (e) He is too busy to watch TV.

5 **What is the talk mainly about?**

(a) animal actors

(b) hit TV shows

(c) fan mail

(d) animal comedians

(e) animals that watch TV

6 **What kind of talk is this?**

(a) a farewell speech

(b) a commercial

(c) a movie actor's lines

(d) a wedding speech

(e) an award acceptance speech

7~8

7 **What is the relationship between the speakers?**

(a) girlfriend and boyfriend

(b) husband and wife

(c) brother and sister

(d) friends

(e) classmates

8 **What type of show are they probably watching?**

(a) a thriller

(b) a drama

(c) a comedy

(d) a documentary

(e) a reality show

DICTATION 2

● **Listen and fill in the blanks.**

1   M   Everybody, please welcome… Stella Avery!
     W   Hi!
     M   Welcome, Stella.
     W   Thanks, Frank.
     M   It's _______________________ , hasn't it? You look great, as always.
     W   Thanks. I do what I can.
     M   So, you've got a big movie _______________________ . Isn't that right?
     W   Yes, Frank. It's _______________ this Friday. It's going to be great.
     M   How was the _________ ?
     W   Just fantastic. The cast was so great _______________________ , and I just had a blast.
     M   That's lovely, Stella. So, everyone, Stella's new movie, *Starlight Romance*, _______________ this Friday. Go check it out.

---

2   W   There's _______________________ that movies are big money. But how big? Well, on top of the world… um… list, is *Titanic*, which made over $600 million. The second-highest-grossing film was made 30 years earlier, in 1977. *Star Wars Episode 4* made an out-of-this-world $461 million. Another big _____________ was the big mean _________ Shrek in *Shrek 2*, which pulled in $437 million. Yet another strange creature made _______________ . He was E.T., and he went home with $435 million.

3~4   M   What do you usually watch on TV, June?
      W   Honestly, I don't watch a lot of TV. There's _______________________ _____________ .

      M   Really? You don't watch TV?
      W   Well, once in a while I'll watch the news or a _____________ .
      M   Wow. I wish I were more like you. I watch about 3 hours of TV a day. I need my game shows, sitcoms, and _______________ .
      W   That's too much, Tim. You'd better _______________ .
      M   Yeah, I know, but it's _________ .

5 W Often, the   actors from TV programs and movies are not even human. Animal actors   in bringing light-hearted comedy as well as action to viewers. Eddie, the dog on the hit show *Frasier*, got   fan mail every week as did the killer whale from *Free Willy*. Animal lovers everywhere were saddened when Bart the bear, who starred in several films,   recently. These animals   the screen and made viewing movies more enjoyable.

6 M Oh, my goodness! I certainly didn't   on this stage tonight. Thank you so much! It is an   ! First, I want to thank my family for their   . I also want to thank the   and the   and everyone who worked so hard on this film. Finally, I'd like to thank my   , who helped me and   so much. I couldn't have won this without everyone's help. Thank so much!

7~8 M Hey, Jamie.   ! Mom and Dad left, and it's about to start!

    W Oh, great. I can't miss the season finale!

    M I hope Gary wins it all.

    W   ! I hope Gale gets the $1,000,000.

    M Whatever! She   at all on the island. Gary did all the work!

    W Yeah, but she's smarter. She won most of the challenges.

    M Okay, if Gary wins, you have to   this week.

    W Sure, and if Gale wins, you do my homework this week.

    M Deal.

Spring Is the Nicest Season

GET READY

Key Words & Expressions

Listen to the sentences and fill in each blank with the words on the list.

1   Fall is my favorite season. The weather is __________, and the leaves are beautiful.

2   Getting enough __________ can help you stay happy.

3   __________ can do billions of dollars worth of damage to a city.

4   Hey, don't forget your umbrella! I heard on TV that it's __________ to rain!

5   __________ __________ is a major problem which is affecting Earth.

6   Tomorrow, Las Vegas will be a __________ 40 degrees Celsius.

7   I think England has the worst weather. All that rain and __________ is horrible.

8   In very hot or cold places, plants and animals adapt to live in the __________ temperatures.

9   A __________ happens when a certain place doesn't get any rain for a long period of time.

10 What's the __________? Should I wear a sweater or just a light jacket?

harsh	fog	sunlight	refreshing	supposed
drought	forecast	global warming	scorching	hurricanes

Questions & Responses

● Match the questions with the responses.

1 What's the weather like where you live?

2 Do you get snow there?

3 What's the most beautiful season there?

4 Have there been any natural disasters?

5 Did you happen to hear tomorrow's forecast?

6 Should I bring my umbrella?

a Yes, it'll be overcast and cool.

b It's warm all year round.

c Fall is the most beautiful season.

d We usually get a few snowfalls a year.

e Nope. It seems to be clear.

f Yes, we had a hurricane last year.

● Listen and check your answers.

● Now practice with your friends.

● **Listen and take notes.**

Lives in: the east coast of Canada

→ pretty __________ weather

Winter weather: __________

Summer weather: __________

● **Based on your notes, answer the question.**

Q Which of the following is true?

(a) There are many snowy days in spring in Canada.

(b) It does not often rain in Canada.

(c) Winter in Canada is not too cold.

(d) The weather in Canada often changes.

■ **Listen again and fill in the blanks.**

Weather's a crazy thing where I live on the east __________ of Canada. One minute it can be cold, __________, and rainy, and the next minute it's a __________ spring day. It's pretty __________. The winters are pretty cold. Actually, they're __________, but it's all worth it when summer arrives. It can get hot, but not __________. There's always a nice __________ off the ocean.

● **Listen and take notes.**

A James
- from Australia
- winters are ___________
- beautiful summers

B Kate
- from ___________
- summer is too hot and dry
- spring is the best season

C Sandra
- from ___________
- plays ___________ sports
- nice summers

D Randy
- lives in Dubai, UAE
- very ___________ and ___________
- people use air conditioners

● **Based on your notes, answer the following questions.**

1 **What do the speakers mainly talk about?**

(a) their country's climate
(b) the best seasons
(c) traveling to other countries
(d) extreme weather

2 **Mark T (true) or F (false).**

(1) Australian winters are very cold. ______
(2) Sandra likes Alaskan summers. ______
(3) Dubai can get very hot and humid. ______

■ **Listen again and check your answers.**

Plus⁺ Question

Q1. Summers in Greece are ___________.

(a) cool and windy
(b) not too hot
(c) hot and dry
(d) hot and humid

Q2. Where do people go on hot days in Dubai?

(a) to the beach
(b) inside
(c) to the islands
(d) to the mountains

● **Listen and answer the questions.**

1 Which picture best describes the boy?

(a)　　　(b)　　　(c)　　　(d)

2 Which of the following is true?

(a) Russian winters are cool and foggy.

(b) Scott likes cold weather.

(c) English weather is very warm.

(d) Sophie likes English weather.

3~4

3 Who did Georgia go to Death Valley with?

(a) by herself

(b) her hiking club

(c) her family

(d) a tour group

4 Which is NOT true of Death Valley?

(a) It has good hiking.

(b) It has a good beach.

(c) It has nice sunsets.

(d) It has history.

Note taking

1

2
- Russian weather:
  very _______ in winter
- English weather:
  it _______ a lot, and it's
  often _______ and
  _______.

3~4

7-5

Listen and answer the questions.

1   What are the speakers' jobs?

(a) weather reporters　　　　　(b) tornado trackers

(c) lumberjacks　　　　　　　(d) taxi drivers

(e) truck drivers

2   Which of the following is NOT true?

(a) People are happier on sunny days.

(b) Some people have serious problems because of the weather.

(c) Sunlight causes our bodies to produce chemicals.

(d) If you don't get enough sunlight, you might be sad.

(e) Staying in darkness can sometimes be good for you.

3~5

3   What is the talk about?

(a) high winds　　　　　　　(b) hurricane categories

(c) people hurt in a hurricane　　(d) hurricanes in the U.S.

(e) a hurricane that hit Florida

4   What decides the category of a hurricane?

(a) the number of people injured　(b) the damage caused

(c) the wind speed　　　　　　(d) the location

(e) the season

5   Which is the best summary?

(a) A category 2 hurricane caused a lot of damage in Fort Meyers, Florida, yesterday.

(b) Businesses are giving millions of dollars to repair damage done to Fort Meyers, Florida, after a category 2 hurricane.

Note taking

1

2

3~5
A hurricane
- Fort Meyers
- 160km / hour ⟶
  category ____ hurricane

DICTATION 1

● **Listen and fill in the blanks.**

1
M _________ out today, Mom?
W It's a nice day.
M What do you mean? I want to know _________.
W It's not too hot and not too cold.
M So, a _________ will be fine?
W Yeah, _________.
M Well, I'll see you after school.
W Sure. Oh, wait!
M What?
W _________ just in case. The clouds are a little dark out there.
M Thanks.

2
M What do you think the _________ is, Sophie?
W Probably a really cold place like Russia.
M Yeah, I heard their winters are _________.
W You _________. What about you, Scott?
M I heard the _________ England is pretty bad.
W Really?
M Yeah, it rains a lot, and it's often _________ and _________.
W Actually, I love that kind of weather. It _________ a murder mystery novel.
M You're strange!

3~4
M So, tell us about your vacation, Georgia. Where did you go?
W I took my family to Death Valley _________ in California.
M You took them to a place called Death Valley?
W Yeah, it's actually very beautiful. It gets some of the _________ on Earth, and it's very dry.
M Then why did you go there?
W There's great hiking, _________, and lots of _________. And even though it's so hot, there are lots of plants and animals to see.
M Really?

W Yeah, the life there has ___________ the ___________. I saw some of the greatest sunsets ___________!

Exercise Step 2

● Listen and fill in the blanks.

1

M Okay, Anna! ___________ and get in the van!

W I'm coming!

M ___________ my tracker, it's heading northeast at 100 km/hour.

W Here we go!

M Wait, there's a tree in the road up ahead. We'll have to turn around!

W ___________. I'll turn around and take another road.

M Hurry, we're going to lose it!

W I'm ___________. There it is!

M Keep going, but be careful.

W No kidding! Are you ___________ this?

2

M How do you feel on a warm, sunny day ___________ a cold, cloudy day? If you feel worse on the colder day, you're not alone. Scientific studies have shown that our moods are very much ___________. When in sunlight, our bodies produce ___________ that ___________ and more alert. So if you're in darkness too long, you could find yourself getting sad. For some people, the emotional problems are more serious than for others, but there's no doubt that a sunny day ___________ to most people's faces.

3~5

M A hurricane ___________ Fort Meyers, Florida, yesterday, leaving damaged homes and businesses ___________. The winds reached 160 km/hour, which made it a category 2 hurricane. There are now millions of dollars worth of repairs to be done to the many buildings that were damaged. Roofs ___________ of houses, and cars ___________. Luckily, no one was killed during the hurricane, and there were only a few serious injuries.

PRACTICE TEST

1 Which picture describes the woman's story?

(a)  (b)  (c) 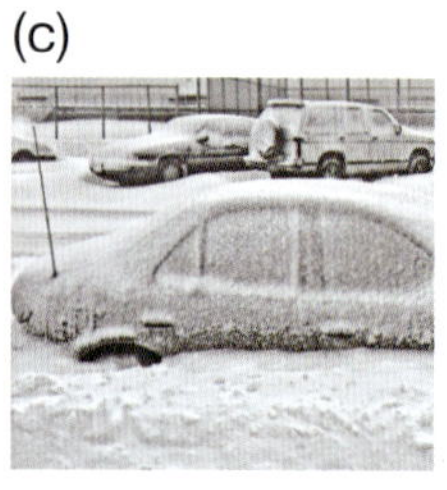 (d)  (e) 

2 Write the temperatures of each region.

Vancouver: _______ degrees

Calgary: _______ degrees

Winnipeg: _______ degrees

Toronto: _______ degrees

Quebec: _______ degrees

3~4

3 What season is it now?

(a) winter   (b) summer

(c) fall   (d) spring

(e) We don't know.

4 What might Terry say next?

(a) to lose is to win   (b) the sky is the limit

(c) let's agree to disagree   (d) when in Rome, do as the Romans do

(e) the ball is in your court

5 **What should people NOT do?**

(a) stay inside

(b) drink water

(c) do exercise

(d) stay in air conditioning

(e) check on elderly neighbors

6 **What kind of talk is this?**

(a) microwave instructions

(b) a car review

(c) a weather report

(d) a snowstorm alert

(e) a product advertisement

7 **What are the speakers doing?**

(a) joking around

(b) making a plan

(c) debating

(d) brainstorming

(e) fighting

8 **What is Jimmy's point of view?**

(a) Something has to be done.

(b) Don't worry about it.

(c) The environment doesn't matter.

(d) Global warming isn't real.

(e) It's not a problem.

DICTATION 2

● **Listen and fill in the blanks.**

1 W I remember it like it was yesterday. I'm talking about that long, long drought in the 1930s. Being from Saskatchewan, I'm __________ __________ hot, dry weather, but this was different. The ground __________ __________ until nothing would grow. The land is all we had to __________ __________ in those hard times, but it wouldn't produce anything. We didn't get __________ __________ __________ rain for years. I don't know how we __________ __________ it, but we did.

2 W Good morning, Canada. I'm Janet Smith, and here's your __________ for today. It's a comfortable spring day in Vancouver today with temperatures __________ about 18 degrees. It seems winter still has a __________ __________ Calgary, where it's a __________ 11 degrees. Winnipeg is the same, except colder. It's only 8 __________ there. Toronto will be 12 degrees and rainy today. Quebec is not doing too well. It's only 5 degrees there.

3~4 M What's your __________ __________, Terry?
W I love weather just like this, so summer __________ __________ __________.
M Why is that? I find it too hot. I'm sweating!
W No way. It's great. I love rollerblading by the sea and surfing.
M I __________ __________ the heat.
W Well then, what about you, Ron?
M Winter is the best season. The snow is beautiful, and the weather is __________.
W Refreshing? I don't think sub-zero temperatures are refreshing.
M You've just got to __________ __________ __________ __________. That's all.
W I suppose _______________________________.

5 W This is a   . Weather France warns all citizens to stay indoors whenever possible,   in an air-conditioned room. Drink lots of water and do not   . Cases of heatstroke are rising. Elderly people are advised not to go outside at all. Check on your   from time to time. This heat wave is likely to be over in the next week, so   until then.

6 M Do you hate getting into a   in the winter? Who doesn't? Now you can   your life for only $29.99! Quick De-icer is the cure for your wintertime blues. You just have to have the Quick De-icer   your local mechanic, and then you'll   . 10 minutes before you leave your home, simply press "quick de-ice" on the handy remote control from inside your home! When you open your car door, you'll   by a warm and toasty interior! Order Quick De-icer today!

7~8 M What are your views on   , Rita?

W I think it's something that has to be stopped before it's too late.

M But seriously, nothing really bad is going to happen in our lifetimes. The temperatures are   .

W That may be true, but what if everyone says that? Plus, what about the damage to the environment now? Many   are almost gone, and animal   , too. What about you, Jimmy? You don't agree?

M Well, I agree that it's a problem, but there's very little I can do about it as one person, so I choose   about it.

I Enjoy Bird Watching

GET READY

Key Words & Expressions

● Listen to the sentences and fill in each blank with the words on the list.

1 I enjoy __________ like hiking and mountain biking.

2 Gale has always __________ cooking ever since she was a kid.

3 Yoga is a __________ hobby among young people.

4 Sometimes it's more interesting to collect something __________, like gum wrappers or pen caps, that no one else collects.

5 To me, __________ things like movie posters or coins is really boring.

6 Some people's successful __________ began with a simple childhood hobby.

7 Lots of kids play sports and are __________ __________ art, music, and collecting things.

8 __________ and baking are popular hobbies because you get to eat the results.

9 I'd like to __________ __________ photography as hobby.

10 I'm really __________ music. I play the piano and write my own songs.

collecting	unique	trendy	take up	into
involved in	activities	cooking	careers	enjoyed

Questions & Responses

● Match the questions with the responses.

1	What are your hobbies?	a	Yes, my hobby is film-making, and that's what I do!
2	Do you collect anything?	b	I'm definitely an outdoor person.
3	Are you an indoor or an outdoor person?	c	I enjoy painting and bird watching.
4	Is your hobby related to your job?	d	Yes, my knitting group meets twice a month.
5	Do you share your hobby with friends or family?	e	I collect salt and pepper shakers.
6	Is your hobby expensive?	f	Unfortunately, yes, it is.

● Listen and check your answers.

● Now practice with your friends.

● **Listen and take notes.**

Hobbies: - collecting
             -
             -

Collections: - stickers
             -
             -

● **Based on your notes, answer the question.**

Q **What does the speaker mainly talk about?**

(a) her stamp collection

(b) her various hobbies

(c) her interest in blogging

(d) her reason for collecting things

■ **Listen again and fill in the blanks.**

I've always had too many __________. I especially love collecting things. So far, I have a sticker __________, a __________ collection, and a postcard collection. It was easy to start my collections because people sometimes gave me things like stickers or coins. Then I __________ more about them, so I got more __________ them. I also like reading and __________, but my true love is __________.

● **Listen and take notes.**

A Mark
- into ___________ ___________
- has done many martial arts
- watches ___________ ___________ films

B Hannah
- into ___________: likes doing ___________ and ___________
- made candles and decorated them with dried flowers

C Pete
- collects movie posters, especially ___________ ___________ posters
- has some ___________ posters

D Brandy
- into ___________
- does sketches and sews clothes
- wants to be a ___________ ___________

● **Based on your notes, answer the following questions.**

1 **What do the speakers mainly talk about?**
   (a) their hobbies   (b) their futures
   (c) movies   (d) school clubs

2 **Mark T (true) or F (false).**
   (1) Hannah can paint and do ceramics.   ______
   (2) Mark likes watching horror films.   ______
   (3) Brandy sews her friends' clothes.   ______

■ **Listen again and check your answers.**

Plus⁺ Question

Q1. Which martial art has Mark NOT done?
(a) judo
(b) kung fu
(c) hapkido
(d) taegwondo

Q2. What is special about Pete's old movie posters?
(a) They're worth a lot of money.
(b) They're like new.
(c) They're signed.
(d) They're of his favorite movies.

EXERCISE

8-4

● **Listen and answer the questions.**

1 **Which one is the Inverted Jenny?**

(a) 

(b) 

(c) 

(d) 

2 **Check T (true) or F (false).**

(1) Alexis ordered a new car.   T   F

(2) Battery-powered cars are more expensive than   T   F
gas-powered ones.

(3) Alexis is saving her money.   T   F

(4) Battery-powered cars are faster than gas-powered ones.   T   F

3~4

3 **What does Deanna think about bird watching?**

(a) It's stressful.

(b) It's exciting.

(c) It's cool.

(d) It's boring.

4 **"I'll take a rain check" roughly means** ___________________.

(a) I think it's going to rain.

(b) Maybe next time.

(c) I'll check the weather.

(d) I'll join you.

1
Inverted Jenny
- is a very rare ________
- was printed in ________
  with a picture of an
  ________ on it

2

3~4

● **Listen and answer the questions.**

1 **According to the dialog, how does the woman stay thin?**

   (a) She gives away her baked goods.

   (b) She exercises.

   (c) She bakes low-fat goods.

   (d) She only eats a little.

   (e) She gives Neil her baked goods.

2 **Which of the following is NOT true?**

   (a) Knitting is inexpensive.

   (b) Knitting is relaxing.

   (c) Knitting is a good way to lose weight.

   (d) Some stars knit.

   (e) Knitting is a new trend.

3~5

3 **What is the talk mainly about?**

   (a) collecting unique things   (b) boring hobbies

   (c) inexpensive hobbies   (d) finding an interesting hobby

   (e) making art from junk

4 **What kind of materials does the speaker suggest using?**

   (a) everyday materials   (b) expensive materials

   (c) artistic materials   (d) rare materials

   (e) garbage

5 **Which is the best summary?**

   (a) If you're bored, try taking up a unique, yet inexpensive hobby.

   (b) Unique people tend to make art out of garbage, so give it a try.

Note taking

1

2
Knitting is now the new
yoga; it is good for the
__________ and helps you
__________.

3~5

DICTATION 1

● **Listen and fill in the blanks.**

1

M You look excited. What's up?

W Oh, I just got a new stamp ______________________ .

M You collect stamps? That sounds boring.

W ____________ . It's really interesting. Have you heard of the Inverted Jenny?

M No, what's that?

W It's a very ____________ ____________ . It was printed in 1918 with a ____________ ____________ airplane on it.

M So, what's so special about that?

W They printed the airplane ____________ ____________ . Now those stamps are worth around $300,000 each!

2

M Hey, Alexis. ____________ ____________ your new remote-controlled car yet?

W Nope, but I ordered it.

M What ____________ ____________ car is it? Battery-powered or gas-powered?

W ____________ . The gas-powered ones are too expensive.

M Yeah, but they're faster.

W Yeah, I know. I'm saving my money to get one. But don't worry, Jacob. I'll still ____________ when we race.

M Yeah, right! Think again!

3~4

M I'm going bird watching this weekend, Deanna. ____________ ____________ ?

W Bird watching? I'd rather ____________ ____________ .

M Huh? There are so many cool birds around this time of year. Come on!

W Where exactly?

M ____________ ____________ . There are so many types of birds in the wetlands.

W What do we do once we're there?

M Just look for types of birds and try to photograph them.

W Sorry, Dave. I'll ____________ .

Exercise Step 2

● **Listen and fill in the blanks.**

1

M Wow, Sheryl! These cookies are ____________ !

W I'm glad you like them, Neil.

M ____________ have you been baking?

W Since I was a kid. I just love it. I love making cookies, cakes, brownies. Pretty much any ____________ !

M But you're so thin! How do you make all this delicious food and not get fat?

W I ____________ what I make. I give it to others.

M I see. Well, next time you have something to ____________ , give me a call.

2

M The newest trend ____________ is knitting! Every since Angelina Jolie and Jennifer Aniston ____________ holding ____________ , everyone is into it! Knitting is now the new yoga; it is good for the mind and ____________ . Plus, you can give your friends and family handmade gifts of knitted pieces. A hand-knit sweater is more comfortable than a store-bought one. And, most importantly, knitting will probably ____________ far less than other trendy hobbies. ____________ !

3~5

M Do you find that average hobbies ____________ ? Why don't you try something a little different? It doesn't have to be expensive. Just ____________ . For example, collect something that's ____________ , but you haven't noticed, like toothpaste caps. Or make a sculpture ____________ lying around the house. Make art from magazine ____________ . Remember, doing ____________ makes you a unique person!

PRACTICE TEST

1 Which picture is the HandyShot 120?

(a)  (b)  (c)  (d)  (e) 

Level up

2 Fill in the graph.

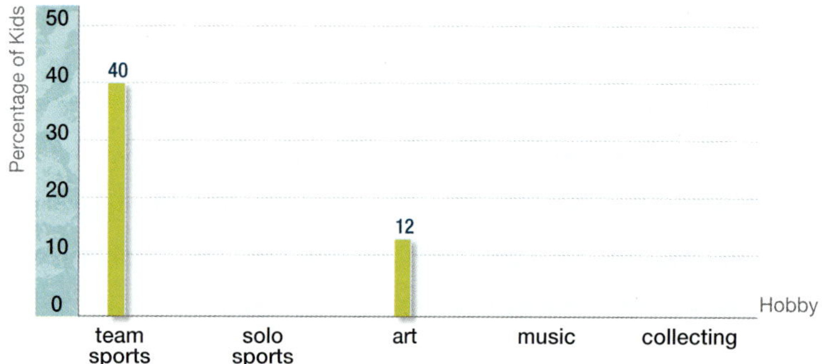

3~4

3 What are they doing tomorrow?

(a) playing sports

(b) cooking

(c) knitting

(d) collecting stamps

(e) hiking

4 What is probably their motto?

(a) Go for broke.

(b) It's better to be safe than sorry.

(c) Practice makes perfect.

(d) It takes two to tango.

(e) Don't rock the boat.

5 How does the speaker feel?

(a) pleased

(b) jealous

(c) bored

(d) sad

(e) curious

6 What is the main idea of the talk?

(a) Sometimes, great success begins with a childhood hobby.

(b) It's very rare when a person becomes famous from doing a hobby.

(c) Steven Spielberg is one of the most famous directors in history.

(d) David Beckham wanted to be a soccer player when he was a child.

(e) Even if your dream seems difficult it is worth doing.

7~8

7 What does Joan NOT use herbs for?

(a) scented oils

(b) medicine

(c) tea

(d) soap

(e) cooking

8 You can guess from the dialog that ________________.

(a) Joan has been growing plants for a long time

(b) Louis doesn't have a hobby

(c) growing herbs is a common hobby

(d) Joan doesn't go out very often

(e) Joan just started growing herbs

DICTATION 2

● **Listen and fill in the blanks.**

1 W The HandyShot 120 is the perfect camera for people who want to _____________ _____________ as a hobby but don't want to spend too much money. It has a 3X zoom and macro lens. There's even a manual mode. Large, _____________ cameras make taking photos _____________ _____________, but with the HandyShot 120, anyone can be a photographer, even beginners! Happy _____________!

---

2 W What are the most popular hobbies for kids these days? For American kids ages 8 to 15 _____________ _____________ _____________ last summer, here are the results. Sports of any kind ranked the highest, with 40% of kids _____________ _____________ _____________ team sports. Next were solo sports like swimming and cycling. 30% of kids do solo sports. _____________ _____________ _____________, with 12% of kids. After that was music, with 10% of kids _____________ _____________ _____________ or singing. Finally, 8% of kids collect something or another. Who said kids are lazy?

3~4 M All right. Here's the map. _____________ _____________ do you want to take tomorrow?
W Let's take the easiest one. It's _____________ _____________ _____________, so it'll be slippery.
M Yeah, that's a good idea. We'll take the easiest trail.
W I'll _____________ _____________ _____________ if you bring the water.
M Sounds good. Bring some rain ponchos, too.
W For sure. I can't wait to _____________ _____________ my new boots.
M Yeah, it'll be fun.
W See you bright and early at 7:30!

---

5 W Dear Diary. Today was not a good day. I came home from school and _____________ to work on my model airplane, but I found it _____________ little pieces. I've been working on that airplane _____________ _____________. It really hurt to see it like that. My brother says he didn't do it, so that only leaves the cat. Who do I believe? There's _____________ _____________ but start over.

6 M It's important to take kids' hobbies seriously. Of course, some kids ________
________ ________ hobbies very quickly, but other kids do a hobby because of a
________ ________. Take film director Steven Spielberg for example. As a child,
his hobby was ________ ________. Now, he's one of the ________ ________
directors in history. David Beckham is another example of a child who followed his
hobby to success. Even if you don't care for a child's hobby, ________ ________.
It might pay off.

7~8 M What's all this, Joan?
W Oh, it's my ________ ________. It's a bit of a hobby now.
M I didn't know you ________ ________. Are they
________ ________?
W No, not really, Louis. And they're really useful.
M What do you use them for?
W I use them in cooking, in teas, and in soaps and to make ________ ________.
M That's ________ ________. What do I need to start?
W Just some ________ and a place with good sunlight.
M Is that all?

I Love the Holidays

GET READY

Key Words & Expressions

○ Listen to the sentences and fill in each blank with the words on the list.

1   People often __________ each other Valentine's Day cards on February 14.

2   __________ and its symbols came to North America from Ireland and Scotland.

3   Come and join us for our __________ Easter Egg Hunt at the Parkview Mall!

4   __________ __________ is a fun day when a groundhog comes out of its hole and tells us when spring will arrive.

5   Many families have __________ once a year as families get together to spend time.

6   In America, women have __________ __________ so that they can get moms-to-be gifts for the baby.

7   Many people find themselves eating too many __________ around the holidays.

8   People usually ring in the New Year with noisemakers and by __________ __________ with champagne.

9   On April Fool's Day, people sometimes play mean __________ on each other.

10 On St. Patrick's Day, many people wear green and __________ by eating Irish food.

baby showers	treats	annual	Halloween	reunions
Groundhog Day	celebrate	making toasts	jokes	send

Questions & Responses

● **Match the questions with the responses.**

1. What's your favorite holiday? •
2. Do you do anything special on your birthday? •
3. Does your country have any unique holidays? •
4. Where do you celebrate important holidays? •
5. How do you ring in the New Year? •
6. Do you celebrate Christmas? •

a Yes, we have Children's Day on May 5.

b I like Thanksgiving the best.

c No, I don't. I'm Buddhist.

d Yes, I usually go out to dinner with my family.

e We usually count down and make a toast to the New Year.

f We usually go to my parents' hometown and stay with my grandparents.

● **Listen and check your answers.**

● **Now practice with your friends.**

BASIC DRILL

9-2

● **Listen and take notes.**

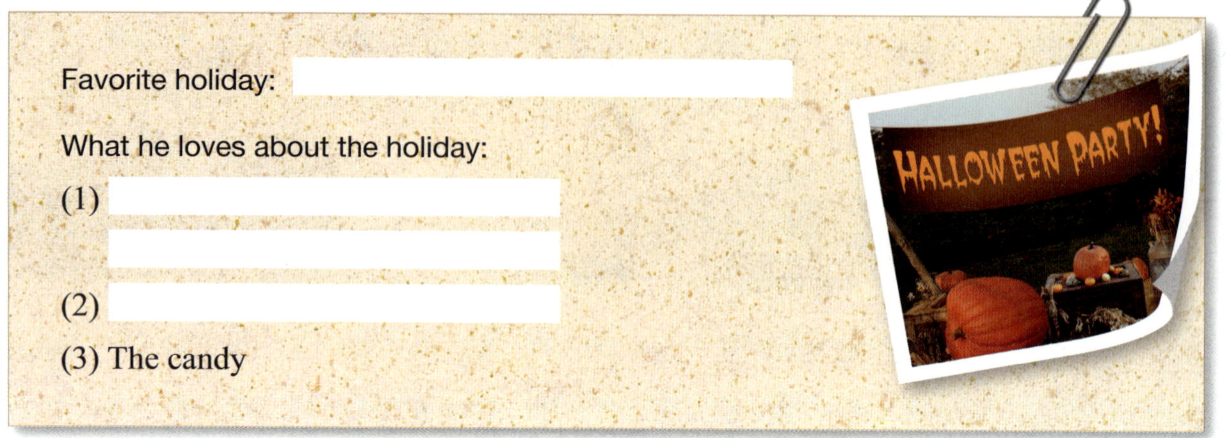

Favorite holiday: ___________

What he loves about the holiday:

(1) ___________

____

(2) ___________

(3) The candy

● **Based on your notes, answer the question.**

Q **Which of the following is true about the speaker?**

(a) He prefers Christmas to Halloween.

(b) He is afraid of haunted houses.

(c) He sometimes gets scared easily.

(d) He really enjoys Halloween parties.

■ **Listen again and fill in the blanks.**

Everyone always says that their favorite holiday is __________, but I'm different. Sure, Christmas is great, but to me Halloween is the best __________. I love getting __________ __________ in scary __________ and trying to scare other people. Halloween __________ are awesome, and, of course, the candy is the best part. Sometimes my dad and I make a __________ house in the garage. __________ is definitely my favorite time of year.

9-3

● **Listen and take notes.**

A Kyle

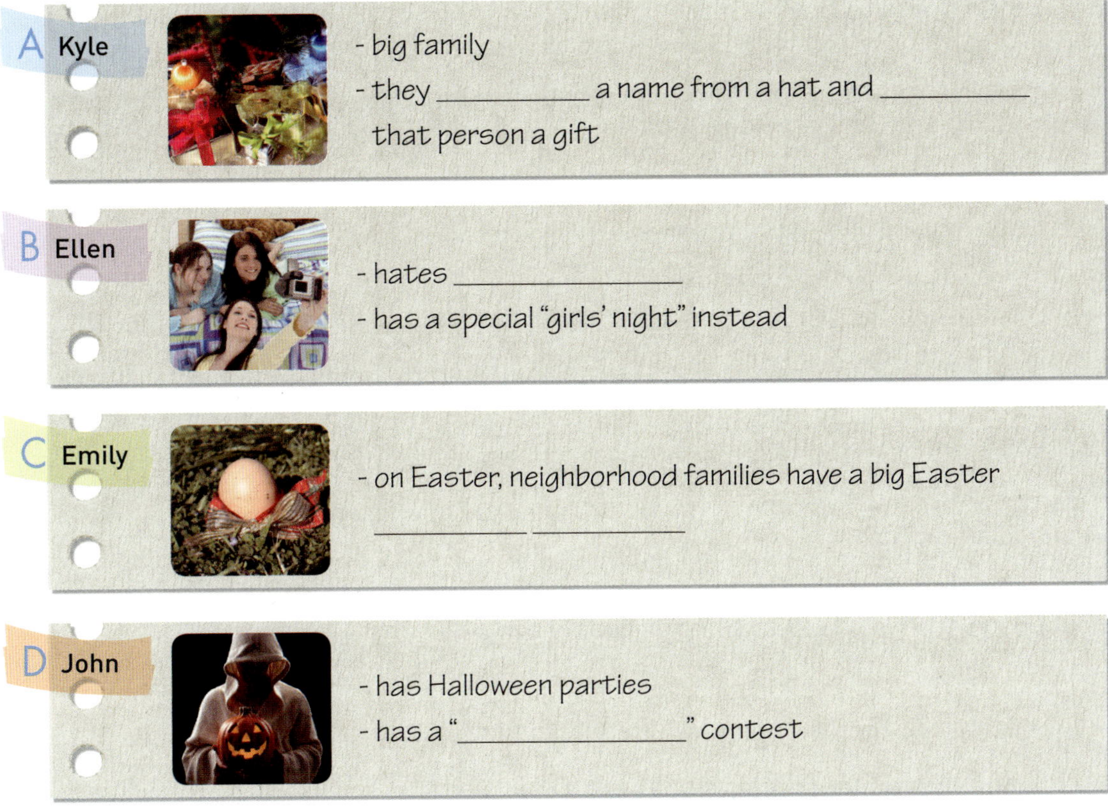

- big family
- they ____________ a name from a hat and ____________
  that person a gift

B Ellen

- hates ________________
- has a special "girls' night" instead

C Emily

- on Easter, neighborhood families have a big Easter
  ____________ ____________

D John

- has Halloween parties
- has a "________________" contest

● **Based on your notes, answer the following questions.**

1 What do the speakers mainly talk about?

(a) holidays they dislike
(b) their favorite holidays
(c) common traditions on holidays
(d) unique ways they celebrate holidays

Plus⁺ Question

Q1. Ellen hates
________________.

(a) Valentine's Day
(b) Christmas
(c) Halloween
(d) Now Year's Day

2 Mark T (true) or F (false).

(1) Emily's parents hide the Easter eggs.   ______
(2) John holds a costume contest on Halloween. ______
(3) Kyle's family doesn't buy Christmas gifts.   ______

■ **Listen again and check your answers.**

9-4

● **Listen and answer the questions.**

1 What is the woman going to buy?

(a)　　　　　　(b)　　　　　　(c)　　　　　　(d)

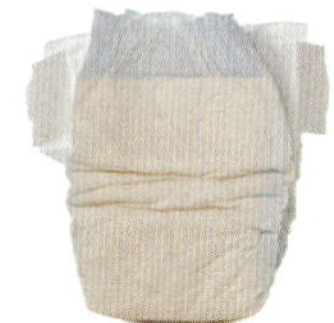   

2 Which of the following is NOT true?

(a) February 2 is Groundhog Day.

(b) Eric loves Groundhog Day.

(c) If it's cloudy, spring will come early.

(d) If the groundhog sees his shadow, spring will come early.

 3~4

3 What is the relationship between the speakers?

(a) friends

(b) brother – sister

(c) husband – wife

(d) father – daughter

4 How does the boy feel?

(a) angry

(b) disappointed

(c) scared

(d) bored

Note taking

1

2

3~4

9-5

● **Listen and answer the questions.**

1 Who sent Larry the card?

(a) his girlfriend

(b) Beth

(c) He doesn't know.

(d) Sarah

(e) Melanie

2 Check T (true) or F (false).

(1) The Irish platter includes stew and fried potatoes.　T　F

(2) St. Patrick's Day is on March 17.　T　F

(3) Irish Eyes Restaurant usually celebrates St. Patrick's Day.　T　F

(4) The first 10 people at the door will get a free meal.　T　F

(5) The Irish platter is 50% off all night.　T　F

3~5

3 What is the talk mainly about?

(a) Christmas in North America

(b) how to avoid stress at Christmas

(c) family problems at Christmas

(d) the stressful parts of Christmas

(e) buying gifts at Christmas

4 Which of the following is NOT mentioned as a cause of stress?

(a) weight gain

(b) cooking Christmas dinner

(c) money spent on gifts

(d) finding the perfect gifts

(e) family members who don't get along

5 Which is the best summary?

(a) For some people, Christmas is more stressful than fun for many reasons, such as buying gifts, being with family members and gaining weight.

(b) People in North America, where Christmas means gifts, get too stressed out about buying gifts at Christmas, because it pays a lot for all the gifts.

Note taking

1

2

3~5
The Christmas holiday can be a very ___________ time for some people.
- reasons:

DICTATION 1

● **Listen and fill in the blanks.**

1

M What are we shopping for, Flora?

W My friend Nikki is ____________________ on Sunday. I need to pick up a gift.

M Okay, I can help. Hmm… What about this little baby dress?

W Um, no, ____________ a boy.

M Well, why not get her something useful like some baby bottles, ____________, or ____________?

W Good idea. I'll get her a few cute bottles. Wait here.

2

M Happy Groundhog Day, Wendy!

W Oh yeah, it's February 2, ____________? I never remember Groundhog Day.

M Really? I always do. I can't wait to ____________!

W How does it work again?

M If the groundhog comes out, ____________, and goes back to sleep, we'll have six more weeks of winter.

W And if not?

M If it's cloudy out or he decides to ____________, we'll have an early spring.

W And you believe that, Eric?

M The ____________, Punxsutawney Phil, is hardly ever wrong.

3~4

W Hey, Al. What's up?

M Um… not much. What's up with you?

W Oh, nothing. ____________ a burger?

M Uh, Valerie… Are you forgetting something?

W I ____________. Why?

M Well, it's my birthday.

W Oh! Oh no! I ____________! I'm so sorry! Are you mad?

M No, but we've been friends for so long, so…

W I'm sorry, Al. It totally ____________. I'll make it up to you. I promise.

Exercise Step 2

● **Listen and fill in the blanks.**

1

M Look at this, Beth.

W What is it?

M It's a Valentine's Day card.

W That's nice.   ?

M It doesn't say.

W What do you mean?

M It says "Dear Larry. Be Mine. From your   ." It doesn't have a name.

W No name?

M Yeah.   , huh?

W Maybe it was Melanie or Sarah. A lot of people like you, you know.

M Oh, come on.

W Well, you should feel good. I didn't   for Valentine's Day.

2

M This Wednesday, March 17, is St. Patrick's Day!   , Irish Eyes Restaurant is getting   . The party starts at 7:00 p.m. The first 3 people at the door will   , and the next 10 will get 50% off. Speaking of meals, our special is the Irish   : Irish stew with mashed potatoes and soda bread. Later on, we'll enjoy some traditional Irish songs and dancing.   the fun this Wednesday!

3~5

M The Christmas holiday can be a very   for some people, especially in North America, where Christmas means gifts. First of all, it's difficult to find the perfect   . Second, it's often difficult to pay for all those gifts! Also, many people find getting together with their families a stressful event, especially if some family members   . Add to this all those holiday   and the thought of   , and you can see that Christmas isn't such a happy holiday for everyone.

PRACTICE TEST

1 **Which is NOT mentioned as a symbol of Halloween?**

(a)   (b)   (c)   (d)   (e)

Level up

2 **When is Thanksgiving? Circle the date.**

11 November

Sun	Mon	Tue	Wed	Thur	Fri	Sat
1	2	3	4	5	6	7
8	9	10	11	12	13	14
15	16	17	18	19	20	21
22	23	24	25	26	27	28
29	30					

3~4

3 **What is the relationship between Hailey and Devon?**

(a) co-workers

(b) teammates

(c) brother – sister

(d) classmates

(e) exercise partners

4 **How does Hailey feel at the end of the dialog?**

(a) upset

(b) sad

(c) excited

(d) afraid

(e) confused

5 **Where did the custom of wearing a white wedding dress start?**

(a) China

(b) Spain

(c) France

(d) the U.S.

(e) England

6 **What kind of talk is this?**

(a) an advertisement for a telephone company

(b) a New Year's speech

(c) an advertisement for a new restaurant

(d) some advice on how to start the new year

(e) an advertisement for a New Year's party

7~8

7 **How do the speakers feel?**

(a) bored

(b) happy

(c) excited

(d) angry

(e) suspicious

8 **How often do they have family reunions?**

(a) twice a year

(b) on birthdays

(c) at Christmas

(d) once a year

(e) once a month

DICTATION 2

● **Listen and fill in the blanks.**

1 W Back in the 1800s, people from Scotland and Ireland going to North America
___________ their special days and traditions with them. One of these was Halloween.
People in North America quickly ___________ ___________ ___________ ___________ .
Now, kids go door to door saying "trick-or-treat" and then receive candy. The colors
of Halloween are orange and black, and the ___________ of Halloween are usually
___________ ___________ ___________ . They include, for example, pumpkins, black
cats, bats, and witches.

2 W Thanksgiving is an important holiday in the U.S. and ___________ ___________
___________ ___________ Thursday of November. It is only a one-day holiday, but
family members often travel from around the country to be together for ___________
dinner. Usually, families eat ___________ ___________ for dinner. It is also important
because it ___________ the beginning of the shopping season for the Christmas
holiday.

3~4 M Hey, Hailey. What's up?
　　　W Not much, Devon. Are you ___________ ___________ the science test today?
　　　M Science test? It ___________ ___________ . Didn't you hear?
　　　W What? It was cancelled? Oh, wow! That's great!
　　　M Hailey…
　　　W What?
　　　M ___________ !
　　　W Huh? Are you kidding me? So the test is still on?
　　　M Yeah, I was just ___________ ___________ ___________ .
　　　W That was a ___________ joke, Devon. See you…

5 W Do you ever ___________ ___________ so many brides wear white? Actually, many
modern Western wedding traditions have their ___________ ___________ England.
This is where the tradition of wearing a white dress comes from. Queen Victoria is
the one who ___________ ___________ in 1840. At the time, many people
admired her wedding photo, and now people from many countries, from Spain to
China, ___________ ___________ white on their wedding day.

6 M This Saturday is New Year's Eve, and you know what that means! The Mandarin Hotel is having its   New Year's Eve Bash! For only \$75   , you can have dinner and enjoy live music as you ring in the New Year. You will also get noisemakers and a glass of champagne   the beginning of a brand new year. Come and join us this Saturday and start next year   !

7~8 M Hey.

W Hey.

M Another family   .

W Yep, another one.

M Why does our family   anyway? Every summer it's the same thing.

W I don't know. I guess it's a tradition.

M Not everyone enjoys it though.

W   .

M Did you see Aunt Diane and Uncle Nick?

W Yeah. Fighting   .

M What do we do now?

W I don't know.   to find some food.

I'd Like a One-way Ticket to New York

GET READY

Key Words & Expressions

● Listen to the sentences and fill in each blank with the words on the list.

1   I'd like two __________ tickets to Vancouver, please.

2   Some people enjoy thrilling __________ __________.

3   We went canoeing and hiking, and we __________ __________.

4   Can I have your ticket and identification, please? Here is your __________ __________.

5   Budgeting your money is one of the most important things to do when __________ __________ __________.

6   When you __________, make sure you know a few important phrases in the country's language.

7   I'd rather spend a vacation on the beach than visit boring __________ __________.

8   The Eiffel Tower is one of the most famous __________ in the world.

9   The Grand Canyon is one of the most often visited __________ __________.

10 It's best to __________ lightly on any trip.

natural sites	camped out	one-way	travel	historical sites
planning a trip	adventure vacations	boarding pass	landmarks	pack

Questions & Responses

● **Match the questions with the responses.**

1	Do you enjoy traveling?	**a**	I've been to America and Australia.
2	What's the hardest part about traveling?	**b**	I wouldn't go to Russia. It's too cold.
3	Where have you traveled?	**c**	Yes, I try to go away once a year.
4	Where would you like to travel?	**d**	Language is definitely the hardest part.
5	Do you like traveling by plane?	**e**	I'd love to go to South America.
6	Is there anywhere you don't want to go?	**f**	I don't like it, but I have no choice. The world is so big!

● **Listen and check your answers.**

● **Now practice with your friends.**

BASIC DRILL

Listen and take notes.

Last summer's trip: California

This summer's trip: __________

What does the speaker do on trips?:

____

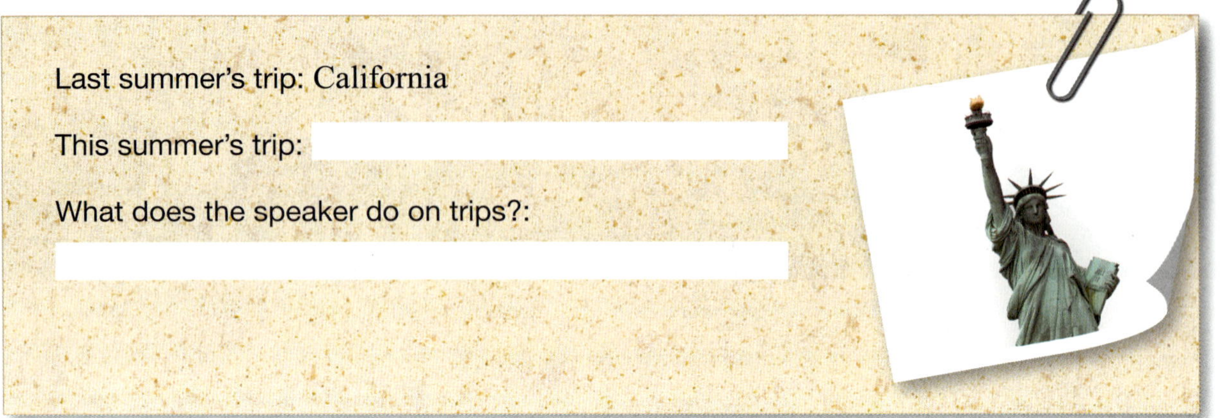

Based on your notes, answer the question.

Q Which of the following is true?

(a) The speaker's family is going to Europe this summer.

(b) The speaker took some pictures in New York.

(c) The speaker likes to visit different places.

(d) The speaker has more than a dozen key chains.

Listen again and fill in the blanks.

Every summer, my family goes on a __________ somewhere different. I love __________, so I really look forward to this time. Last summer, we went to California, and this summer we're going to New York. This summer's trip is going to be great because I just got a new __________. I can't wait to go __________ downtown and snap some photos! I also buy __________ wherever I go. So far, I have 11 key chains all from different __________. My dream is to go to __________ someday, so I'll have to start saving my money now!

10-3

● **Listen and take notes.**

A **Sam**

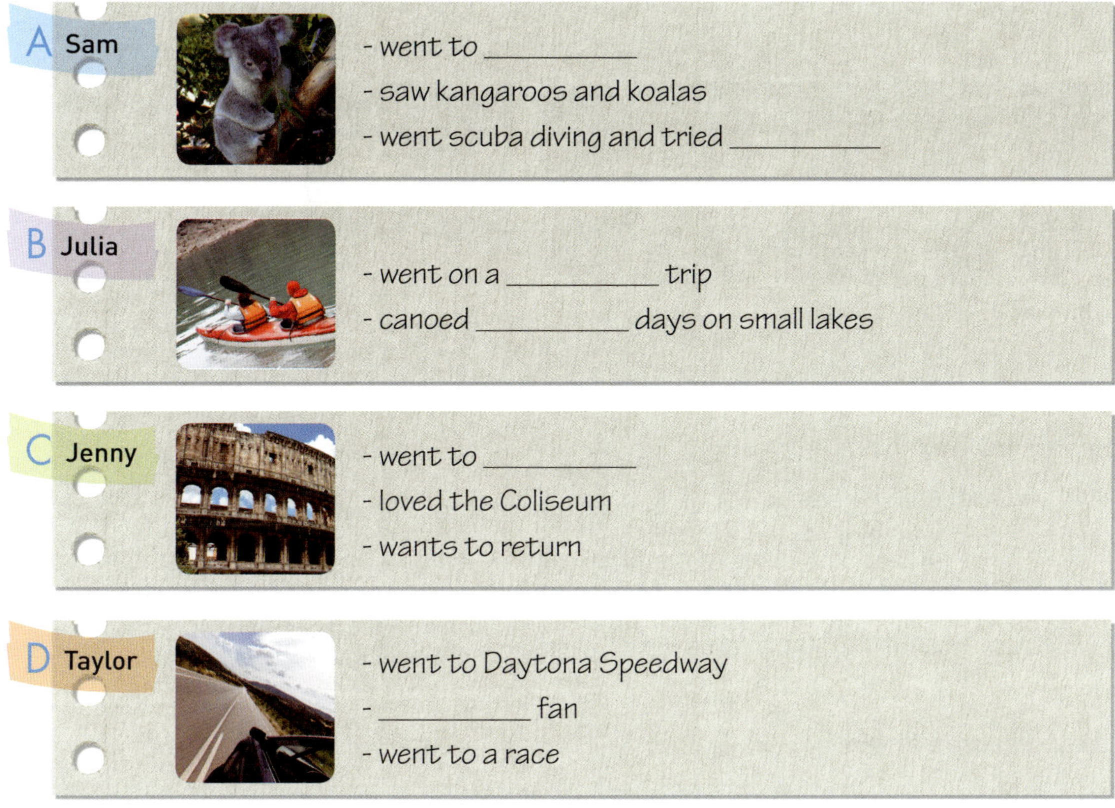

- went to ____________
- saw kangaroos and koalas
- went scuba diving and tried ____________

B **Julia**

- went on a ____________ trip
- canoed ____________ days on small lakes

C **Jenny**

- went to ____________
- loved the Coliseum
- wants to return

D **Taylor**

- went to Daytona Speedway
- ____________ fan
- went to a race

● **Based on your notes, answer the following questions.**

1 **What do the speakers mainly talk about?**

(a) hot vacation spots
(b) family vacations
(c) their favorite places
(d) their favorite trips

2 **Mark T (true) or F (false).**

(1) Sam tried surfing in Australia. ______
(2) Julia went canoeing for four days. ______
(3) Taylor is a racing fan. ______

■ **Listen again and check your answers.**

Plus⁺ Question

Q1. Who did Julia travel with?

(a) her parents
(b) her friends
(c) her gym class
(d) her relatives

Q2. What did Taylor enjoy seeing on his trip?

(a) the track and the cars
(b) the Coliseum
(c) the beach
(d) his favorite racing star

EXERCISE

● **Listen and answer the questions.**

1 What are they going to do?

(a)  (b)  (c)  (d) 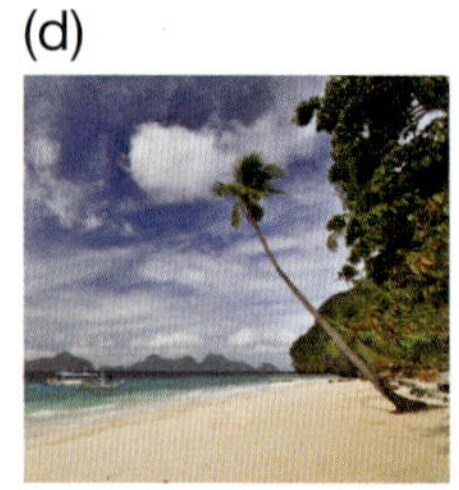

2 Check T (true) or F (false).

(1) The woman is traveling alone. T F

(2) The woman is returning to Calgary. T F

(3) It isn't possible to travel on June 2. T F

(4) The woman wants to sleep on the train. T F

`3~4`

3 What do they disagree about?

(a) what to do in Turkey

(b) what beaches to visit

(c) what historical site to visit

(d) which coast to visit

4 Kelly is more interested in __________, but Mike is more interested in __________.

(a) big cities, the coast

(b) Turkish culture, parties

(c) historical sites, beaches

(d) mosques and museums, fishing

Note taking

1

2
Ticket information
- Destination: __________
- One-way ticket
- Date: __________
- Number of people: ____
- Type of train: __________

3~4

10-5

● **Listen and answer the questions.**

1 **How does the man feel?**

(a) calm

(b) angry

(c) relieved

(d) ashamed

(e) uninterested

2 **Which of the following is true?**

(a) Thrilling vacations are the best.

(b) People enjoy different types of vacations.

(c) Vacations cause stress.

(d) Relaxing on the beach is the best kind of vacation.

(e) Relaxing in the real world is the best vacation.

3~5

3 **What is the speaker's job?**

(a) wedding planner

(b) restaurant owner

(c) taxi driver

(d) tour guide

(e) stuntman

4 **When did Annie Taylor go over the falls?**

(a) 1920   (b) 1902   (c) 1901

(d) 19 years ago   (e) 1915

5 **Which is the best summary?**

(a) The man encourages people to go over the falls.

(b) The man introduces Niagara Falls to visitors.

Note taking

1

2

3~5

DICTATION 1

● **Listen and fill in the blanks.**

1　M　Bad news. The weather doesn't ______________________. It's raining.

　　W　Oh, no. We came to Thailand to go to the beaches.

　　M　I know, but this isn't very good beach weather.

　　W　What does your travel book say we can do around here?

　　M　Okay, ______________________ … There are elephant rides, a ______________,
　　　　a market, a tiger zoo… What do you think?

　　W　I guess if we go to a temple, at least we can ______________________ the
　　　　rain.

　　M　True. Let's ______________________ and then grab a nice dinner.

2　W　Hello, I'd like a ticket from Calgary to Vancouver.

　　M　Trains ______________ 8:00 a.m. daily. What day would you like to leave?

　　W　In two weeks ______________, on June 2.

　　M　Okay. Just yourself traveling, ma'am?

　　W　Yes.

　　M　Return or ______________?

　　W　One-way, please.

　　M　Would you like a regular seat or a sleeper?

　　W　A ______________, please.

　　M　Okay, that's $350.

　　W　Can I pay by credit card?

　　M　Sure.

3~4　W　There's just so much to see in Turkey. I think we'll have to choose ______________
　　　　______________________ because we can't do it all. So, what's
　　　　most important to you, Kelly?

　　W　I really want to see all the mosques and museums in Istanbul. I'd also like to see the
　　　　______________________ of Ephesus.

　　M　But I'm more of a beach person. There are supposed to be some gorgeous beaches
　　　　______________________.

　　W　We can go to beaches anywhere. The ______________________ are far more interesting.

　　M　Can't we do both?

　　W　I don't think we'll have time, Mike.

Exercise Step 2

● **Listen and fill in the blanks.**

1

M What are you taking?

W Well, I'm trying to pack lightly. Just __________ __________ __________ __________ __________, __________, and a bathing suit.

M Are you bringing shampoo?

W Yeah, I've __________ __________ __________ __________.

M Okay. Where's my beach towel?

W It's in the __________.

M Do you have the tickets?

W Yes, I've got everything __________ __________.

M What about our passports?

W I've got mine. Where's yours?

M Don't you have it? Oh, no!

W Don't worry. I was just joking. I've __________ __________ right here.

2

M You're tired and __________ and need a vacation, right? __________ that the type of vacation you choose is the most important decision. Sure, the __________ __________ __________ on a beach with a cold drink and a book is great for some, but others might find that boring. For some, __________ __________, like a trek in the jungle or bungee jumping, might be a better choice. You have to consider how you personally __________ __________ stress so that you will feel relaxed when you return to the "real world."

3~5

M Okay, everyone, if you __________ __________ on your right, you'll see the world-famous Niagara Falls. This is the Canadian Falls, __________ __________ the Horseshoe Falls. In 2 minutes, we'll be __________ __________ to the American Falls, which includes the Bridal Veil Falls. The first person to __________ it was Annie Taylor __________ __________. She barely survived. Since her stunt, about 15 other people have tried the same thing, but __________ __________.

PRACTICE TEST

1 Which site is it?

(a)  (b)  (c)  (d)  (e) 

2 Check the correct information and fill in the blanks.

Package Tour

Day 1: transfer to (1) _______________; take a city tour
(Cuzco / Lima)

Day 2: Machu Picchu guided tour in (2) _______________
(English / Spanish)

Day 3: Pisac village and market

Day 4: return to Lima

3~4

3 Where are the speakers?

(a) at a train station

(b) on a plane

(c) at the airport

(d) at a bus terminal

(e) at a restaurant

4 What does the woman need to show the man?

(a) her ticket and identification

(b) her boarding pass

(c) her bags

(d) her money

(e) her seat number

5 You're going to Europe for five days, and you have $550. What is the best budget per day?

(a) $15

(b) $110

(c) $50

(d) $55

(e) $15

6 What is the talk mainly about?

(a) learning a new language

(b) being polite

(c) finding a good phrasebook

(d) learning travel phrases

(e) tough situations while traveling

7~8

7 What is the woman's problem?

(a) She doesn't have enough money.

(b) She can't find the travel Internet site.

(c) She doesn't know where to go.

(d) She doesn't like trying new foods.

(e) She can't find a travel partner.

8 Which expression best suits the man's final advice?

(a) Beggars can't be choosers.

(b) You're barking up the wrong tree.

(c) Don't count your chickens before they hatch.

(d) It's a blessing in disguise.

(e) A journey begins with a single step.

DICTATION 2

● **Listen and fill in the blanks.**

1 w Built from 1887 to 1889, this is ___________ sights in the world. It was designed by Gustave Eiffel for a World Fair and ___________ over 200 million visitors. It stands 325 meters tall and ___________ every seven years. It is the tallest building in Paris, but not in France. These days, there is a light show every night ___________, and there is an ice rink on the first floor.

2 w On day one of our trip to Peru, after arriving in Lima, we will ___________ to the city of Cuzco. We will take a ___________ after lunch. On day two, we will take a 6:00 a.m. train to Machu Picchu, an ancient city ___________ the Incas. We will provide an English-speaking guide for you. ___________ in your fee. On day three, we will visit the village of Pisac and see its famous market. On day four, we will ___________ Lima.

3~4 w Can I have your ticket and ___________, please?

w Sure.

M How many bags do you have?

w Two.

M Okay, ___________ here. Would you like a window or an aisle seat?

w Um, a window seat, please.

M Okay. Here is your ___________. Go to Gate 39 by 4:50 p.m. Your flight leaves at 6:00.

w Are there ___________?

M No, not that I know of.

w Thank you.

5 w ___________ your money is an important part of every vacation. While we'd all like to stay at luxury hotels, ___________ the best restaurants, and buy ___________, for most of us, that's impossible. The easiest way to take the ___________ traveling is to budget your money.

how much money you have, and divide it by the number of days you'll be traveling. That will give you a   of how much money you can spend per day.

6   M   Language is always   when traveling. If the place you're traveling to does not have English as an   , consider learning some basic phrases before you go. Phrases like "Please" and "Thank you"   more polite to local people. Phrases like "Where's the bathroom?" can   in a tough situation. If you don't have time to study the language, bring a phrasebook with you just   .

7~8   M   How's your trip planning going, Dawn?
W   Oh,   , Sid.
M   What do you mean?
W   Well, I haven't found a good   .
M   Really? What about Whitney?
W   She's busy then.
M   Paula?
W   She never   new foods.
M   Jessica?
W   She doesn't want to go to the same places that I do.
M   Did you try looking   ? There are some sites that will match you with travel partners.
W   Go with a stranger?
M   Well, it's better than not going   !

Dogs Are My Favorite Animals

GET READY

Key Words & Expressions

● Listen to the sentences and fill in each blank with the words on the list.

1 Cats are my favorite animals because they're __________ and elegant.

2 Owning pets can __________ stress and illness.

3 Most dog lovers prefer their pets because they are __________ and dependable.

4 __________ have to learn all about different types of animals.

5 Cat and dog lovers will never agree about which makes a better __________.

6 Some __________ of dogs and cats can cost thousands of dollars.

7 I really love animals. They're so cute, and they all have their own __________, just like people.

8 Most kids like going to the zoo and watching the monkeys __________ around.

9 I don't know how anyone could own a __________ like an iguana. They're creepy!

10 A kid should only get a pet if he or she is responsible enough to __________ __________ __________ one.

personalities	smart	vets	lizard	breeds
loyal	goof	reduce	pet	take care of

Questions & Responses

● Match the questions with the responses.

1	Do you like animals? ●	**a** Cleaning up after them is the hardest part.
2	What's your favorite animal? ●	**b** If they are responsible enough, yes.
3	Have you had many pets? ●	**c** Yes, especially cats.
4	Are you allergic to any pets? ●	**d** Fish. I think it's really relaxing to watch them.
5	What's the hardest thing about having a pet? ●	**e** Just a dog when I was growing up.
6	Should kids have pets? ●	**f** No, luckily I don't have any allergies.

● Listen and check your answers.

● Now practice with your friends.

● **Listen and take notes.**

Past pets: ________________

Favorite animal: dogs

Dream: ________________

● **Based on your notes, answer the question.**

Q What is the main reason the speaker wants to be a veterinarian?

(a) He wants to make a lot of money.

(b) He wants to take care of his pets.

(c) He wants to work with animals.

(d) He wants to understand animals' personalities.

■ **Listen again and fill in the blanks.**

A lot of kids love __________, but I really love animals. In my life, I've had two dogs, three cats, six fish, two __________, and two __________. I love __________ __________ of them and getting to know their different personalities. Dogs are my favorite animals because they're so __________ and __________. I'm going to be a __________ when I grow up, so I can work with animals all the time. That's my dream.

11-3

● **Listen and take notes.**

A **Isaac**
- likes ___________
- thinks they are ___________

B **Maria**
- likes lions
- thinks they are ___________ but ___________
- thinks male lions are ___________

C **Hannah**
- likes ___________
- likes the rattlesnake's sound

D **Eric**
- likes ___________
- watches them at the zoo

● **Based on your notes, answer the following questions.**

1 **What do the speakers mainly talk about?**

(a) animals at the zoo
(b) their favorite animals
(c) beautiful animals
(d) their dream pets

2 **Mark T (true) or F (false).**

(1) Isaac thinks wolves are gentle. ______
(2) Maria thinks male lions are cute. ______
(3) Eric likes the monkeys at the zoo. ______

■ **Listen again and check your answers.**

Plus⁺ Question

Q1. What does Hannah like about snakes?

(a) their babies
(b) their loyalty
(c) the patterns on their bodies
(d) their mysteriousness

Q2. What is Eric's dream?

(a) to have a pet monkey
(b) to be a zookeeper
(c) to go to the zoo
(d) to work with monkeys

EXERCISE

● **Listen and answer the questions.**

1 **What do iguanas eat? Check TWO pictures.**

(a)   (b)   (c)   (d)

2 **Which of the following is NOT true?**

(a) Louise will have to bathe and train the dog.

(b) Louise thinks she can take care of a dog.

(c) Taking care of a dog is difficult.

(d) Louise's Dad thinks she's too young to have a dog.

3~4

3 **According to the dialog, why does Rudy like cats?**

(a) They're smart.

(b) They're active.

(c) They're clean.

(d) They're quiet.

4 **Why does Darla want to end the conversation?**

(a) She has to go.

(b) She hates cats.

(c) Rudy makes her angry.

(d) They will never agree.

Note taking

1
Jane has _______ iguanas.
- They're _______
- Feeds them _______

2

3~4
Dogs vs. Cats
- Dogs are loyal, _______
- Cats are smarter, _______

11-5

● **Listen and answer the questions.**

1 **What is the monkey doing?**

(a)　　　　　(b)　　　　　(c)　　　　　(d)　　　　　(e)

2 **Check T (true) or F (false).**

(1) Some pets cost thousands of dollars.　　　　　　　　T　F

(2) Labradoodles usually cost around $1,500.　　　　　　T　F

(3) You can adopt a homeless pet for free.　　　　　　　T　F

(4) Labradoodle is another name for a Labrador retriever.　T　F

(5) Dog and cat breeders sell their animals.　　　　　　　T　F

3~5

3 **What kind of talk is this?**

(a) a movie advertisement　　　　　(b) a lecture

(c) a news report　　　　　　　　　(d) a zoo advertisement

(e) a speech

4 **Why couldn't the police shoot the tigers?**

(a) Some animal experts stopped them.

(b) The tigers attacked a police officer.

(c) The tigers were in the forest.

(d) The tigers were too fast.

(e) There were too many people around.

5 **Which is the best summary?**

(a) Two tigers escaped from the San Diego Zoo and have entered a forest near
the zoo.

(b) Two tigers escaped from the San Diego Zoo and are attacking and killing people.

Note taking

1

2

3~5

DICTATION 1

● **Listen and fill in the blanks.**

1
M So, Jane, do you have any pets?
W Yeah, I have two iguanas. They're great.
M Iguanas? That's   !
W Why? They're   but beautiful to watch.
M What do you feed them?
W Just small   and sometimes some fruits and vegetables.
M No mice?
W No, you're   .
M Are they   ?
W Well, in their own way, I guess. They're good around me, but they   at my brother.

2
W Hey, Dad. Do you think I can get a dog?
M Well, Louise, I don't know about that.   a pet is a lot of work!
W Yeah, I know, but I can   .
M Do you think so?
W Yeah, I'll   every day.
M There's more to do than just feeding it. It'll need to be walked every day, and you'll have to   and train it.
W Yes, I know, Dad. I think I can do it.
M All right. I guess you're   . Let's talk more about it later.
W Okay.

3~4
M What do you   Darla, cats or dogs?
W Dogs, definitely. They're loyal,   , dependable, cute, active…
M Dog lovers always say the same things.
W Oh really, Rudy? Well, I can tell you don't   , so why are cats so special?
M It's simple. They're smarter.
W Whatever!
M They are! They're smarter, more   , and so much cuter.

W Let's ____________. I don't think the ____________ issue will ever be resolved.

Exercise Step 2

● **Listen and fill in the blanks.**

1
M Come on! Come on! Look at the monkeys!
W I'm coming. I'm coming.
M Oh, wow. They're ____________ !
W Yeah, the baby is really cute!
M Oh, look at that one! He's ____________ his tongue at us!
W Oh, my gosh. He is!
M Maybe he wants some food. Do you have anything?
W Yeah, here. ____________ .

2
W Are you thinking of ____________ or a cat? You probably ____________ the cost of getting one in the first place. ____________ the pet you want, it could cost you thousands of dollars. Dog and cat ____________ top-quality animals, and they aren't cheap. For example, the ____________ called the Labradoodle, a mix between a Labrador retriever and a poodle, sells for about $2,500. Before going to the pet store, do some research, or, better yet, go to the animal shelter and adopt a ____________ .

3~5
M This is just in! Two tigers have escaped ____________ at the San Diego Zoo and are ____________ the city. So far, they only injured two people as they escaped from the zoo, but the police are worried they could do more damage. Police tried to ____________ at the tigers, but there were too many people in the area. The tigers were last seen ____________ a forest behind the zoo's parking lots. Police and animal experts are doing their best to ____________ .

PRACTICE TEST

1 **How is a vet's job different than a doctor's?**

(a) Vets have to learn about different types of animals.

(b) Vets have to study for years.

(c) Vets have to do a lot of work.

(d) Vets make more money than doctors.

(e) Vets don't work at a hospital.

Level up

2 **Fill in the graph with the animals.**

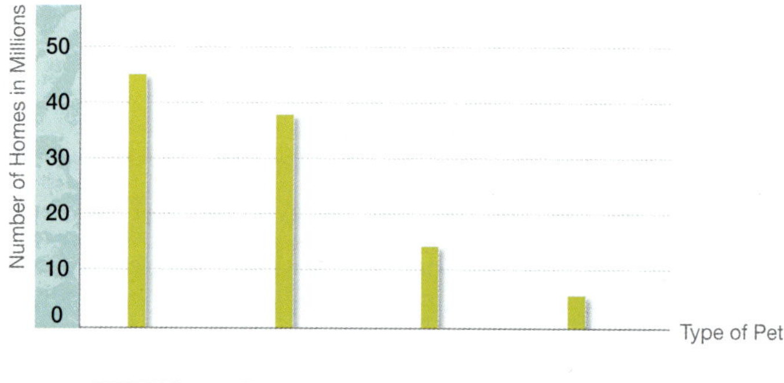

3~4

3 **What does Rick want to do tomorrow?**

(a) have dinner

(b) meet Yolanda's rats

(c) go to the RSA meeting

(d) make baskets

(e) play basketball

4 **What might be the RSA's slogan?**

(a) Rats are the scariest pets in the world.

(b) Rats are creepy, but they're good pets.

(c) Improving rats' image at a time

(d) Helping rats take over the world!

(e) Rats—people's favorite pets for centuries

5 **What is the talk mainly about?**

(a) advantages of having pets

(b) people who need pets

(c) disadvantages of keeping pets

(d) kinds of people who easily get sick

(e) various characteristics of pets

6 **What could be the title of the report?**

(a) Neighbors Find Dead Man

(b) Man Loved Pet Snake

(c) Man Finds Dead Snake

(d) Man Killed by Pet Snake

(e) Snake Reaches 4 Meters Long

7~8

7 **Which of the following is NOT true?**

(a) The mammoth was found in Iceland.

(b) The mammoth is 37,000 years old.

(c) Scientists are keeping the mammoth cold.

(d) The speakers think cloning the mammoth would be cool.

(e) The woman's favorite animal is elephant.

8 **Why does Jeannie find the news interesting?**

(a) Because she loves history

(b) Because she studies mammoths

(c) Because she loves animals

(d) Because it's incredible

(e) Because mammoths will be cloned

DICTATION 2

● **Listen and fill in the blanks.**

1

W What do you ________ ________ ________ when you grow up, Mitch?

M I really want to be a ________ .

W Oh, yeah? That sounds like a lot of work though.

M Yeah, I'll have to ________ ________ ________ .

W I think being a vet would be more difficult than being a doctor. There are so many ________ ________ ________ to learn about!

M That's a good point, Alice. It won't be easy, but I just love animals. I'll do ________ ________ ________ .

2

W Everyone knows that Americans ________ ________ ________ . And it seems that every year, they love them more and more as the number of pet owners is ________ ________ ________ . But what are the most popular pets? Well, you should ________ ________ ________ ________ . Here they are: 45 million homes have a dog. 38 million homes have a cat. 14 million have a fish, and 6.5 million have a bird. It seems that dog is still man's best friend, but cats are ________ ________ !

3~4

M Hey, Yolanda. Do you want to ________ ________ ________ tomorrow?

W Sorry, Rick, but I can't. I'm busy.

M How about ________ ________ ________ ?

W Sorry, I have an RSA meeting tomorrow.

M RSA? What's that?

W The Rat Society of America.

M You like ________ ?

W Yes. In fact, I have three.

M That's just ________ . So, what do you do at your rat meetings?

W We just talk about ways to make the world ________ ________ ________ rats. Do you want to come? You can meet my rats.

M I think I'll pass.

5 W Did you know that ____________________ can actually be good for you?
Recently, there has been a lot of research into the __________ of owning pets, and the
results are surprising. People who own pets go to the doctor ________________.
Sick people who own pets live longer. ________________ that part of the reason
is that pets are always __________ and loyal and do not ________________. If
you were considering getting a pet, it's probably a good idea.

---

6 M Today on Strange News, we ________________________ of a
man who was killed by his own pet. This wasn't any ________________; it was
a 4-meter-long boa constrictor. Neighbors say that the man, Mr. Cruz, had raised
the snake since it was a baby. He would ________________ to play
from time to time, but he always seemed to have ________________.
No one was present ________________, so it is unknown what
________________. "It's sad," said a neighbor. "He loved that snake."

7~8 M ________________ the news from Russia, Jeannie?
W No, Will. What news?
M They found a ________________ in the ice.
W Really? How old is it?
M They think it's 37,000 years old.
W Wow, that's __________! What are they doing with it?
M I think scientists are ________________ so it doesn't
go bad. And they're studying it of course. Wouldn't it be awesome if they could
__________ a mammoth?
W For sure. That's so interesting, especially since elephants are my favorite animals.
Mammoths must have been so cool.

I'm a Big Sports Fan

GET READY

Key Words & Expressions

● Listen to the sentences and fill in each blank with the words on the list.

1 In soccer, my ___________ is defense.

2 Don't be afraid to ___________ ___________ for your school's sports teams.

3 The English sport football is the same as the American sport of ___________.

4 Sometimes ___________ react badly to stress. In the last World Cup, 28 players received red cards.

5 In yesterday's World Cup ___________, Brazil won against Costa Rica 5:2.

6 The champions in ___________ eating are usually small people.

7 The Olympic Games ___________ ___________ every four years in ancient Greece.

8 In baseball, when you're ___________, the most important thing is to keep your eye on the ball.

9 I play hockey in the winter. I'm a ___________.

10 The ___________ game in baseball is called the World Series.

goalie	soccer	position	championship	match
athletes	were held	competitive	try out	batting

Questions & Responses

● Match the questions with the responses.

1 Do you enjoy team sports or individual sports?

2 What's your favorite sport?

3 Have you tried a lot of sports?

4 Do you follow sports news?

5 Who's your favorite athlete?

6 Do you watch sports on TV?

a Barry Bonds is the best.

b I prefer team sports.

c Yes, I read the sports section every day.

d Occasionally, but not golf. It's too boring to watch.

e Yes, I've been on a lot of teams.

f Football is my favorite sport.

● Listen and check your answers.

● Now practice with your friends.

● **Listen and take notes.**

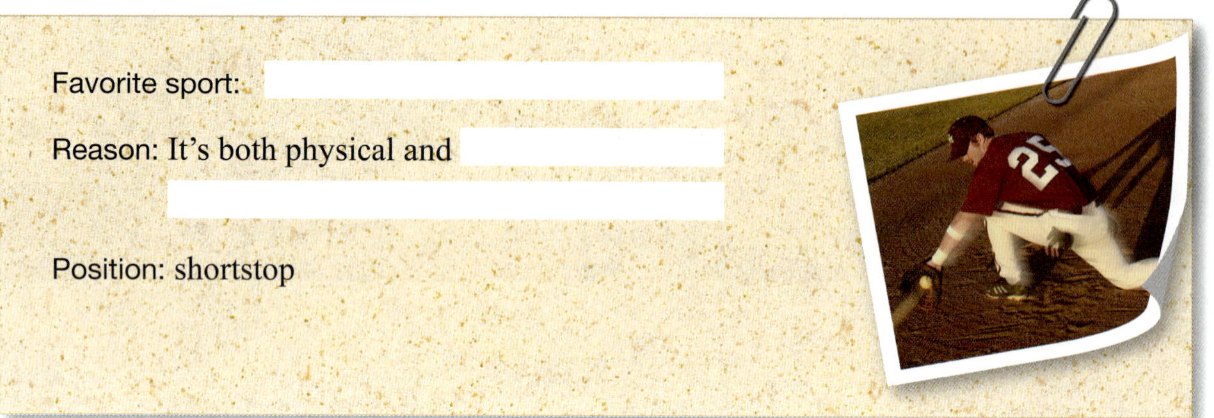

Favorite sport: ____________________

Reason: It's both physical and ____________________
____

Position: shortstop

● **Based on your notes, answer the question.**

Q **Which of the following is true about the speaker?**

(a) He likes the strategy involved in baseball.

(b) He only likes to play team sports.

(c) He is always the best player on his team.

(d) He prefers playing soccer to baseball.

■ **Listen again and fill in the blanks.**

I think I've always like sports because, as a kid, I was always __________ __________ them. I played everything from __________ to tennis to __________. Some I was better at than others, but I always enjoyed being part of a __________. After trying a lot of sports, the one I enjoyed the most and the one I was the best at was baseball. I like it because it's both __________ and it take some thought and __________. I've hit 5 homeruns so far, and my __________ is shortstop.

● 12-3

● **Listen and take notes.**

A Hockey
- __________ sport
- position is __________

B Karate
- good for __________ and __________
- helps with hockey

C Soccer
- position is __________
- has many friends on the team

D Tennis
- takes lessons from a coach
- started __________ __________

● **Based on your notes, answer the following questions.**

1 **What does Sally talk about?**

(a) her favorite sports

(b) the sports she plays

(c) her positions in different sports

(d) the sports she's good at

2 **Mark T (true) or F (false).**

(1) Sally plays forward in hockey. ______

(2) Sally has been playing sports for a long time. ______

(3) Sally plays tennis in the winter. ______

■ **Listen again and check your answers.**

Plus⁺ Question

Q1. Sally plays _____ team sports and _____ individual sports.

(a) 0 / 4   (b) 4 / 0

(c) 1 / 3   (d) 2 / 2

Q2. Why does she do karate?

(a) It's fun.

(b) It improves her strength and balance.

(c) A lot of her friends do it, too.

(d) The gym is near her house.

● **Listen and answer the questions.**

1 What do the cheese rolling winners get?

(a)   (b)   (c)   (d)

2 Check T (true) or F (false).

(1) Americans have their own sport called football.   T   F

(2) "Soccer" is the short form of "football."   T   F

(3) Americans and British use some different words.   T   F

(4) Susan's favorite sport is soccer.   T   F

3~4

3 Where are the speakers going?

(a) a golf course

(b) an ice rink

(c) a race track

(d) a football field

4 What are the "Sabres"?

(a) a type of coat

(b) a hockey player

(c) a brand name

(d) a hockey team

Note taking

1

2

3~4
They are going to _____ games.

12-5

● **Listen and answer the questions.**

1 What's the score?

  (a) 5:5   (b) 2:3   (c) 9:2

  (d) 3:5   (e) 9:5

2 Which of the following is NOT true?

  (a) Olympia, Greece, is the home of the Olympics.

  (b) Women could not be in the Olympics.

  (c) Olympic champions received olive branches.

  (d) The Olympic Games were celebrated every two years.

  (e) The Olympic Games have been around for thousands of years.

`3~5`

3 What is the talk about?

  (a) strange sports

  (b) sports for large people

  (c) Sonia Thomas, a competitive eater

  (d) competitive eating

  (e) dieting

4 What do you need in order to be a competitive eater?

  (a) a stretchy stomach   (b) a good eating habit

  (c) a big body   (d) a small body

  (e) a focused mind

5 Which is the best summary?

  (a) Competitive eaters compete to see who can eat the most. Some of the best competitive eaters are small people.

  (b) Competitive eaters compete to see who can eat the fastest. Small people always do better than big people.

Note taking

1

2
The Olympic Games
- started in ________ in 776 BC
- only ________ were allowed to be in the Olympics
- were held every ________ years

3~5

DICTATION 1

● **Listen and fill in the blanks.**

1 W When you ___________________________, you usually think about baseball, basketball, soccer, and hockey, but if you're ___________________________ these sports, don't worry. There are all kinds of lesser-known sports that you may be good at. For example, ___________________________ has been around for hundreds of years in England. In this sport, a large wheel of cheese is rolled down a steep hill, and the ___________________________. The one who gets to the bottom first wins. He or she also gets the ___________________________ cheese!

2 M What's your ___________ sport, Susan?

W Football.

M I like football, too. The Superbowl is coming up, huh?

W Uh, no, I mean English football. I guess Americans ___________________________.

M Oh, I get it. I ___________________________ Americans and British have different names for the same sport.

W I think it ___________________________ a long time. The British used the word "soccer" as the ___________________________ of the word "association." I guess it caught on with the Americans.

M Cool, I didn't know that. It's ___________________________ because we have a totally different sport called football.

W Yeah, I know.

3~4 M Are you ___________________________?

W Yep. Just let me grab some ___________________________.

M This'll be fun. I love going to hockey games.

W Yeah, me too. ___________________________ hot chocolate at the game.

M For sure.

W Are you wearing your Sabres coat?

M Of course. I have to ___________________________.

W Okay, let's go. I've got the tickets.

Exercise Step 2

● **Listen and fill in the blanks.**

1
W Are you still watching that game?
M _______ _______ _______ _______. It's the World Series!
W Huh?
M The championship game!
W Okay. When will it _______ _______? I want to watch my soap opera.
M Well, it's the _______ _______ the _______ _______. There are 3 balls and 2 strikes, and the score is 5:5. It'll be over soon enough!
W It had better be. It's the _______ _______ of my show, too.

2
W The Olympic Games _______ _______ all over the world today, but they started in a little place in _______ called Olympia in the year 776 BC. The ancient Greeks _______ their Olympic games every four years, and the games were considered a very important event. Only men _______ _______ to be in the Olympics, and they _______ _______ for the important festival. The winners were given an _______ _______.

3~5
M One sport that definitely isn't for everybody is _______ _______. Competitive eaters _______ _______ eating contests to see who can eat the most of a _______ _______ _______ food. The interesting thing about this sport is that you don't need to be a big person to win. Some of the _______ _______ are very thin, small people. You just need a stomach that _______ _______. For example, one of the best competitive eaters, Sonia Thomas, is only 44kg, but she can eat 5kg of cheesecake in 9 minutes!

PRACTICE TEST

1 **What are the speakers watching?**

(a) golf

(b) figure skating

(c) baseball

(d) volleyball

(e) soccer

2 **Fill in the graph.**

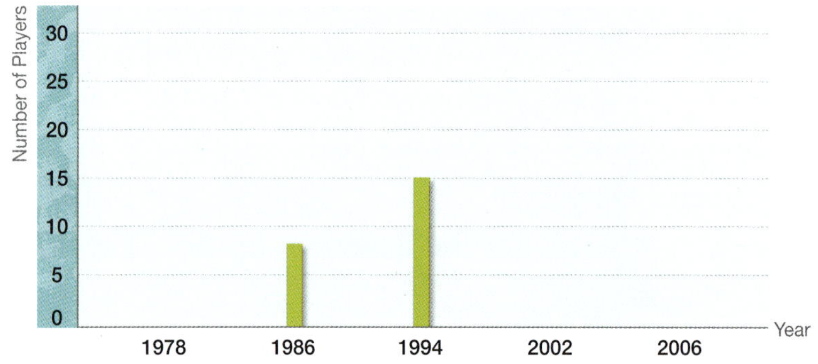

3~4

3 **What is the relationship between Ada and the man?**

(a) player – fan

(b) student – teacher

(c) player – coach

(d) daughter - father

(e) girlfriend – boyfriend

4 **What does "break a leg" mean?**

(a) Don't break your leg.

(b) Good luck.

(c) Hurry up.

(d) Hit the ball.

(e) Break the bat.

5   **What was NOT a rule for women's baseball in the 1940s?**

(a) They had to wear makeup.

(b) They played on a smaller field.

(c) They wore skirts.

(d) They used a special ball.

(e) They threw the ball underhanded.

6   **How is speed golf different than regular golf?**

(a) You play on a team.

(b) You play early in the morning.

(c) You complete a longer golf course.

(d) You have a time limit.

(e) You run from hole to hole.

7~8

7   **How does Greg feel about trying out for the basketball team?**

(a) hopeful

(b) optimistic

(c) terrified

(d) pessimistic

(e) excited

8   **What expression best describes the woman's advice?**

(a) Quitters never win, and winners never quit.

(b) Practice makes perfect.

(c) Blood is thicker than water.

(d) He can't cut the mustard.

(e) Great minds think alike.

DICTATION 2

● **Listen and fill in the blanks.**

1 M Wow, she ___________ great.

W Yeah, that was beautiful. I bet she'll get a perfect score.

M You think? I'm ___________ ___________.

W Here it comes… What? Only 8.2? But she was the best! She didn't ___________ ___________, and her ___________ was perfect!

M I think there's a lot about the ___________ we don't know, Kelly.

W Well, that's not right.

M Of course not, but that's the way it works. Hopefully no one will ___________. Keep your ___________.

2 W There is ___________ that the competition in the World Cup gets tougher and tougher every year. With so much stress on the soccer players to win for their country, they're sure to ___________ and do bad things that earn them red cards. As time ___________, more and more players are getting red cards. In 1978, 3 players received red cards. In 1986, 8 players ___________. In 1994, 15 players were given red cards. 2002 saw 17 players sent off the field. And, finally, in the most ___________, 25 players were given the ___________ red card.

3~4 M Are you ready, Ada?

W Yeah.

M Okay, go out there and ___________ best shot. Hit one out of the park for me and your mom.

W I will.

M And remember to ___________ on the ball. Never take your eye off the ball. Got it?

W Yeah, yeah! I ___________!

M Okay, go on. You're almost ___________.

W Thanks.

M ___________!

5 W The first ___________ was founded in the U.S. in 1943. Many male baseball players ___________ in World War II, so women were happy to keep the sport alive. But there were some "special" rules for women players. For example, they had to wear skirts, and they ___________. They also played on a smaller field and threw the ball ___________. Although this was a strange introduction for women into professional baseball, these first women players ___________ the way for women athletes today.

---

6 M Have you ever wanted to play golf, but you didn't have any free time? Try speed golf! It's like regular golf, but you run from hole to hole ___________ your clubs. Your score is a ___________ of the time it takes you to ___________ a regular course plus your ___________. It's great for keeping fit, too! The Speed Golf Association meets on Saturday mornings at 7:00 a.m. at the Greenways Golf Course. Come and ___________!

7~8 W Are you ___________ for the basketball team this year, Greg?
M Oh, I don't know.
W What do you mean?
M I think I'm going to ___________.
W What? But you love playing basketball.
M I know, but all the guys are taller than me this year. I'm not ___________.
W Well, you can't be the best every year. And how do you know ___________?
M Yeah, I guess so.
W ___________ yet, Greg.

Academic Listening Builder

다양한 학문 분야의 광범위한 배경지식과 어휘력 향상에 효과적인 듣기 프로그램

- 인문학, 예술, 사회과학, 자연과학, 생명과학에 속하는 다양한 학문 분야별 강의 수록
- 토플에서 다뤄지는 주제를 반영한 광범위한 듣기 주제 포함
- 주요 학문 분야 소개와 진로 탐색 질문을 통한 학습자 동기 유발과 과목 이해도 향상
- 학술적인 강의 이해에 필요한 기본 어휘 학습과 어휘 확장 활동을 통한 어휘력 증강
- 특목고 대비, 토플 입문, 수능 대비에 적합한 교재

교재	구성	페이지	가격
Academic Listening Builder ①	교재 + MP3 CD 1개	244 pages	16,000원
Academic Listening Builder ②	교재 + MP3 CD 1개	244 pages	16,000원
Academic Listening Builder ③	교재 + MP3 CD 1개	244 pages	16,000원

Listen to the MAX

탄탄한 듣기 실력을 다지고자 하는 상위권 중학생들을 위한 3단계 리스닝 훈련서

- 갈수록 범위가 넓어져가고 있는 영어듣기 시험에 대비하기 위한 시험에 잘 나오는 16개의 다양한 토픽을 수록
- 각 토픽 별로 꼭 알아두어야 하는 단어와 표현을 집중 학습
- 1~3권을 학습해나갈수록 길고 어려워지는 지문과 다양하고 풍부한 유형의 문제들
- Dictation Test를 통한 기본 리스닝 실력 다지기

교재	구성	페이지	가격
Listen to the MAX ①	교재 + 해설집 + 무료 MP3 다운로드	본책 152 pages + 해설집 80 pages	15,000원
Listen to the MAX ②	교재 + 해설집 + 무료 MP3 다운로드	본책 160 pages + 해설집 98 pages	17,000원
Listen to the MAX ③	교재 + 해설집 + 무료 MP3 다운로드	본책 176 pages + 해설집 108 pages	17,000원

Listening AVIATOR RUN 1

Answer Book

Listening AVIATOR RUN 1

Answer Book

DARAKWON

It's Great to Meet You

Answers

GET READY p. 8~9

Key Words & Expressions

1 Welcome to   2 after school   3 listening to
4 class   5 great to meet   6 grew up
7 lives in   8 subject   9 enjoys
10 take photos

Questions & Responses

1 e   2 d   3 f   4 c   5 b   6 a

BASIC DRILL p. 10~11

Step 1 ● 13 / 9 / gym, art / reading comic books, playing basketball

　　Q (c)

　　■ name, years, area, grade, subjects, hobbies, shoot baskets

Step 2 A California / cold weather
　　B acting / drama club
　　C 15 / hiking
　　D fishing
　　1 (c)   2 (1) T   (2) T   (3) F

Plus⁺ Question   1 (b)   2 (d)

EXERCISE p. 12~13

Step 1　1 (c)   2 (1) F (2) T (3) F (4) F   3 (a)   4 (b)
Step 2　1 (a)   2 (c)   3 (a)   4 (c)   5 (a)

PRACTICE TEST p. 16~17

1 (a)
2

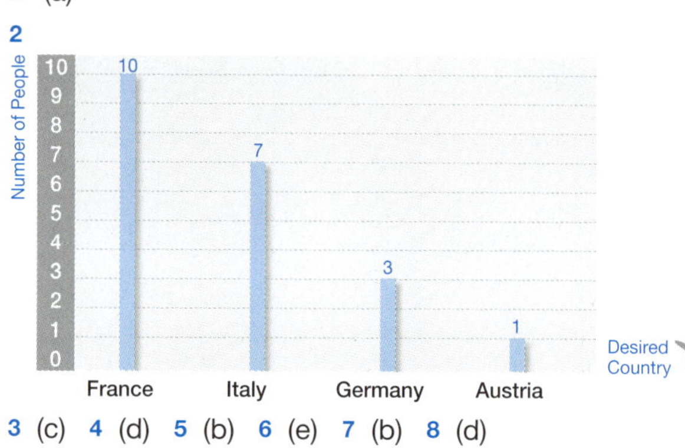

3 (c)   4 (d)   5 (b)   6 (e)   7 (b)   8 (d)

* Dictation 1, 2의 정답은 각 Script의 밑줄친 부분임.

Scripts and Translations

GET READY

Key Words & Expressions

다음 문장을 듣고 보기 박스에서 알맞은 단어를 골라 빈칸을 채우시오.

1 이 동아리에 온 걸 환영해! 뭘 그리고 싶니?

2 내 여동생은 꽤 뛰어난 테니스 선수야. 그애는 방과 후에 매일 연습을 하지.

3 전 록음악 듣고 영화 보는 것을 좋아해요.

4 피터랑 저는 켈리 선생님 과학 수업을 같이 들어요.

5 만나서 반가워요. 언제 한번 전화주세요.

6 전 작은 동네에서 자랐어요. 다소 지루했죠.

7 젠킨스 부인은 모퉁이에 있는 큰 집에 살아요.

8 그가 제일 좋아하는 과목은 음악인데요. 역사는 형편 없어요.

9 글로리아는 야외 스포츠를 즐겨. 항상 하이킹을 하거나 수영을 한다니까.

10 난 학교 신문 동아리에서 쓸 사진을 찍어.

Questions & Responses

질문에 어울리는 대답과 연결하시오.

1 어디에 살아?　　　　　　　ⓔ 네바다 주 해밀턴에 살아.

2 몇 살이니?　　　　　　　　ⓓ 열일곱 살이야.

3 취미가 뭐야?　　　　　　　ⓕ 하이킹하고 음악 듣는 걸 좋아해.

4 가장 좋아하는 수업은 뭐야?　ⓒ 음악과 수학이 가장 좋아.

5 너네 학교 이름은 뭐니?　　　ⓑ 캐니언 고등학교야.

6 학교 생활은 어때?　　　　　ⓐ 좋아. 학교 생활을 즐기고 있어.

들고 정답을 확인하시오.

친구와 함께 연습하시오.

Basic Drill Step 1

다음을 듣고 메모하시오.

M Hi there. My name is Sean Brownson, and I'm 13 years old. I live in Niagara Falls, Canada, which is a pretty cool area. I just started grade nine at Laura Secord High School. So far, high school is difficult, but I like it. Gym and art are my favorite subjects. My hobbies are reading comic books and playing basketball. On the weekend, my friend Alex and I get together and shoot baskets.

▶ pretty 꽤, 상당히 so far 지금까지 shoot (스포츠) 골을 향해 (공을) 던지다

남　안녕, 내 이름은 션 브라운슨이고 열세 살이야. 나는 캐나다의 나이아가라 폭포 지역에 사는데, 진짜 멋진 곳이지. 나는 로라 세코드 고등학교에서 9학년이 된 지 얼마 안 됐어. 아직까지는 고등학교 과정이 어렵지만 마음에 들어. 체육과 미술이 내가 가장 좋아하는 과목이야. 취미는 만화책 읽는 것과 농구하는 거야. 주말에는 내 친구 알렉스랑 함께 모여 농구를 해.

메모를 바탕으로 다음 문제에 답하시오.

Q 화자는 주로 무엇에 관해 이야기하고 있는가?

  (a) 고등학교 과정이 어려운 이유

  (b) 가장 좋아하는 수업들

  (c) 고등학교 생활

  (d) 취미와 소일거리

■　다시 듣고 빈칸을 채우시오.

Basic Drill　Step 2

다음을 듣고 메모하시오.

W1　Hi, I'm Diane. My friends just call me Di. I grew up in Wisconsin, but now I live in California. I don't like cold weather, so I just love California. The beaches are great.

M1　My name is Steve, and I go to Rosemont High School. At first, I didn't like high school, but it's going better now. I love acting, so I joined the drama club.

W2　I'm Clare, and I'm 15 years old. I love outdoor sports like hiking and mountain biking. Camping is my favorite thing to do, and I usually do that twice a year with my family.

M2　Hello, I'm Derek. I live in a beautiful little town called Bellevue. Some people think it's a boring town, but I love it. My hobby is fishing. There's a nice river near my home where I like to fish.

▶ **beach** 해변　**acting** 연기　**outdoor sports** 야외 스포츠

여1　안녕, 나는 다이앤이야. 내 친구들은 그냥 다이라고 불러. 위스콘신에서 자랐지만 지금은 캘리포니아에서 살아. 나는 추운 날씨를 싫어해서 캘리포니아가 좋아. 해변도 정말 멋져.

남1　내 이름은 스티브고, 로즈먼트 고등학교에 다녀. 처음엔 고등학교가 싫었는데 지금은 나아지고 있어. 연기하는 걸 좋아해서 연극반에 들었지.

여2　나는 클레어고 열다섯 살이야. 하이킹이나 산악 자전거 타기 같은 야외 스포츠를 좋아해. 캠핑은 내가 가장 좋아하는 일이라서 보통 일 년에 두 번 가족들과 캠핑을 가.

남2　안녕, 나는 데렉이야. 벨레뷰라는 아름답고 자그마한 동네에 살아. 어떤 사람들은 이곳이 지루한 동네라고 생각하지만, 나는 정말 맘에 들어. 내 취미는 낚시야. 우리 집 근처에 멋진 강이 있는데, 거기서 낚시하는 걸 좋아해.

메모를 바탕으로 다음 문제에 답하시오.

1 화자들은 주로 무엇에 관해 이야기하고 있는가?

  (a) 자기들의 학교 생활

  (b) 야외 활동

  (c) 자기들이 좋아하는 것과 싫어하는 것

  (d) 학교 동아리

2 맞으면 T, 틀리면 F를 쓰시오.

  (1) 다이앤은 추운 날씨를 좋아하지 않는다.

  (2) 스티브는 연극반 회원이다.

  (3) 데렉은 자기 집 근처에 있는 강에서 수영을 한다.

다시 듣고 정답을 확인하시오.

Plus⁺ Question

1 클레어가 가장 하기 좋아하는 것은 무엇인가?

  (a) 스키타는 것　　　　(b) 캠핑하는 것

  (c) 스포츠 경기하는 것　(d) 해변에 가는 것

2 데렉은 자기 동네가 __________고 생각한다.

  (a) 지루하다　　　　(b) 너무 작다

  (c) 너무 조용하다　　(d) 아름답다

EXERCISE　Step 1

듣고 문제에 답하시오.

❶

W　Hi. Is this the photography club meeting?

M　Yes, it is. Come on in.

W　Oh, good. Sorry I'm late.

M　No problem. Tell us about yourself.

W　Okay. My name's Tammy. I'm in the 10th grade, and I love taking photos.

M　Then you're in the right place! Great to meet you.

W　I'm happy to be here. Oh, should I bring my camera to meetings?

M　Sure. We'll start taking pictures right away.

▶ **grade** 학년　**take photos/pictures** 사진을 찍다　**bring** 가져오다 **right away** 곧, 즉시

여　안녕. 여기가 사진 동아리 모임이니?

남　응, 맞아. 어서 들어와.

여　그렇구나. 늦어서 미안해.

남　괜찮아. 네 소개 좀 해줘.

여　그래. 내 이름은 태미야. 10학년이고 사진 찍는 걸 좋아해.

남　그럼 제대로 온 거네! 만나서 반가워.

여　나도 여기 오게 돼서 좋아. 그럼, 모임에 카메라를 가져와야 하니?

남　물론이지. 당장 사진 촬영을 시작할 거야.

1 태미가 모임에 필요한 것은 무엇인가?

(a) 　(b) 　(c) 　(d) 

❷

M　Thanks, Janice, for letting me interview you.

W　It's my pleasure.

M　Tell us about your life before you were a famous actress.

W　Oh, wow, well… I had a great childhood. I grew up in small-town Australia. I moved to New York when I was 14.

M　What were your favorite subjects in school?

W　I was really good at math and science. I was terrible at history.

M　Did you enjoy acting as a child?

W　Yes, I did. My friends and I put on plays for our neighbors. It was great fun.

▶ interview 인터뷰하다   childhood 어린 시절   put on plays 연극을 상연하다   neighbor 이웃

남　인터뷰할 수 있게 해줘서 고마워요, 재니스.
여　별 말씀을요.
남　유명 여배우가 되기 전의 삶에 대해 얘기 좀 해주세요.
여　음, 글쎄요. 멋진 유년 시절을 보냈죠. 호주의 작은 마을에서 자랐고요. 열네 살 때 뉴욕으로 이주했어요.
남　학교 다닐 때 가장 좋아하던 과목은 뭐였어요?
여　수학이랑 과학을 정말 잘했어요. 역사는 아주 형편없었죠.
남　어릴 때도 연기하는 걸 좋아했어요?
여　네, 좋아했어요. 친구들이랑 전 이웃분들을 모셔놓고 연극을 공연했었죠. 정말 즐거웠어요.

2　맞으면 T, 틀리면 F에 체크하시오.
(1) 재니스는 미국에서 태어났다.
(2) 재니스는 과학을 좋아했다.
(3) 재니스는 선생님이다.
(4) 재니스는 어릴 때 영화에서 연기했다.

3~4

W　Can I sit here?
M　Sure, go ahead.
W　What are you reading?
M　It's a gaming magazine.
W　Cool. I love gaming. My favorite game is *Dark Worlds*.
M　Really? Me too! My handle is *darkboy12*.
W　Nice. Online, I'm *gamegirl1991*.
M　Awesome. So, what's your real name?
W　It's Jane. You?
M　Troy. Are you new at this school?
W　Yeah, I just moved here from Cleveland.

▶ go ahead. 어서, 먼저 해.　magazine 잡지　handle 통신용 별명; 손잡이　awesome 아주 멋진　move 이사하다

여　여기 앉아도 되니?
남　그럼. 어서 앉아.
여　뭐 읽고 있어?
남　게임 잡지야.
여　멋진걸. 나는 게임을 좋아해. 가장 좋아하는 게임은 〈다크월드〉야.
남　정말? 나도 그런데! 내 온라인 이름은 '다크보이12'야.
여　좋다. 온라인에서 나는 '게임걸1991'이야.
남　아주 멋져. 그럼, 진짜 이름은 뭐야?
여　제인. 너는?
남　트로이. 이 학교로 전학 왔니?
여　응, 클리블랜드에서 이사온 지 얼마 안 됐어.

3　화자들의 온라인상 이름은 무엇인가?
(a) 다크보이12와 게임걸1991
(b) 다크보이1919와 게임걸12
(c) 다크걸12와 게임월드1991
(d) 다크보이12와 다크걸1919

4　트로이와 제인 둘 다 무엇을 하기 좋아하는가?
(a) 인터넷 서핑　　　　(b) 온라인 게임 하기
(c) 잡지 읽기　　　　　(d) 온라인 채팅 하기

Exercise　Step 2

들고 문제에 답하시오.

W　Oh, hello. You moved in yesterday, didn't you? I'm Cindy.
M　Yes, that's right. I'm Daniel.
W　Nice to meet you, Daniel. Welcome to the apartment building. I'm upstairs in number 602.
M　I moved to number 502. Nice to meet you, too.
W　So, are you from Wellington?
M　Yes, I grew up here.
W　No way! Where?
M　Down on Drake Road.
W　What? On Drake Road? I used to live in the big house on the corner!
M　Are you serious? Wow! What a small world!

▶ upstairs 위층　on the corner 모퉁이에　used to (과거에) ~하곤 했다, ~했었다

여　안녕하세요. 어제 이사오셨죠? 저는 신디에요.
남　예, 맞습니다. 저는 대니얼입니다.
여　만나서 반가워요, 대니얼. 이 아파트에 이사온 걸 환영합니다. 저는 위층 602호에 살아요.
남　저는 502호에 이사왔어요. 저도 반갑습니다.
여　그럼, 웰링턴 출신이세요?
남　네, 여기서 자랐어요.
여　그럴 리가! 웰링턴 어디요?
남　드레이크 로드 아래쪽이요.
여　네? 드레이크 로드요? 저 그 모퉁이에 있는 큰 집에서 살았어요!
남　정말이요? 와! 세상 정말 좁네요!

1　화자들의 관계는 무엇인가?
(a) 이웃　　　　　　　　(b) 동료
(c) 남자친구와 여자친구　(d) 어머니와 아들
(e) 교사와 학생

2

M　Hey, guys! We have a new player this week. This is my cousin Andrew. He's 16, just like me. We don't see each other often because he lives in New Zealand. He's visiting London for two weeks, so I thought he could play soccer with us today. What do you think? He's a great soccer player, so don't worry. Oh, you should see him on a skateboard! He's so cool! Well, enough talking. Let's get this game started!

▶ cousin 사촌　cool 멋진　enough 충분히　Let's get ~ started! ~을 시작하자!

남　얘들아! 이번 주에는 새로 들어온 선수가 있어. 내 사촌 앤드류인데 나와 같은 열여섯 살 동갑이야. 앤드류가 뉴질랜드에 살아서 서로 자주 보지는 못해. 2주 동안 런던을 방문하는 중이라서 오늘 우리랑 함께 축구를 할 수 있을 거라고 생각했지. 어떻게 생각해? 앤드류는 축구를 정말 잘하니까 걱정마. 아, 앤드류가 스케이트보드 타는 모습도 봐야 하는데! 정말 멋지거든! 음, 얘기는 충분히 한 것 같다. 우리 경기 시작하자!

2 다음 중 사실이 <u>아닌</u> 것은?

(a) 화자와 앤드류는 사촌이다.

(b) 화자와 앤드류는 열여섯 살이다.

(c) 앤드류는 런던에 산다.

(d) 앤드류는 스케이트보드를 잘 탄다.

(e) 화자와 앤드류는 축구를 한다.

3~5

W Hi, Sandra! Thanks for your letter. It's great to be your pen pal. My name's Julie. I'm 12 years old, and I'm in the 9th grade. I live in Cape Town, which is a very pretty city in South Africa. A lot of people come to Cape Town to go surfing and to go on safari. You can see some pretty cool animals here! I'd love to hear more about your home. What's it like in Alaska? Write back soon! Your new friend, Julie.

▶ safari 〈사냥 등의〉 원정 여행

여 안녕, 샌드라! 편지 고마워. 너와 펜팔이 돼서 참 좋다. 내 이름은 줄리야. 열두 살이고 9학년이지. 난 남아프리카의 매우 멋진 도시인 케이프 타운에 살아. 많은 사람들이 서핑하고 사냥 여행을 가려고 케이프 타운에 오지. 여기서 매우 멋진 동물들을 볼 수가 있어! 네 고향에 대해서 더 많이 듣고 싶다. 알래스카는 어떠니? 곧 답장해줘! 너의 친구, 줄리.

3 줄리는 주로 무엇에 관해 이야기하고 있는가?

(a) 자기 고향   (b) 야생 사냥 여행

(c) 알래스카에서의 생활   (d) 펜팔이 되는 것

(e) 여행하는 것

4 줄리에 대해 뭐라고 추측할 수 있는가?

(a) 전혀 사냥 여행을 가지 않는다.

(b) 여행하는 것을 좋아한다.

(c) 알래스카를 가본 적이 없다.

(d) 케이프 타운을 정말로 좋아하는 것은 아니다.

(e) 알래스카로 이사가고 싶어한다.

5 내용을 가장 잘 요약한 것은 무엇인가?

(a) 줄리는 알래스카에 사는 새 펜팔 샌드라에게 편지를 쓴다.

(b) 줄리는 케이프 타운 방문에 관심이 있는 자기 친구, 샌드라에게 편지를 쓴다.

PRACTICE TEST

들고 문제에 답하시오.

1

M I'm Tom. I'm 16 years old, and I'm from Ottawa, the capital of Canada. I love to draw pictures in my free time. I usually draw pictures of characters from animated movies. For example, I can draw a lot of Disney characters. I take a special drawing class on weekends. Maybe you'll see my drawings in some animated movies some day.

▶ capital 수도   draw 그리다   character 〈만화의〉 캐릭터: 등장인물   animated movies 만화영화

남 나는 탐이야. 열여섯 살이고 캐나다의 수도인 오타와 출신이지. 여가 시간에 그림 그리는 것을 좋아해. 대개 만화영화 캐릭터를 그려. 예를 들면, 디즈니 캐릭터를 많이 그릴 수 있어. 주말엔 그림 특강을 들어. 언젠가 어떤 만화영화에서 내 그림을 볼 수 있을 거야.

1 탐은 주로 무엇을 그리는가?

(a)    (b)    (c) 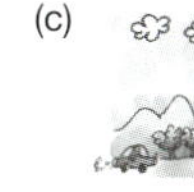

(d)    (e) 

2

W Hi, I'm Alison. This is my first time at the travel club.

M Welcome. I'm Tony.

W Glad to meet you. So, Tony, what does the travel club do?

M Every year we go on a different trip.

W Oh, wow! That's great. Where are we going this year?

M Well, we took a vote last week. 10 people want to go to France, 7 people want to go to Italy, 3 people want to go to Germany, and 1 person wants to go to Austria.

W Looks like we're going to France. Great!

▶ take a vote 표결에 부치다

여 안녕, 나는 앨리슨이야. 여행 동아리에 처음 나왔어.

남 어서 와. 나는 토니야.

여 만나서 반가워. 토니, 여행 동아리에서 무엇을 하니?

남 우리는 해마다 다른 곳으로 여행 가.

여 와, 좋다! 올해는 어디 갈 거니?

남 음, 지난주에 투표를 했는데, 10명은 프랑스, 7명은 이탈리아, 3명은 독일, 1명은 오스트리아에 가고 싶어하지.

여 프랑스로 갈 것 같네. 좋다!

Level up

2 그래프에 여행 동아리 투표 결과를 나타내시오.

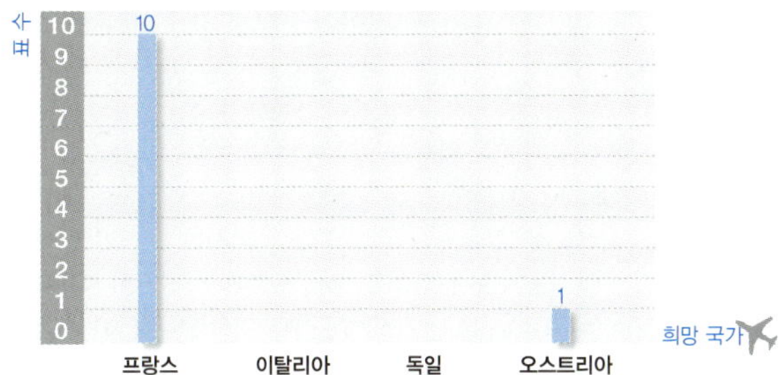

3~4

W Can I sit here?

M Sure, why not?

W Thanks. When does this class start?

M Um, I think in five minutes.

W   Ugh, I hate the first day of school.
M   Me too. By the way, I'm James.
W   I'm Lucy. How are your classes so far?
M   Not good at all. Gym is okay, but everything else is terrible.
W   Sorry to hear that. My classes aren't looking good, either.
M   Oh, no. The teacher's coming.

▶ **hate** 싫어하다   **by the way** 그런데   **gym** 체육

여   여기 앉아도 되니?
남   그럼, 물론이지.
여   고마워. 이 수업 언제 시작해?
남   음, 5분 뒤에 시작할 것 같은데.
여   아, 난 수업 첫날이 싫어.
남   나도 그래. 참, 나는 제임스야.
여   나는 루시야. 지금까지 들은 수업은 어땠니?
남   다 별로야. 체육은 괜찮지만 다른 것들은 다 끔찍해.
여   유감이다. 내 수업들도 좋아 보이진 않아.
남   아, 선생님 오시네.

3   루시와 제임스는 어디에 있는가?

(a) 도서관에   (b) 체육관에   (c) 교실에

(d) 카페테리아에   (e) 운동장에

4   수업에 대한 학생들의 태도는 어떠한가?

(a) 들떠 있다.
(b) 괜찮다고 생각한다.
(c) 맘에 들어 한다.
(d) 좋아하지 않는다.
(e) 선생님을 좋아하지 않는다.

5

M   Thank you for interviewing me. Let me tell you about myself. My name's Bradley Thomas, and I'm in the fifth grade at Glendale Elementary School. I love riding my bike, and I think that will help me in this job. I finish school at 2:30, so I have lots of free time to deliver newspapers. Also, I grew up in this neighborhood, so I know the houses well. I think I'm the perfect person for this job.

▶ **interview** 면접하다   **deliver** 배달하다   **neighborhood** 지역, 인근

남   면접 기회를 주셔서 감사합니다. 제 소개를 하겠습니다. 이름은 브래들리 토마스고요, 그렌델 초등학교 5학년입니다. 저는 자전거 타는 것을 좋아해서, 이 일을 하는 데 도움이 될 것 같아요. 2시 30분에 학교가 끝나니까 신문 배달할 여유시간도 많고요. 또 이 지역에서 자라서, 집들도 잘 알아요. 제가 이 일에 적임인 것 같습니다.

5   브래들리는 무엇을 하고 있는가?

(a) 선생님과 이야기하고 있다.
(b) 면접을 보고 있다.
(c) 전화 통화를 하고 있다.
(d) 친구에게 이야기하고 있다.
(e) 신문을 사고 있다.

6

W   Hello? Oh, hi. Is this Peter Fulling? Hi, I'm Jenny Stewart. I saw your ad in the newspaper about your dog for sale. I understand that you want a good home for your dog. I'm 14 years old, and I'm in high school. I finish school every day at 3:00, so I have plenty of time to walk the dog. I just love dogs. I know I can give your dog a good home. [...] Sure, call me any time after 3:00. Have a good day! Bye!

▶ **ad** 광고   **for sale** 팔려고 내 놓은   **plenty of** 많은

여   여보세요? 안녕하세요. 피터 풀링 씨세요? 예, 저는 제니 스튜어트라고 합니다. 신문에서 개를 판다고 광고 내신 걸 봤어요. 개에게 좋은 가정을 주고 싶어하시는 점 이해합니다. 저는 열네 살이고, 고등학생이에요. 매일 3시에 학교가 끝나니까 개 산책시킬 시간은 충분해요. 저는 정말 개를 좋아해요. 제가 아저씨 개에게 좋은 가정을 줄 수 있을 것 같은데요. 그럼요, 3시 이후에 언제든지 전화하세요. 좋은 하루 보내시고, 안녕히 계세요!

6   피터 풀링이 마지막에 제니에게 뭐라고 말했을 것 같은가?

(a) 내 개를 가져도 된단다.
(b) 넌 내 개한테 맞는 사람이 아니야.
(c) 학교 언제 끝나니?
(d) 통화해서 반가웠다.
(e) 내가 다시 전화해도 되겠니?

7~8

W   Hi. Great party, huh?
M   Yeah, I'm having a great time.
W   That's good. I'm Linda.
M   Hi, Linda. I'm Jack.
W   Very nice to meet you, Jack.
M   Nice to meet you, too. So, how long have you known the host, Alex?
W   He's an old classmate of mine.
M   Is that right? I went to school with Alex, too!
W   Really? That's so weird. Wait a minute. Did you have math with Mr. Watts?
M   Yeah, good old Mr. Watts! Are you Linda Robins?
W   Yes! Jack Powers? This is so weird! Long time no see!

▶ **host** (손님을 접대하는) 주인   **classmate** 학급 친구   **weird** 기묘한   **good old** 그리운; 제법 괜찮은

여   안녕. 파티 근사하지?
남   응, 진짜 재미있어.
여   잘 됐다. 난 린다야.
남   안녕, 린다. 난 잭이야.
여   만나서 매우 반가워, 잭.
남   나도 만나서 반가워. 이 파티를 연 알렉스와 안 지는 얼마나 됐니?
여   알렉스는 내 오랜 반 친구야.
남   그래? 나도 알렉스와 함께 학교를 다녔는데!
여   정말? 신기하네. 잠깐! 혹시 왓츠 선생님 수학 수업 들었니?
남   응. 그 근사하셨던 왓츠 선생님! 그럼 네가 린다 로빈스니?
여   응! 잭 파워스? 정말 희한한 일이네! 오랜만이야!

7 상황을 가장 잘 설명하고 있는 표현은 무엇인가?

(a) 끝이 좋으면 다 좋다.

(b) 세상 참 좁다.

(c) 그는 양의 탈을 쓴 늑대다.

(d) 잠 자는 개를 건드리지 마라. (긁어 부스럼 만들지 마라.)

(e) 눈에서 멀어지면 마음에서 멀어진다.

8 왓츠 씨는 누구인가?

(a) 잭의 친구

(b) 파티 주최자

(c) 린다의 오랜 학급 친구

(d) 선생님

(e) 알렉스의 아버지

Unit 2   I Go to the Gym Every Day

Answers

GET READY   p. 20~21

Key Words & Expressions

1 goes off	**2** lead	**3** morning person
4 exercise	**5** get enough sleep	
6 homework	**7** every day	**8** on my way
9 tired of	**10** getting up	

Questions & Responses

1 d   **2** b   **3** a   **4** f   **5** e   **6** c

BASIC DRILL   p. 22~23

Step 1   • toast with juice / 8:00 / 9:00

   Q (b)

   ■ get up, Every day, take a shower, usually, catch the bus, hang out

Step 2   **A** hockey practice   **B** in the morning

   C tired, 9:00   **D** football / basketball

   1 (b)   **2** (1) F (2) T (3) T

Plus⁺ Question   **1** (d)   **2** (d)

EXERCISE   p. 24~25

Step 1   **1** (b)   **2** (c)   **3** (d)   **4** (c)

Step 2   **1** (c) → (d) → (a) → (e) → (b)   **2** (1) T (2) T (3) F (4) F (5) T   **3** (d)   **4** (b)   **5** (a)

PRACTICE TEST   p. 28~29

1 (d)

2

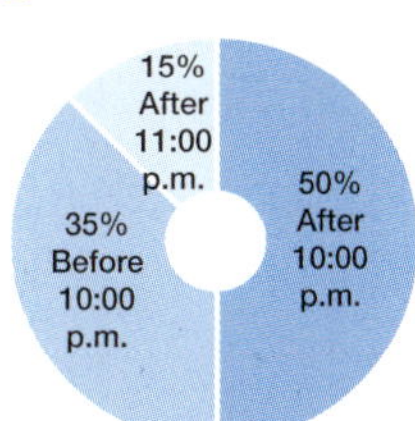

3 (e)   **4** (d)   **5** (a)   **6** (b)   **7** (c)   **8** (d)

* Dictation 1, 2의 정답은 각 Script의 밑줄친 부분임.

Scripts and Translations

GET READY

Key Words & Expressions

다음 문장을 듣고 보기 박스에서 알맞은 단어를 골라 빈칸을 채우시오.

1 나는 보통 알람 시계가 울릴 때 일어나.

2 요즘은 많은 아이들이 바쁘게 삽니다.

3 젝은 아침형 인간이 아니야. 걔는 늘 수업에 늦어.

4 많은 사람들이 일하러 가기 전 아침에 운동합니다.

5 많은 아이들이 너무 늦게 잠자리에 들어서 잠을 충분히 못 자.

6 나는 개 산책시킬 시간이 없어! 해야 할 숙제가 있거든.

7 걔네들은 매일 점심때마다 같은 테이블에 앉아.

8 나는 학교 가는 길에 남동생을 탁아소에 데려다 줘야 해.

9 바쁜 스케줄에 신물이 나. 난 휴가가 필요해.

10 버스를 또 놓쳤다고? 더 일찍 일어나도록 해봐.

Questions & Responses

질문에 어울리는 대답과 연결하시오.

1 몇 시에 일어나니?   ⓓ 7시 30분까지는 일어나려고 해.

2 제일 먼저 뭘 해?   ⓑ 항상 먼저 아침을 먹어.

3 아침식사로 뭘 먹니?   ⓐ 보통 시리얼이랑 과일을 먹어.

4 밤에 샤워하니, 아침에 샤워하니? ⓕ 아침에 해. 그래야 잠이 깨거든.

5 1교시는 언제 시작해? ⓔ 수업은 8시 30분에 시작해.

6 학교엔 어떻게 가니? ⓒ 날씨가 좋을 때는 자전거 타고 가.

듣고 정답을 확인하시오.

친구와 함께 연습하시오.

Basic Drill <u>Step 1</u>

다음을 듣고 메모하시오.

M I get up at about 7:00 a.m. in the morning. Every day, my mom yells upstairs to make sure I'm awake. Then, I take a shower and go downstairs for breakfast, which is usually eggs and toast with juice. I usually have to rush out the door at 8:00 to catch the bus. Luckily, it stops right in front of my house. Once I'm at school, I hang out with my friends until class starts at 9:00.

▶ yell 소리치다 upstairs 위층에 take a shower 샤워를 하다 rush out 급히 달려나가다 hang out 슬슬 거닐다. ~와 어울리다

남 난 아침 7시 정도에 일어나. 엄마는 매일 내가 일어났는지 확인하시려고 위층에다 소리를 지르셔. 그리고 나서 난 샤워하고 아래층에 내려가 아침 식사를 해. 아침은 보통 달걀이랑 토스트에 주스지. 8시면 버스 타려고 후다닥 문밖으로 뛰어나가야 해. 다행스럽게도 버스는 우리 집 바로 앞에 서. 일단 학교에 도착하면 9시에 수업 시작할 때까지 친구들과 시간을 보내.

메모를 바탕으로 다음 문제에 답하시오.

Q 화자에 대한 내용 중 사실인 것은?
   (a) 늘 아침 식사로 시리얼을 먹는다.
   (b) 9시 전에 학교에 도착한다.
   (c) 걸어서 학교에 간다.
   (d) 식사한 후에 샤워한다.

■ 다시 듣고 빈칸을 채우시오.

Basic Drill <u>Step 2</u>

다음을 듣고 메모하시오.

W1 I'm Cindy. I think I have a busier day than most people. I have to get up every morning at 5:00 a.m. to go to hockey practice before school. It's tough some days, especially in the winter.

M1 I'm Cameron. I'm not a morning person. When my alarm clock goes off, I always turn it off and go back to sleep. I'm sometimes late for school because of that.

W2 My name's Bev. I have a full schedule, so I'm usually very tired when evening comes. I often go to bed at 9:00 p.m. after I study, take a shower, and watch an hour of TV.

M2 I'm Chris. I play a lot of sports, so my evenings are pretty busy. On Mondays and Wednesdays, I play football, on Tuesdays and Fridays, I play basketball, and on Thursdays, I coach a kids' soccer team.

▶ tough 힘든 morning person 아침형 인간 go off (알람 등이) 울리다 turn off 끄다

여1 난 신디라고 해. 난 대부분의 사람들보다 더 바쁜 하루를 보내는 것 같아. 학교 가기 전에 하키 연습하러 가려면 매일 아침 5시에 일어나야 돼. 어떤 날은 참 힘들어. 겨울에 특히 더 그래.

남1 난 캐머론이야. 아침형 인간이 아니지. 알람시계가 울리면 늘 꺼버리고 다시 잠이 들어. 그것 때문에 가끔 학교에 지각해.

여2 내 이름은 베브야. 하루 스케줄이 꽉 차 있어서 저녁이 되면 보통 엄청 피곤해. 대개 공부하고 샤워하고 텔레비전 한 시간 정도 보고 나서 밤 9시에 잠자리에 들어.

남2 난 크리스야. 운동을 많이 해서 저녁에는 굉장히 바빠. 월요일과 수요일에는 미식축구를 하고, 화요일과 금요일에는 농구를 해. 목요일에는 어린이 축구팀 코치도 하지.

메모를 바탕으로 다음 문제에 답하시오.

1 화자들은 주로 무엇에 관해 이야기하고 있는가?
   (a) 스포츠
   (b) 자신들의 일상 스케줄
   (c) 아침에 일어나는 것
   (d) 자신들의 학교 생활

2 맞으면 T, 틀리면 F를 쓰시오.
   (1) 신디는 방과 후에 하키 연습을 한다.
   (2) 크리스는 미식축구와 농구를 한다.
   (3) 카메론은 때때로 학교에 지각한다.

다시 듣고 정답을 확인하시오.

Plus⁺ Question

1 캐머론의 문제는 무엇인가?
   (a) 잠을 잘 수가 없다.
   (b) 너무 바쁘다.
   (c) 알람시계가 없다.
   (d) 아침에 일어날 수가 없다.

2 베브가 잠자리에 들기 전에 하지 <u>않는</u> 일은 무엇인가?
   (a) 공부하기
   (b) 텔레비전 보기
   (c) 샤워하기
   (d) 음악 듣기

EXERCISE <u>Step 1</u>

듣고 문제에 답하시오.

1

M Hey, Lauren! What's up?

W Hey, Dan! What are you doing here?

M I come to this gym every day after work around 6:00.

W Oh, really? I'm usually here in the morning… most days by around 7:00.

M Ah, that's why we haven't seen each other here before.

W Yeah, I guess so.

M I wish I could exercise before work like you, but I'm just not a morning person. I also start work at 8:00 a.m.

W Gotcha. I start at 9:30, so I have a bit more time.

▶ gym 체육관 Gotcha. 알겠어요.

남 안녕, 로렌! 잘 지내요?

여 안녕, 댄! 여긴 어쩐 일이에요?

8

남 일 끝나고 6시 정도에 매일 이 체육관에 와요.

여 어, 그래요? 난 보통 아침에 여기 오는데. 대개 한 7시까지 와요.

남 아, 그래서 우리가 전에 여기서 본 적이 없는 거군요.

여 예, 그런 것 같네요.

남 나도 당신처럼 일하기 전에 운동할 수 있으면 좋으련만. 내가 아침형 인간이 아니라서요. 게다가 일도 오전 8시에 시작하고요.

여 그렇군요. 전 일이 9시 30분에 시작해서 시간이 좀 더 있어요.

1 화자들은 어디에 있는가?

(a)  (b)  (c)  (d) 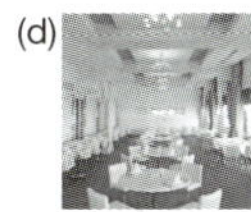

2

W Some days, I'm so busy that I forget to brush my teeth! I have three kids, so I have to get up at 6:00 a.m. every morning to get them ready for school. While they're getting dressed, I make them breakfast and pack their lunches. We usually get out the door by 8:15. I never have time to eat breakfast. I drop them off at school, and then I go to work. I usually pick up a coffee and a muffin on the way there.

▶ brush one's teeth 이를 닦다 get dressed 옷을 입다 pack 싸다 drop off 차에서 내려주다

여 어떤 날은 너무 바빠서 전 양치질하는 것도 잊어버린다니까요! 아이가 셋이라서 매일 아침 6시에는 일어나 애들 학교 갈 준비를 시켜야 해요. 애들이 옷을 입는 동안 전 아침을 차리고 도시락을 싸지요. 보통 8시 15분에는 집에서 나와요. 전 아침 먹을 시간이 전혀 없어요. 애들을 학교에 내려주고 나서 회사에 가요. 보통 회사 가는 길에 커피 한 잔과 머핀 하나를 사지요.

2 다음 중 화자에 대한 내용 중 사실이 아닌 것은?

(a) 아이가 셋이다.

(b) 아침 6시에 일어난다.

(c) 아이들과 아침식사를 한다.

(d) 아침 8시 15분에 집을 나선다.

3~4

W Excuse me, Mr. Harris. Sorry I'm late.

M Tina, you're late again?

W Yes, I'm sorry. I missed the bus again this morning.

M Why do you miss it so often?

W Well, I have to walk my little brother to his school in the morning. Sometimes he's a little slow.

M Where's his school?

W It's on Woodlawn Road.

M The number 12 bus stops on Woodlawn Road. Try that one tomorrow.

W I will. Thanks, Mr. Harris.

▶ late 늦은 miss 놓치다

여 해리스 선생님, 늦어서 죄송해요.

남 티나, 또 늦은 거니?

여 예, 죄송해요. 오늘 아침에도 버스를 놓쳤어요.

남 왜 그렇게 버스를 자주 놓치는 거야?

여 그게, 아침에 남동생을 학교까지 걸어서 데려다 줘야 하는데요, 가끔 걔가 좀 굼떠요.

남 동생 학교가 어디 있는데?

여 우드론 로드요.

남 12번 버스가 우드론 로드에 서니까 내일은 그 버스를 타보렴.

여 그럴게요. 고맙습니다, 해리스 선생님.

3 다음 중 사실이 아닌 것은?

(a) 티나는 걸어서 남동생을 학교까지 데려다 준다.

(b) 해리스 씨는 티나의 선생님이다.

(c) 티나의 남동생은 우드론 로드에 있는 학교에 다닌다.

(d) 해리스 씨는 티나의 남동생을 가르친다.

4 왜 티나는 버스를 자주 놓치는가?

(a) 너무 늦게까지 잠을 잔다.

(b) 너무 느리게 걷는다.

(c) 남동생을 학교까지 데려다 줘야 한다.

(d) 12번 버스가 너무 일찍 온다.

Exercise Step 2

듣고 문제에 답하시오.

1

M I don't have a normal daily schedule. You see, I'm a night guard at a bank. I start work at 11:00 p.m. and finish at 7:00 a.m. I have to stay up all night. At first, it was hard, but now I don't mind it. After work, I go straight home and take a bath. Then, I sleep until about 3:00 p.m. Then, I get up, make dinner, and relax for a few more hours until work starts again.

▶ normal 정규의, 보통의 daily schedule 하루 일과 guard 수위, 경비원 stay up 일어나 (자지 않고) 있다 mind 싫어하다, 신경쓰다

남 제 하루 일과는 보통과는 달라요. 보시다시피 은행 야간 경비원이거든요. 밤 11시에 근무를 시작해서 오전 7시에 끝나요. 밤새 깨어 있어야 하죠. 처음에는 힘들었지만 지금은 아무렇지 않아요. 일이 끝나면 바로 집에 가서 목욕하고 오후 세 시 정도까지 잡니다. 그런 다음 일어나서 저녁 식사를 준비하고 다시 일을 시작하기 전까지 몇 시간 더 쉬지요.

1 그림을 순서에 맞게 놓으시오.

(a)  (b)  (c) 

(d)  (e) 

2

W Welcome to *Celebrity Snapshot*! Today, we're taking a peek into the life of Brandy Williams, a rising actress. What's it like to be Brandy? Well, it's actually not that easy. Every morning, she gets up at 6:30 a.m. After a quick breakfast, she jogs for 1 hour and then does yoga for another hour. After that, she heads to the set of her TV drama, *Double Time*. Most days, she works until 9:00 p.m. And you thought being a celebrity was easy?

▶ **celebrity** 명사, 유명인 **snapshot** 엿봄, 훔쳐보기 **peek** 엿보기 **actress** 여배우 **jog** 조깅하다 **head to** ~을 향하다

여 안녕하세요. 〈유명인 훔쳐보기〉 시간입니다! 오늘은 떠오르는 신예 여배우 브랜디 윌리엄스의 생활을 한번 살펴보겠습니다. 브랜디처럼 산다는 건 어떤 것일까요? 글쎄요, 실제로 그렇게 만만치만은 않네요. 매일 아침 6시 30분에 일어나서 아침식사를 얼른 끝내고 한 시간 동안 조깅을 한 다음 또 한 시간 동안 요가를 합니다. 그런 다음 TV 드라마 〈더블 타임〉 세트장으로 향합니다. 거의 매일 밤 9시까지 일하죠. 유명인으로 사는 게 쉬울 거라고 생각하셨나요?

2 맞으면 T, 틀리면 F에 체크하시오.
(1) 브랜디는 하루에 두 시간 운동한다.
(2) 브랜디는 매일 아침 일찍 일어난다.
(3) 브랜디는 팝 가수다.
(4) 브랜디는 〈더블 타임〉이라는 영화에 나온다.
(5) 브랜디는 밤 9시까지 일한다.

3~5

M I have a slightly different day than most kids. I go to a regular school in the morning, but at 1:00, I take a bus to another school. It's a school for kids studying to be chefs. I take all sorts of cooking classes. My favorite class is called World Foods. Anyway, I study at that school until 7:00 in the evening. I have a longer day than other kids, but I love what I'm learning. I can't wait to work in a restaurant overseas some day.

▶ **slightly** 조금 **chef** 요리사 **overseas** 해외의 **all sorts of** 모든 종류의, 온갖

남 전 대부분의 아이들과는 조금 다르게 하루를 보내요. 아침에는 일반 정규 학교에 가지만 1시가 되면 버스를 타고 다른 학교에 갑니다. 그곳은 요리사가 되려고 공부하는 아이들이 다니는 학교예요. 전 온갖 요리 수업을 다 들어요. 제가 제일 좋아하는 수업은 '세계의 음식' 수업이에요. 아무튼 그 학교에서 저녁 7시까지 공부해요. 다른 애들보다 더 긴 하루를 보내지만 지금 제가 배우는 것을 정말 좋아해요. 언젠가 해외에 있는 레스토랑에서 어서 빨리 일해 보고 싶다니까요.

3 소년은 어떤 학교를 다니는가?
(a) 과학학교
(b) 예술학교
(c) 식당경영학교
(d) 요리학교
(e) 음악학교

4 소년은 요리 외에 무엇에 관심이 있는 것 같은가?
(a) 역사
(b) 여행
(c) 패션
(d) 글짓기
(e) 예술

5 내용을 가장 잘 요약한 것은 무엇인가?
(a) 소년은 요리사가 되고 싶은 아이들을 위한 특수학교에 다닌다.
(b) 소년은 언젠가 다른 나라에서 식당을 운영하고 싶어한다.

PRACTICE TEST

듣고 문제에 답하시오.

W Dear Diary. It's June already. That means it's almost summer vacation. I'm really excited about that. My schedule is so boring now: I get up, go to school, do my homework… I'm so sick of studying. It'll be great to sleep late every morning and ride my bike to the beach. Well, I'd better go to bed now. Another week starts tomorrow!

▶ **vacation** 방학 **be sick of** 싫증이 나다

여 일기야 안녕. 벌써 6월이네. 곧 여름방학이 온다는 뜻이구나. 그 생각을 하면 정말 신난다니까. 지금 내 일정은 정말 지루하기 짝이 없어. 일어나서 학교 가고, 숙제하고… 공부하는 게 너무 지겨워. 매일 아침 늦게까지 자고 해변에 자전거 타고 가면 정말 근사할 텐데. 아, 이제 잠자리에 들어야겠다. 내일은 또 다른 한 주가 시작되니까!

1 다음 중 사실인 것은?
(a) 지금은 7월이다.
(b) 화자는 공부를 좋아한다.
(c) 여름방학은 8월에 시작한다.
(d) 화자는 여름방학을 학수고대하고 있다.
(e) 화자의 현재 일정은 지루하지 않다.

M This week, on *Your Health*, we will look at the busy lives of our children. These days, kids are busier than ever with school, after-school activities, and sometimes extra classes. Because of this, they are not getting enough sleep. We surveyed 100 kids aged 13~15 and found out that 50% go to bed after 10:00 p.m. and 15% go to bed after 11:00 p.m. That means that many kids are not getting the sleep they need.

▶ **after-school** 방과 후의 **extra class** 과외수업 **survey** 조사하다 **mean** 의미하다

남 이번 주, 〈당신의 건강〉에서는 우리 아이들의 바쁜 일상을 살펴보겠습니다. 요즘에는 아이들이 수업이다, 방과 후 활동이다, 때때로 과외수업이다 해서 그 어느 때보다도 바쁩니다. 이 때문에 잠도 충분히 자지 못하고요. 저희가 13세부터 15세까지의 아이들 100명을 대상으로 조사했는데, 50%가 밤 10시 이후에 잠자리에 들고, 15%는 11시 이후에 잠자리에 드는 것으로 나왔습니다. 이는 많은 아이들이 필요한 잠을 제대로 못 자고 있다는 의미이기도 합니다.

2 원 그래프를 완성하시오.

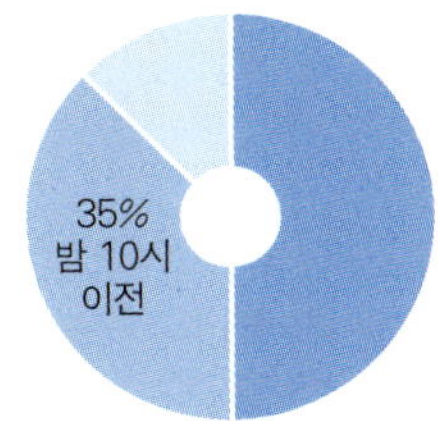

3~4

M Hey, let's get some lunch.

W Sure. What are they serving today?

M Um, what day is it? Thursday? Then it's spaghetti and meatball day.

W Right… Ugh, it's so gross.

M Let's go sit down.

W Hey! Someone's in our spot!

M Don't they know that's our table?

W Oh, well. Let's sit somewhere else.

M What class do you have after lunch?

W It's Thursday, so… science. I don't like Thursdays.

M Me neither. Ugh, this spaghetti is disgusting. Want to grab a burger after school?

W Sure, good call.

▶ serve 음식을 내다 gross 지겨운: 불쾌한 spot 장소. 지점 somewhere 어딘가에 disgusting 메스꺼운 grab 먹다 good call 잘 내린 결정

남 야, 점심 먹자.
여 그래. 오늘은 뭐가 나올까?
남 음, 오늘 무슨 요일이지? 목요일? 그럼 스파게티랑 미트볼 나오는 날인데.
여 맞아. 아, 너무 지겨워.
남 가서 앉자.
여 야, 누가 우리 자리에 앉아 있어!
남 쟤들은 저기가 우리 자리인 줄 모르나?
여 글쎄, 다른 데 앉자.
남 점심 이후 수업은 뭐야?
여 목요일이니까, 과학 수업. 난 목요일이 싫어.
남 나도 그래. 어우, 이 스파게티 역겨워. 수업 끝나고 햄버거 먹을래?
여 그래, 좋아.

3 화자들은 어디에 있는가?
(a) 패스트푸드점   (b) 과학 실험실
(c) 공공 도서관   (d) 교실
(e) 교내 식당

4 화자들에 대해 추측할 수 있는 것은 무엇인가?
(a) 학교에서 나오는 음식을 좋아한다.
(b) 친구가 아무도 없다.
(c) 점심 먹으러 밖에 나간다.
(d) 매일 점심을 같은 자리에서 먹는다.
(e) 목요일마다 과학 시험이 있다.

5

M I don't go to school. Actually, I am what you call "home-schooled." My mom teaches me. My friends all say, "Oh, Daniel, you're so lucky!" but I think I work harder than they do. I study all the regular subjects, and I get lots of homework. I never watch TV during the day, even at lunchtime. I even have tests, just like at a school.

▶ home-school 자택에서 교육하다 lucky 운이 좋은 subject 과목

남 난 학교에 다니지 않아. 사실 사람들이 말하는 '홈 스쿨링'으로 교육을 받아. 엄마가 날 가르치시지. 친구들은 다들 "야, 대니얼, 너 진짜 좋겠다!"라고 하지만 내가 걔네들보다 더 열심히 공부하는 것 같아. 모든 정규과목을 다 공부하고, 숙제도 많거든. 낮 시간에 텔레비전을 절대 안 봐. 심지어 점심시간에도 안 본다니까. 학교에서처럼 시험도 치지.

5 다음 중 사실이 아닌 것은?
(a) 대니얼은 점심시간에 텔레비전을 볼 수 있다.
(b) 대니얼은 숙제를 해야 한다.
(c) 대니얼은 집에서 공부한다.
(d) 대니얼은 시험을 본다.
(e) 대니얼은 자기가 친구들보다 더 열심히 공부한다고 생각한다.

6

M Hey, Mom.

W You're late, Luke. Your dinner's cold.

M Yeah, I had to stay after class.

W And I see your room is a big mess.

M I'm too busy to clean my room!

W Busy? With what?

M I go to school early every day for volleyball practice. Then I come home, eat dinner, do my homework, and watch TV. I have no time!

W Well, find some time! You have to clean your room every day. Or…

M Or what?

W Or you're not getting your allowance!

▶ mess 엉망진창 practice 연습 allowance 용돈

남 엄마.
여 늦었구나, 루크. 저녁이 다 식어버렸네.
남 예, 수업 끝나고 남아 있어야 했어요.
여 네 방을 보니까 정말 엉망이더구나.
남 전 방 청소를 하기엔 너무 바빠요!
여 바빠? 뭣 때문에?
남 배구 연습하러 매일 일찍 학교 가죠, 그 다음에 집에 와서 저녁 먹고, 숙제하고, 텔레비전 보고. 시간이 없다고요!
여 그럼 시간을 찾으면 되겠네! 매일 방 청소를 하든가, 아니면…
남 아니면 뭐요?
여 아니면 용돈을 안 받든가!

6 소년은 대화가 끝나고 어떤 심정이겠는가?
(a) 만족해한다.   (b) 좌절감을 느낀다.
(c) 기뻐한다.   (d) 자부심을 느낀다.
(e) 신이 난다.

W I'm doing a project on careers. Can I ask you some questions?
M Sure, go ahead.
W Okay. About what time do you get up in the morning?
M At about 4:30 a.m. I eat breakfast and start work by 5:15.
W Why so early?
M I have to start work when the sun comes up. I feed the animals and let them out. Then, I go to work in the fields.
W What time do you finish?
M Around 6:00 in the evening.
W That's a long day!
M Well, it comes with the job.

▶ career 직업 come up 떠오르다 feed 먹이를 주다 come with ~에 부수되다, ~에 으레 따르다

여 직업과 관련해 과제를 하고 있는데요, 몇 가지 여쭤봐도 될까요?
남 그럼요. 물어보세요.
여 좋아요. 아침에 몇 시쯤 일어나세요?
남 한 4시 30분쯤이요. 5시 15분까지 아침식사하고 일을 시작하죠.
여 왜 그렇게 일찍 하세요?
남 해가 뜨면 일을 시작해야 하거든요. 가축들 먹이를 주고 밖으로 내보내고요. 그런 다음 밭으로 일하러 가죠.
여 몇 시에 일을 마치세요?
남 저녁 6시쯤에요.
여 진짜 힘드시겠어요!
남 뭐, 그 일을 하다 보니 그렇네요.

7 남자의 직업은 무엇이겠는가?
   (a) 정원사   (b) 사무직 근로자
   (c) 농부   (d) 수의사
   (e) 양봉업자

8 남자의 일정과 가장 잘 어울리는 표현은 무엇인가?
   (a) 일석이조.
   (b) 더디더라도 착실히 하면 결국 이긴다.
   (c) 즐거울 때는 시간이 빨리 간다.
   (d) 일찍 일어나는 새가 벌레를 잡는다.
   (e) 미모는 거죽 한 꺼풀.

Unit 3 — She's Quiet but Nice

Answers

GET READY p. 32~33

Key Words & Expressions

1 get along   2 Optimists   3 bully
4 personality   5 outgoing   6 hardworking
7 good points   8 selfish   9 get to know
10 Perfectionists

Questions & Responses

1 c   2 a   3 f   4 e   5 d   6 b

BASIC DRILL p. 34~35

Step 1 ● Laura Trent / Second grade / outgoing
   Q (a)
   ■ best friend, jumping rope, different, quiet, shy, outgoing, get along

Step 2 A brothers   B funny / clown
            C grades / captain   D insult / loser
   1 (b)   2 (1) F (2) F (3) F

Plus⁺ Question 1 (b)

EXERCISE p. 36~37

Step 1 1 (1) Optimist (2) Pessimist   2 (d)   3 (a)
            4 (d)

Step 2 1 (b)   2 (1) T (2) T (3) F (4) T (5) F   3 (d)
            4 (b)   5 (b)

PRACTICE TEST p. 40~41

1 (e)

2

	Good points	Bad points
	- hardworking	- too picky
	- perfectionist	- can sometimes waste time
	- team player	
	- people person	

3 (c)   4 (e)   5 (d)   6 (a)   7 (e)   8 (c)

* Dictation 1, 2의 정답은 각 Script의 밑줄친 부분임.

GET READY

Key Words & Expressions

다음 문장을 듣고 보기 박스에서 알맞은 단어를 골라 빈칸을 채우시오.

1 남동생과 나는 아주 달라서 우리는 같이 잘 못 지내.

2 낙관론자는 모든 것의 좋은 면을 보는 행복한 사람들이지.

3 세레나는 우리 반 왈가닥이야. 다른 아이들에게 자기 숙제를 하도록 시킬 때도 있다니까.

4 네 성격과 잘 맞는 직업을 골라야 해.

5 외향적인 사람이라면, 그룹을 지어 이야기하면 가장 쉽게 언어를 배울 수 있죠.

6 우리 회사에 입사할 근면하고, 사람들과 팀을 이뤄 일할 수 있는 사람을 찾고 있습니다.

7 몇몇 성격 테스트는 자신의 장점과 단점을 파악하도록 도와준다는 면에서 좋아요.

8 돈으로 행복을 살 수는 없어요. 돈은 사람들을 냉정하고 이기적으로 만들 수 있지요.

9 그 사람에 대해서 잘 알게 될 때까지 그 사람에 대해 판단하지 마세요.

10 완벽주의자들이 일은 잘하지만 때때로 사소한 것에 너무 스트레스를 받기도 하죠.

Questions & Responses

질문에 어울리는 대답과 연결하시오.

1 제일 친한 친구가 누구니?   ⓒ 그 애 이름은 벤 그르니에야.

2 너희들은 친구가 된 지 얼마나 됐니?   ⓐ 우린 6년 간 알고 지냈어.

3 그는 어떤 사람이에요?   ⓕ 어떤 때는 조용하기도 하지만 농담하는 것도 좋아해요.

4 너희들은 어떻게 만났니?   ⓔ 태권도 동아리에서 만났어.

5 너희들은 싸우거나 말다툼한 적 있니?   ⓓ 아니, 한 번도 없어. 우린 항상 잘 지내.

6 왜 그 사람과 제일 친해요?   ⓑ 저를 위해 늘 그 자리에 있으니까요.

듣고 정답은 확인하시오.

친구와 함께 연습하시오.

Basic Drill   Step 1

다음을 듣고 메모하시오.

W   My name's Laura Doyle. My best friend's name is also Laura, but her last name is Trent. Isn't that cool? We've been friends since second grade. I was jumping rope alone when she asked to join me. Even though we have the same name, we're pretty different. I'm quiet and shy, but she's outgoing. I call her a chatterbox sometimes, but she knows I'm joking. We get along so well.

▶ cool 멋진, 근사한   jump rope 줄넘기를 하다   outgoing 외향적인   chatterbox 수다쟁이   get along 사이 좋게 지내다

여   제 이름은 로라 도일이에요. 저의 제일 친한 친구 이름도 로라인데요, 성은 트렌트죠. 멋지지 않아요? 우린 2학년 때부터 친구예요. 제가 혼자서 줄넘기를 하고 있었는데 그 애가 저와 같이 하자고 하는 거예요. 이름은 같지만 우린 정말 많이 달라요. 전 조용하고 수줍음을 타는데, 그 애는 외향적이거든요. 제가 가끔 그 친구를 수다쟁이라고 부르기도 하지만 그 애도 제가 농담으로 그런다는 걸 알아요. 우린 아주 사이 좋게 잘 지내요.

메모를 바탕으로 다음 문제에 답하시오.

Q   로라는 가장 친한 친구를 어떻게 만나게 되었는가?

   (a) 그들은 어떤 활동을 함께 하기 시작했다.

   (b) 선생님께서 소녀를 로라에게 소개하셨다.

   (c) 그들은 서로 옆집에 살았다.

   (d) 그들은 같은 스포츠 팀에서 경기를 했다.

■   다시 듣고 빈칸을 채우시오.

Basic Drill   Step 2

다음을 듣고 메모하시오.

M   I get along with most people. I guess you could say I'm pretty easygoing. I have a lot of friends. My best friend is Tony. We're so close that we're like brothers. Sometimes we act so much alike people ask if we're related!

Another close friend of mine is Rick. Rick's a funny guy. He always cracks jokes in class. Everyone loves him for that. The teachers don't though. He sometimes gets into a bit of trouble by being the class clown.

Alan is pretty cool. He's actually my cousin, but he's also a friend. I really look up to him. He gets good grades, he's captain of the baseball team, and he's a swimming instructor. Everyone likes him.

The only person I don't get along with is Jesse. Jesse never has anything nice to say. He always insults other people. Once he pulled my chair out while I was sitting down. What a jerk. I don't let him bother me. He's just a loser.

▶ get into trouble 꾸지람 듣다: 곤경에 처하다   easygoing 태평한, 마음 편한   alike 서로 같은, 비슷한   related 친족의: 관련된   crack 농담 등을 하다: 길라진 금   clown 어릿광대: 익살꾼   look up to ~을 존경하다, 쳐다보다   grade 성적   instructor 강사   insult 모욕하다   jerk 얼간이, 바보   bother 괴롭히다

남   전 사람들 대부분이랑 잘 지내요. 아마 절 성격이 둥글둥글한 사람이라고 생각할 거예요. 제겐 친구가 많아요. 제일 친한 친구는 토니예요. 진짜 친해서 마치 형제 같아요. 때로는 너무나 똑같이 행동해서 사람들이 우리보고 친척 간이냐고 물어보기도 한답니다!

가깝게 지내는 또 다른 친구는 릭이에요. 릭은 정말 재미있는 친구죠. 늘 수업시간에 농담을 해서 모두 그 애를 좋아해요. 하지만 선생님들은 그렇지 않죠. 반에서 익살 떠는 것 때문에 가끔 꾸지람을 듣기도 한답니다.

앨런은 아주 멋진 애에요. 사실 제 사촌인데, 친구기도 하지요. 전 정말로 그 애를 존경해요. 성적도 우수하고, 야구팀 주장이면서, 수영 강사이기도 해요. 모두가 앨런을 좋아해요.

제가 친하게 지내지 못하는 유일한 사람은 바로 제시에요. 제시 그 녀석은 좋게 말해줄 만한 구석이 전혀 없다니까요. 그 애는 늘 다른 사람들에게 모욕을 줘요. 한 번은 제가 앉으려고 하는데 걔가 제 의자를 뒤로 뺐어요. 뭐

그런 얼간이가 다 있는지. 전 걔가 절 귀찮게 굴지 못하도록 해요. 진짜 쓸모 없는 녀석이에요.

메모를 바탕으로 다음 문제에 답하시오.

1 화자는 주로 무엇에 관해 이야기하고 있는가?
   (a) 자기와 가장 친한 친구들
   (b) 자기 주변의 사람들
   (c) 자기의 영웅
   (d) 자기의 성격

2 맞으면 T, 틀리면 F를 쓰시오.
   (1) 화자와 토니는 형제간이다.
   (2) 앨런은 야구팀 코치를 맡고 있다.
   (3) 제시는 좋은 아이이다.

다시 듣고 정답을 확인하시오.

Plus⁺ Question

1 왜 릭은 학교에서 꾸지람을 듣는가?
   (a) 광대처럼 옷을 입는다.
   (b) 농담을 너무 많이 한다.
   (c) 다른 사람들에게 모욕감을 준다.
   (d) 다른 아이들을 괴롭힌다.

EXERCISE Step 1

듣고 문제에 답하시오.

 **1**

W Some people are <u>optimists</u>, and some people are pessimists. Optimists always see the good side of things. They enjoy life. For them, "the glass is <u>half full</u>." Pessimists, on the other hand, are usually very <u>negative</u>. They often complain about minor things. For <u>pessimists</u>, "the glass is half empty." Pessimists have to be careful. New studies show that pessimists have more health problems and do not live as long as optimists. Remember, <u>the way you think</u> can affect your body.

▶ optimist 낙관론자 pessimist 비관론자 negative 부정적인 complain 불평하다

여 어떤 사람들은 낙관론자고, 어떤 사람들은 비관론자입니다. 낙관론자들은 항상 사물의 좋은 면을 보고, 인생을 즐깁니다. 그 사람들에게는 유리잔에 물이 반이나 채워져 있는 것입니다. 반면, 비관론자들은 대개 상당히 부정적입니다. 사소한 일에 자주 불평을 하죠. 비관론자들에게는 유리잔에 물이 반이나 비어 있는 것이지요. 비관론자들은 조심해야 합니다. 새로 발표된 연구 결과를 보면 비관론자들에게 건강상 문제가 더 많고 낙관론자들만큼 장수하지 못한다고 합니다. 사고방식이 신체에 영향을 끼친다는 점을 명심하세요.

1 어떤 사람이 낙관론자이고 어떤 사람이 비관론자인가? 그림에 표시하시오.

(1) 

(2) 

2

M Let's go the <u>other way</u>.
W Why? What's wrong, Carl?
M I just saw Alex. I'd rather not run into him.
W You guys <u>don't get along</u>?
M Nope.
W What happened?
M I have no idea. I was at the park the other day, and I saw him there. So I said, "Hey, Alex. What's up?" Then he <u>got angry</u>.
W What did he do?
M He <u>came up to me</u> and tried to start a fight. I just walked away.
W Whoa.
M Yeah, weird, huh? I think he's <u>a bit strange</u>.
W I think you're right. He doesn't have many friends.

▶ run into ~와 우연히 마주치다 the other day 일전에, 며칠 전에 weird 이상한

남 다른 길로 가자.
여 왜? 뭐가 잘못됐어, 칼?
남 나 방금 알렉스를 봤어. 그 애랑 안 마주치고 싶어.
여 너네 사이가 안 좋아?
남 응, 안 좋아.
여 무슨 일이었어?
남 모르겠어. 요전 날 공원에 있다가 거기서 알렉스를 봤거든. 그래서 "야, 알렉스, 어떻게 지내?" 라고 물었는데 화를 내더라고.
여 걔가 어떻게 했는데?
남 나한테 다가오더니 싸움을 걸려고 하는 거야. 난 그냥 가버렸지.
여 그래?
남 그래, 좀 이상하지? 내 생각엔 걔 좀 이상한 것 같아.
여 네 말이 맞는 것 같은데. 걔는 친구도 별로 없잖아.

2 다음 중 사실이 아닌 것은?
   (a) 칼과 알렉스는 사이좋게 지내지 않는다.
   (b) 칼은 공원에서 알렉스에게 인사했다.
   (c) 알렉스는 친구가 많지 않다.
   (d) 칼은 알렉스랑 싸우고 싶었다.

3-4

W Hi, I'm Mrs. Hill.
M Oh, yes. Emma's mother, <u>correct</u>?
W Yes, that's right.
M Nice to meet you. Well, you'll be happy to hear that Emma is <u>doing just fine</u> in my class.
W Oh, that's good.
M Yes, she <u>pays attention</u> and works hard. She is well-liked by her classmates.
W She enjoys your English class a lot.
M Good. The only problem is she's <u>a bit shy</u>.
W Oh, I see.
M Yes, she's extremely quiet, and she doesn't raise her hand often. I hope she can <u>improve</u> on this because she's a smart girl.
W I'll talk to her about that. Thank you.

▶ **pay attention** 열중하다 **shy** 수줍은 **extremely** 매우, 정말로 **raise** 들어 올리다 **improve** 개선하다

여 안녕하세요, 힐입니다.
남 아, 예. 엠마 어머님 맞으시죠?
여 예, 맞습니다.
남 만나 뵙게 되어서 반갑습니다. 엠마가 제 수업 시간에 참 잘한다는 얘길 들으시면 기쁘실 거예요.
여 오, 좋네요.
남 네, 수업 시간에 집중하고 열심히 공부합니다. 반 아이들도 엠마를 참 좋아해요.
여 엠마가 선생님 영어 수업을 참 좋아하더라고요.
남 다행이네요. 엠마의 유일한 문제는 수줍음을 좀 탄다는 거예요.
여 아, 그렇군요.
남 네. 너무 조용하고, 수업 시간에 손을 자주 안 들어요. 똑똑한 아이니까 이 점을 고칠 수 있으면 좋겠습니다.
여 제가 엠마랑 그 얘기를 해볼게요. 감사합니다.

3 전체적으로 봤을 때 엠마는 __________________.

(a) 좋은 학생이다 　　　　　(b) 학급에서 익살을 떤다

(c) 외향적인 소녀다 　　　　(d) 깡패같다

4 엠마의 문제점은 무엇인가?

(a) 영어 수업을 좋아하지 않는다.

(b) 수업 시간에 너무 시끄럽다.

(c) 친구가 많지 않다.

(d) 수업 시간에 말을 별로 안 한다.

Exercise **Step 2**

듣고 문제에 답하시오.

M　When learning a new language, it's important to remember that <u>your personality affects</u> how you learn. <u>Introverted</u>, or quiet people tend to like to study by themselves. They need more time to think before they speak. <u>Extroverted</u>, or outgoing people learn better by talking in groups. There is no "correct" way to learn a language. So <u>don't feel disappointed</u> if you prefer to study quietly alone or to talk out loud in groups. Find out what works best for you and <u>keep learning</u>.

▶ **personality** 성격 **introverted** 내향적인 **tend to** ~하는 경향이 있다 **by oneself** 자기 혼자서 **extroverted** 외향적인

남 새로운 언어를 배울 때, 성격이 배우는 방식에 영향을 끼친다는 점을 기억하는 게 중요합니다. 내향적인, 즉 조용한 사람들은 혼자서 공부하는 걸 좋아하는 경향이 있어요. 말하기 전에 생각할 시간이 더 필요하죠. 외향적인, 즉 사교적인 사람들은 그룹으로 말할 때 더 잘 배우죠. 언어를 배울 때 '올바른' 방법이란 없습니다. 그러니 혼자 조용히 공부하는 걸 더 좋아하든 여러 사람들이랑 크게 말하는 것을 더 좋아하든 실망하지 마세요. 자기한테 어느 쪽이 제일 효과적인지 알아낸 다음 계속 배워나가세요.

1 남자의 청중은 누구일 것 같은가?

(a) 내향적인 사람

(b) 새로운 언어를 배우는 사람

(c) 외향적인 사람

(d) 교사

(e) 과학자

W　Sometimes my little brother and sister drive me crazy. Since I'm the oldest, I'm always stuck <u>taking care of</u> them when my parents aren't home. My brother, Jeff, is all right. He usually <u>behaves</u>. But my sister, Julie, is pretty wild. While my brother and I are pretty <u>relaxed and quiet</u>, she's the total <u>opposite</u>. She's so loud, and she never listens to me. She sometimes <u>pushes</u> my brother <u>around</u>, too. I don't know how we're so different, but we are.

▶ **drive** ~한 상태에 빠뜨리다 **take care of** ~을 돌보다 **behave** 예의 바르게 행동하다 **relaxed** 느긋한 **opposite** 정반대의 **push around** 괴롭히다

여 때때로 남동생과 여동생이 절 미치게 만들어요. 제가 장녀라서 부모님께서 집에 안 계실 때는 늘 꼼짝없이 그 애들을 돌봐야 해요. 남동생 제프는 그래도 괜찮아요. 대개 얌전하게 굴거든요. 하지만 여동생 줄리는 정말 천방지축이에요. 남동생과 제가 느긋하고 조용한 반면, 여동생은 완전히 그 반대예요. 목소리도 너무 크고 제 말을 절대 안 들어요. 가끔 제프를 괴롭히기도 하고요. 어쩜 이렇게 서로 다를 수 있는지 모르겠지만 우리는 정말 달라요.

2 맞으면 T, 틀리면 F에 체크하시오.

(1) 화자에게 남동생과 여동생이 있다.

(2) 제프는 예의 바르게 군다.

(3) 줄리는 느긋하고 조용하다.

(4) 화자가 때때로 제프와 줄리를 돌본다.

(5) 화자와 줄리는 어느 면에서는 비슷하다.

M　My hero is Jim Carrey. He's a Canadian movie star who <u>had a tough life</u> but made it big. When he was a kid, his parents were very poor. They sometimes had no home, so they lived in their car. But Jim had <u>special talents</u>. When he wasn't working, he did his <u>comedy</u> act in nightclubs. People loved him. Now, he's a <u>celebrity</u> and a millionaire. He's my hero because he never <u>gave up</u>, so he achieved his dream.

▶ **tough** 힘든 **make it big** 성공하다 **talent** 재능 **millionaire** 백만장자 **give up** 포기하다 **achieve** 이루다, 성취하다

남 제 영웅은 짐 캐리에요. 힘들게 살았지만 대성한 캐나다 출신의 영화배우죠. 짐이 어렸을 때 그의 부모님이 매우 가난했대요. 때로는 집도 없어서 자동차 안에서 살기도 했고요. 하지만 짐에게는 특별한 재능이 있었어요. 일을 안 할 때는 나이트클럽에서 코미디 연기를 했어요. 사람들이 짐을 무척이나 좋아했죠. 이제 그는 유명인사에 백만장자가 되었어요. 절대 포기하지 않았고, 자신의 꿈을 이뤘기 때문에 짐은 제 영웅이랍니다.

3 어렸을 때 짐 캐리는 __________지만, __________ 했다.

(a) 성공했지만 가난했다.

(b) 부자였지만 웃겼다.

(c) 가난했지만 관대했다.

(d) 가난했지만 재능이 있었다.

(e) 재능이 있었지만 인기가 많았다.

4 화자는 어떤 사람을 가장 존경하는가?

   (a) 웃긴 사람   (b) 포기하지 않는 사람

   (c) 돈을 많이 버는 사람   (d) 똑똑한 사람

   (e) 다른 사람을 돕는 사람

5 내용을 가장 잘 요약한 것은 무엇인가?

   (a) 화자의 꿈은 짐 캐리처럼 코미디언이 되는 것이다. 짐 캐리가 어렸을 때 그랬던 것처럼 화자도 가난하기 때문이다.

   (b) 화자의 영웅은 캐나다 출신 영화배우로 가난하게 시작했으나 크게 성공한 짐 캐리이다.

PRACTICE TEST

듣고 문제에 답하시오.

M We're looking for salespeople to work at our store, Suits 'R' Us. These positions require people who are not afraid to talk to others. So we're looking for people who are outgoing and hardworking. You also have to have an interest in men's fashion since part of your job will be helping men find the right suits. If you're a people person and are ready for a challenge, contact us at 555-3945.

▶ **suit** 슈트, 정장 **position** 직장, 직 **require** 필요로 하다 **outgoing** 사교성이 풍부한, 외향성의 **have an interest** ~에 관심을 갖다 **people person** 사교적인 사람 **challenge** 도전

남 저희 슈트 'R' Us 매장에서 근무할 판매사원을 찾습니다. 이 일을 하려면 사람들과 말하는 것을 두려워하지 않아야 합니다. 그래서 외향적이면서 근면한 사람을 찾고 있지요. 또한 업무의 일부가 남자 고객들에게 맞는 정장을 찾도록 도와주는 것이라서 남성 패션에도 관심이 있어야 합니다. 사교적이고, 도전할 준비가 된 사람이라면 555-3945로 연락주세요.

1 어떤 곳에서 새 직원을 찾으려고 하는가?

(a)   (b)   (c)

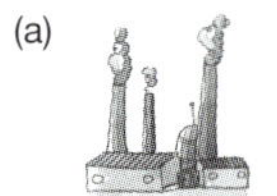 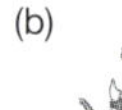  

(d)   (e)

W Okay, Mr. Peterson, tell me about yourself.

M Sure. Well, I'm very hardworking. I'm a perfectionist, so when I do something, I do it right. I'm also a team player. I work well with others. You could say I'm a people person.

W Good. That's what we're looking for. Now, what about your bad points?

M My bad points?

W Yes, what are you not good at?

M Hmm, well… I'm sometimes too picky.

W Explain.

M Well, like I said, I'm a perfectionist, so I sometimes

waste time trying to get things perfect.

W Good answer.

▶ **hardworking** 근면한 **perfectionist** 완벽주의자 **picky** 까다로운 **waste** 낭비하다

여 좋아요. 피터슨 씨, 당신 얘기를 해보세요.

남 네. 음, 전 굉장히 부지런하고, 완벽주의자입니다. 그래서 뭔가 할 때 늘 제대로 해내죠. 또한 사람들과 조화를 이뤄 일하는 타입이기도 합니다. 다른 사람들이랑 일도 잘해요. 사교적인 타입이라고 보실 수 있습니다.

여 좋네요. 저희가 찾는 사람이 그런 사람이거든요. 자, 그렇다면 단점은 무엇이 있을까요?

남 제 단점이요?

여 네, 그다지 잘 하지 못하는 점은 뭔가요?

남 음, 글쎄요. 때때로 너무 까다롭게 굴기도 합니다.

여 더 설명해주세요.

남 저기, 말씀 드렸듯이 제가 완벽주의자라서 일을 완벽하게 하려다 시간을 좀 허비하기도 하지요.

여 아주 확실한 답이네요.

Level up

2 피터슨 씨의 장점과 단점을 써서 차트를 완성하시오.

장점	단점

3-4

M How was school today, Katie?

W Good. Social studies was cool. We took a personality test.

M Oh, yeah? What did you find out about yourself?

W Mostly stuff I already knew. I'm outgoing, and I like helping people, I'm good at solving problems… stuff like that. I'm not very organized though.

M I see.

W Yeah, so at the end, the test tells you what kinds of jobs you'd be good at. I guess I'd make a good teacher or social worker.

M I agree with the test. You'd make an excellent teacher.

▶ **social studies** 사회과목 **organized** 계획된; 조직적인 **be good at** ~을 잘하다 **make** ~이 되다; 만들다

남 오늘 수업은 어땠어, 케이티?

여 좋았어. 사회 수업이 아주 재미있었어. 성격 테스트를 했거든.

남 아, 그래? 너에 대해서 뭘 알아냈니?

여 대부분은 이미 내가 알고 있는 것들이었어. 외향적이고, 남들 도와주는 거 좋아하고. 문제 해결에도 능하고, 뭐 그런 것들. 그렇지만 내가 아주 계획적인 사람은 아니라는 거야.

남 그렇구나.

여 응, 그리고 끝에 가니까 어떤 직업에서 능력을 발휘할 수 있을 것인지 얘기해 주는데, 난 좋은 선생님이나 사회 복지사가 될 것 같아.

남 그 테스트 결과에 나도 동의해. 넌 멋진 선생님이 될 거야.

3 케이티의 단점은 무엇인가?

   (a) 너무 외향적이다.

   (b) 도움이 되지 않는다.

   (c) 계획적이지 못하다.

(d) 문제를 해결하지 못한다.

(e) 말을 너무 많이 한다.

4　케이티는 선생님이 되어야 한다. 왜냐하면 ___________.

(a) 계획적이지 못하기 때문이다

(b) 그것이 케이티의 꿈이기 때문이다

(c) 케이티의 엄마가 케이티가 선생님이 되길 바라기 때문이다

(d) 케이티가 사회과목을 좋아하기 때문이다

(e) 케이티가 사람들을 도와주는 것을 좋아하기 때문이다

❺

W　I really enjoyed the movie *The Family Man*. It's about a rich man, Jack Campbell, who is very <u>selfish</u> and unhappy. He wakes up one morning to find that he has a <u>regular</u> life. He has a wife, kids, a <u>regular</u> <u>job</u>, and not a lot of money. Over time, he slowly <u>changes</u> <u>into</u> a more loving and <u>generous</u> person as well as a good dad. This movie really shows how even very cold and selfish people can become better, happier people.

▶ selfish 이기적인　generous 관대한

여　전 〈패밀리 맨〉이란 영화를 참 재미있게 봤어요. 잭 캠벨이라는, 부자지만 아주 이기적이고 불행한 남자에 관한 이야기예요. 그는 어느 날 아침에 깨어나서 자기가 보통 사람들처럼 살고 있는 걸 알게 되죠. 부인과 아이들, 꼬박꼬박 나가야 하는 직장이 있지만 돈은 많지 않은 그런 삶이요. 시간이 지나면서 잭은 좋은 아빠에 사랑이 넘치고 관대한 사람으로 서서히 변해가요. 이 영화는 정말 냉정하고 이기적인 사람조차도 어떻게 더 나은, 행복한 사람으로 변화할 수 있는지 보여줘요.

5　영화 〈패밀리 맨〉에 어울리는 슬로건은 무엇이라고 생각하는가?

(a) 돈이 세상을 굴러가게 한다.

(b) 돈은 모든 악의 근원이다.

(c) 돈이 적을 만든다.

(d) 돈으로 행복을 살 수 없다.

(e) 돈이 당신의 인생을 변화시킬 수 있다.

❻

W　So what do you think of that new kid? What's her name?

M　Um… Lisa, I think.

W　Yeah, Lisa.

M　I don't know. She seems okay.

W　Really? She <u>seems</u> <u>quiet</u>.

M　Yeah, well, maybe she's just shy. Or maybe she <u>just</u> <u>seems</u> <u>that</u> <u>way</u> because she's at a new school.

W　Yeah, you could be right. I don't really know her yet.

M　Why don't you <u>introduce</u> yourself?

W　Maybe I'll sit with her at lunch and see <u>what</u> <u>she's</u> <u>like</u>.

M　I think she'd like that. Let me know how it goes.

▶ introduce 소개하다　what the doctor ordered (바로) 필요한 것, 갖고 싶었던 것

여　저기 새로 온 애 어떻게 생각해? 저 여자애 이름이 뭐니?

남　음, 리사인 것 같은데.

여　그래, 리사.

남　모르겠어. 괜찮은 애인 것 같은데.

여　그래? 조용한 것 같아.

남　그러게. 음, 그냥 수줍음을 타는 것일 수도 있지. 아니면 새로 전학 와서 그렇게 보이는 것일 수도 있고.

여　그래, 네 말이 맞겠다. 나도 아직 저 애를 잘 몰라.

남　네 소개를 해보지 그래?

여　점심 때 쟤랑 앉아서 어떤 애인지 봐야겠어.

남　그래 주면 쟤가 좋아하겠지. 어떻게 되어 가는지 알려줘.

6　소년의 충고를 가장 잘 표현한 것은 무엇인가?

(a) 겉만 보고 판단하지 마라.

(b) 세상 일이 다 그런 거지.

(c) 한 귀로 듣고 한 귀로 흘려라.

(d) 그게 바로 내가 원했던 거야.

(e) 말만 그렇지 실제로는 고약하지 않아.

7~8

M　Kelly, who do you <u>take</u> <u>after</u>, your mom or your dad?

W　Hmm, I think I look more like my dad, but my personality is more like my mom's.

M　How so?

W　Well, I'm really good at math and science, like my mom. She's an <u>engineer</u>.

M　Oh, I didn't know that.

W　Yeah, she <u>designs</u> airplanes.

M　Cool!

W　Yeah. But my dad is different. <u>He's</u> <u>into</u> history. He loves watching those <u>historical</u> <u>dramas</u> on TV. He also likes to paint.

M　Yeah, you sound more like your mom.

W　Definitely.

▶ take after ~을 닮다　be into ~에 관심을 가지다　Definitely. (구어) 물론, 그럼.

남　켈리, 넌 엄마, 아빠 중에서 누굴 닮았니?

여　음, 외모는 아빠 쪽을 닮은 것 같은데, 성격은 엄마랑 더 비슷해.

남　어떻게?

여　글쎄, 난 엄마처럼 수학이랑 과학은 정말 잘하거든. 엄마가 엔지니어셔.

남　아, 그건 몰랐어.

여　흥. 우리 엄마, 비행기 설계하신다.

남　멋지다!

여　맞아. 그런데 우리 아빠는 달라. 아빠는 역사에 참 관심이 많으셔. 텔레비전에서 하는 역사 드라마 보는 것을 좋아하시지. 또 그림 그리는 것도 좋아하셔.

남　그러게. 넌 진짜 엄마를 더 닮은 것 같다.

여　맞아.

7　켈리 엄마의 직업은 무엇인가?

(a) 비행기를 조종한다.　　　(b) 비행기를 수리한다.

(c) 과학을 가르친다.　　　(d) 수학자다.

(e) 엔지니어다.

8　다음 중 사실이 아닌 것은?

(a) 켈리는 엄마를 닮았다.

(b) 켈리는 수학을 좋아한다.

(c) 켈리의 아빠는 역사책을 쓰신다.

(d) 켈리의 엄마는 비행기를 설계한다.

(e) 켈리의 외모는 아빠를 닮았다.

Answers

GET READY   p. 44~45

Key Words & Expressions

1 picky   2 Would you like   3 specialty
4 grocery store   5 amazing   6 baked
7 diets   8 starving   9 ingredients
10 fried

Questions & Responses

1 b   2 f   3 e   4 a   5 d   6 c

BASIC DRILL   p. 46~47

Step 1   • Thai food / Pad Thai noodles / junk food like hamburgers and French fries
   Q (d)
   ■ try, sweet, spicy, type, dish, junk food, unhealthy

Step 2   A Japanese   B spicy curries
   C spaghetti, pizza   D junk food / three times
   1 (b)   2 (1) F   (2) T   (3) F

Plus⁺ Question   1 (a)   2 (c)

EXERCISE   p. 48~49

Step 1   1

shopping list

two steaks
some potatoes
carrots
broccoli
a loaf of bread
some ice cream

   2 (c)   3 (b)   4 (c)

Step 2   1 (1) Today   (2) 1990   2 (1) F (2) T (3) F (4) F (5) T   3 (e)   4 (d)   5 (a)

PRACTICE TEST   p. 52~53

1 (a)

2

Shakin' Chicken Order Sheet

Address: 52 Douglas St.
Items: a 5-piece chicken combo, a French fries, a potato salad, a bottle of soda, a small bucket of chocolate ice cream

Total: $16.00

3 (b)   4 (e)   5 (c)   6 (d)   7 (b)   8 (e)

* Dictation 1, 2의 정답은 각 Script의 밑줄친 부분임.

Scripts and Translations

GET READY

Key Words & Expressions

다음 문장을 듣고 보기 박스에서 알맞은 단어를 골라 빈칸을 채우시오.

1 난 입맛이 까다롭진 않지만 양념이 많이 들어간 음식은 안 좋아해.

2 기다리시는 동안 마실 것 좀 드릴까요?

3 브레드는 많은 음식을 요리할 수 있는데, 특별히 잘하는 건 태국 음식이야.

4 식료품점에서 빵이랑 우유 좀 사다 줄 수 있어요?

5 새로 생긴 카페에서 파는 와플이 진짜 끝내줘요.

6 일요일마다 갓 구운 애플파이 냄새에 잠이 깼어요.

7 그리스 사람들과 이탈리아 사람들은 음식에 올리브 오일을 많이 넣어요.

8 뷔페 음식이 정말 맛있어 보여. 나 너무 배고픈데 어서 먹자.

9 외국 물품을 파는 슈퍼마켓에서 민속음식 재료를 구할 수 있어.

10 난 튀긴 음식을 안 좋아해서 중국 음식에 그다지 열광하지 않아요.

Questions & Responses

질문에 어울리는 대답과 연결하시오.

1 어떤 종류의 음식을 가장 좋아해?

2 싫어하는 음식이 있니?

3 가장 좋아하는 요리는 뭐니?

4 정크 푸드를 많이 먹니?

5 요리할 줄 알아?

6 새로운 음식 먹어보는 것을 좋아하니?

ⓑ 난 프랑스 음식을 참 좋아해.

ⓕ 글쎄, 난 양념이 많이 든 음식을 안 좋아해.

ⓔ 내가 가장 좋아하는 요리는 푸아 그라야.

ⓐ 아니, 몸에 안 좋잖아.

ⓓ 조금은 하는데, 복잡한 것은 못해.

ⓒ 물론이야. 새로운 음식을 먹어보는 것은 아주 즐거운 일이지.

듣고 정답을 확인하시오.

친구와 함께 연습하시오.

Basic Drill **Step 1**

다음을 듣고 메모하시오.

M I'm never afraid to try new foods. In fact, I find it exciting. I like hot and cold foods and sweet, sour, and even spicy foods. Thai food is my favorite type of food, and Pad Thai noodles is my favorite dish. I don't like junk food like hamburgers and French fries. It's unhealthy. I think home-cooked food is much better.

▶ **sour** 신, 시큼한 **spicy** 매운; 양념을 넣은 **noodle** 국수; 면류 **junk food** 칼로리는 높고 영양가는 낮은 인스턴트 식품류

남 전 새로운 음식을 먹어보는 게 전혀 두렵지 않아요. 사실 아주 신나는 일이라고 생각해요. 뜨겁고, 차갑고, 달고, 시고, 심지어 매콤한 음식까지 모두 좋아해요. 전 태국 음식을 제일 좋아하는데, 팟 타이 누들이 가장 좋아하는 요리에요. 햄버거나 프렌치 프라이 같은 정크 푸드는 좋아하지 않아요. 몸에 안 좋잖아요. 집에서 만든 음식이 훨씬 더 좋다고 생각해요.

메모를 바탕으로 다음 문제에 답하시오.

Q 다음 중 사실인 것은?

(a) 남자는 매우 까다로운 식성을 가진 사람이다.

(b) 남자는 태국 음식을 좋아하지 않는다.

(c) 남자는 햄버거를 정말 좋아한다.

(d) 남자는 새로운 음식을 먹는 것을 좋아한다.

■ 다시 듣고 빈칸을 채우시오.

Basic Drill **Step 2**

다음을 듣고 메모하시오.

W1 I'm June, and my favorite type of food is Japanese. I just tried sushi about a year ago, and I love it! At first, I thought it looked strange, but it's actually very fresh and tasty.

M1 My name's Dwayne. I like most foods and love trying new kinds. My all-time favorite, though, is Indian food. I love the spicy curries. I'd love to learn how to cook Indian food.

W2 Hi, I'm Emma. My favorite dish is authentic Italian

spaghetti with lots of cheese. Pizza's also good. I can't get enough Italian food. I love trying new Italian restaurants.

M2 I'm Jason. My parents are always scolding me for eating too much junk food. I eat it about three times a week. I know it's bad for me, but I can't help it. I love it! Bacon double cheeseburgers are awesome.

▶ **tasty** 맛이 좋은 **authentic** 진정한 **scold** 꾸짖다 **awesome** 최고의, 굉장한

여1 난 준이야. 내가 제일 좋아하는 음식 종류는 일식이야. 약 1년 전에 초밥을 먹어봤는데, 정말 좋아해! 처음에는 이상해 보인다고 생각했어. 하지만 사실 초밥은 무척 신선하고 맛있는 음식이야.

남1 내 이름은 드웨인이야. 난 대부분의 음식을 다 좋아하고, 새로운 음식 먹어보는 것도 참 좋아해. 하지만 내가 항상 최고로 좋아하는 건 인도 음식이야. 매콤한 카레를 아주 좋아해. 인도 음식 만드는 법을 정말 배우고 싶어.

여2 안녕. 난 엠마야. 내가 가장 좋아하는 요리는 치즈가 많이 들어간 정통 이탈리아 스파게티야. 피자도 물론 좋아. 이탈리아 음식은 아무리 먹어도 충분하지 않아. 새로 생긴 이탈리아 식당에 가서 먹는 것도 정말 좋아해.

남2 난 제이슨이야. 우리 부모님은 내가 정크 푸드를 너무 많이 먹는다고 늘 꾸중하셔. 일주일에 세 번 정도 먹거든. 나도 정크 푸드가 안 좋다는 건 알지만 어쩔 수가 없어. 그게 좋은 걸! 베이컨 더블 치즈버거는 정말 기가 막히게 맛있어.

메모를 바탕으로 다음 문제에 답하시오.

1 화자들은 주로 무엇에 관해 이야기하고 있는가?

(a) 자기들의 요리 솜씨　　(b) 자기들이 좋아하는 음식 종류

(c) 정크 푸드와 건강　　(d) 외식하기

2 맞으면 T, 틀리면 F를 쓰시오.

(1) 준은 자기가 초밥을 만든다.

(2) 엠마가 제일 좋아하는 음식은 스파게티이다.

(3) 제이슨은 정크 푸드 먹는 걸 그만두고 싶어한다.

다시 듣고 정답을 확인하시오.

Plus⁺ Question

1 준은 언제 일본 음식을 먹어 보았는가?

(a) 작년에　　(b) 지난 주에

(c) 어렸을 때　　(d) 일본 여행 중에

2 제이슨은 얼마나 자주 정크 푸드를 먹는가?

(a) 매일　　(b) 거의 먹지 않는다.

(c) 일주일에 세 번　　(d) 전혀 안 먹는다.

EXERCISE **Step 1**

듣고 문제에 답하시오.

M Hey, where are you going?

W Oh, I'm just heading to the corner store.

M Really? Can you stop by the grocery store? I need some stuff to make dinner.

W Sure, what do you need?

M Um, pick up two steaks, some potatoes, carrots, broccoli, and a loaf of bread.

W What about dessert?

M   Well, I'll let you choose.

W   Sure. I'll pick up some ice cream then.

▶ grocery store 식료 잡화점   stuff 재료

남   이봐, 어디 가?
여   어, 그냥 저기 모퉁이에 있는 가게 가는 길이야.
남   그래? 그럼 잠깐 식료품점에 들를 수 있어? 저녁거리가 좀 필요한데.
여   그럴게. 뭐가 필요해?
남   음, 스테이크 두 개랑, 감자 조금, 당근, 브로콜리랑 빵 한 덩이.
여   디저트는 뭘로 할 건데?
남   글쎄, 네가 골라봐.
여   그래. 그럼 아이스크림으로 해야겠다.

1   여자의 쇼핑 리스트를 써 넣으시오.

M   Mom, something smells good. What are you making?

W   Oh, it's a recipe from an old cookbook.

M   It smells like cinnamon.

W   Actually, it's gingerbread.

M   Oh, you're making gingerbread cookies?

W   No, I'm making a gingerbread house.

M   Cool! Can I help you?

W   Sure, Greg. When the gingerbread is finished baking, you can help me put the house together and decorate it with icing and candy.

M   Oh, I can't wait!

▶ recipe 조리법   cinnamon 계피   gingerbread 생강 빵[쿠키]   put together 구성하다, 편집하다; 모으다   decorate 장식하다   icing 과자에 입힌 설탕

남   엄마, 뭔가 좋은 냄새가 나는데요. 뭐 만드세요?
여   아, 이거 옛날 요리책에 나와 있는 조리법이야.
남   계피 비슷한 냄새가 나요.
여   사실은 생강 과자야.
남   와, 엄마 지금 생강 쿠키 만드는 거예요?
여   아니, 생강 과자로 집을 만들고 있는 거란다.
남   멋지다! 제가 도와드려요?
여   그래, 그레그. 생강 과자가 다 구워지면 함께 집을 조립하고, 설탕물과 사탕으로 집 장식하는 것을 도와주면 돼.
남   와, 빨리 하고 싶어요!

2   다음 중 사실이 아닌 것은?
  (a) 디저트에서 좋은 냄새가 난다.
  (b) 엄마는 생강 과자 집을 만들고 있다.
  (c) 엄마는 쿠키를 굽고 있다.
  (d) 엄마는 옛날 요리책을 사용하고 있다.

3-4

M   Hey, Laura! So how was your trip to Europe?

W   Oh, it was amazing.

M   Really? What was your favorite part?

W   Well, I'd have to say the food. I just loved the cafés!

M   Oh, really? What did you eat?

W   You mean, what didn't we eat? Ha ha… We ate a lot of fruit, bread, cheese – lovely cheeses – and coffee. We also had some lovely dinners with wine. It was so delicious!

M   Well, I have to admit I'm a little jealous!

▶ admit 인정하다   jealous 질투가 많은

남   여어, 로라! 유럽 여행은 어땠어?
여   진짜 멋졌지.
남   정말? 어떤 점이 가장 좋았어?
여   글쎄, 음식이라고 해야 할 것 같네. 난 카페들이 정말 맘에 들었거든.
남   오, 그래? 뭘 먹었는데?
여   네 말은, 우리가 뭘 안 먹었느냐는 거지? 하하. 과일과 빵, 치즈를 많이 먹었어. 치즈가 정말 맛있었지. 커피도 마셨고. 또 와인을 곁들여 멋진 저녁식사도 했어. 정말 너무 맛있었어!
남   글쎄, 좀 질투가 난다고 인정해야겠는 걸!

3   로라는 주로 ________________에 대해서 이야기하고 있다.
  (a) 유럽 문화   (b) 카페 음식
  (c) 와인   (d) 치즈

4   로라는 저녁식사에 무엇을 곁들였는가?
  (a) 치즈   (b) 빵
  (c) 와인   (d) 커피

Exercise   Step 2
들고 문제에 답하시오.

M   Traditionally, women are the ones who prepare dinner in the kitchen. In the past, men rarely cooked except to make a quick sandwich. But times are changing. Men are spending more time in the kitchen these days. Surveys show that 22% of American men cook dinner in their homes. While 22% may not sound like a lot, it's a historic all-time high. In 1990, only 13% of men cooked.

▶ traditionally 전통적으로   prepare 준비하다   rarely 좀처럼 ~하지 않는   historic 역사상의   all-time high 사상 최고

남   전통적으로 부엌에서 저녁을 준비하는 사람들은 여성들입니다. 과거에는 샌드위치를 재빨리 만드는 것 외에는 남자들은 거의 요리를 하지 않았습니다. 하지만 시대가 바뀌고 있지요. 요즘은 남자들도 부엌에서 더 많은 시간을 보냅니다. 조사에 따르면 미국 남성의 22%가 집에서 저녁을 요리한다고 합니다. 22%가 높게 느껴지는 수치는 아니지만 역사적으로 봤을 때 사상 최고의 수치입니다. 1990년에는 13%의 남성만이 요리를 했죠.

1 각 원 그래프에 해당하는 올바른 시기를 써 넣으시오.

(1)
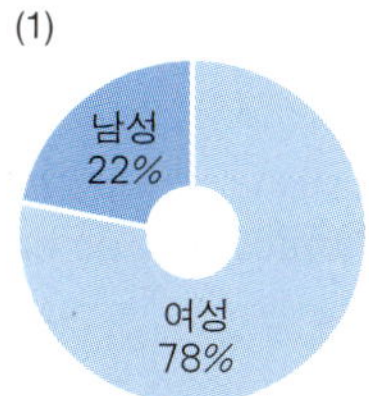

(2)
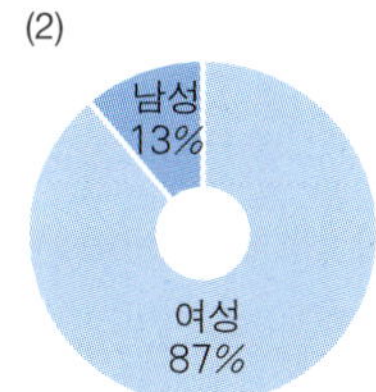

2

W I remember those days on the farm like they were yesterday. I woke up every morning to the smell of freshly baked bread. In those days, my mother made bread daily. Every morning, we had a big breakfast of eggs, potatoes, sausages, toast, and fresh orange juice. I was always hungry again by lunchtime. I couldn't wait to get to the table for meat, vegetables, and hot biscuits. Those smells bring back a lot of memories.

▶ farm 농장 freshly 신선하게 daily 매일, 날마다 bring back ~을 생각나게 하다

여 농장에서 보낸 날들이 마치 어제 일처럼 기억나요. 매일 아침 갓 구운 빵 냄새에 잠이 깼어요. 그 당시에 엄마는 매일 빵을 만드셨죠. 매일 아침, 우리는 계란, 감자, 소시지, 토스트, 신선한 오렌지 주스로 아침을 푸짐하게 먹었어요. 점심 시간이 될 때쯤이면 전 늘 또 배가 고파졌어요. 고기와 채소, 뜨거운 비스킷이 놓인 식탁으로 얼른 가고 싶어 견딜 수가 없었죠. 그런 냄새를 맡으면 많은 기억들이 떠올라요.

2 맞으면 T, 틀리면 F에 체크하시오.

(1) 화자는 매일 빵을 만들었다.
(2) 화자는 매일 아침식사를 푸짐하게 먹었다.
(3) 화자는 점심에 소시지를 먹었다.
(4) 화자는 농장에서의 생활이 잘 기억나지 않는다.
(5) 화자는 점심 시간이 되면 배가 고팠다.

3-5

M Today on *Food Secrets*, we look at the power of olives. Scientists decided to investigate why Greek people typically live longer than other people. They looked at an average Greek person's diet and found that it contains a lot of olive oil. Olive oil has some special powers: It lowers blood pressure and reduces the risk of heart disease. The Greeks put olive oil on everything, from salads to breads to meat. This has resulted in good health for the Greeks.

▶ investigate 조사하다 typically 대체로; 전형적으로 average 평균의, 보통의 diet 일상의 음식물 contain 포함하다; 담고 있다 blood pressure 혈압 risk 위험 result in 결국 ~이 되다

남 오늘 〈음식의 비밀〉에서는 올리브가 지닌 힘을 살펴보겠습니다. 과학자들은 그리스 사람들이 대체로 다른 지역 사람들보다 장수하는 이유를 조사해보기로 했지요. 일반적인 그리스 국민의 식단을 살펴본 그들은 음식에 올리브 오일이 많이 들어 있다는 것을 알게 되었습니다. 올리브 오일에는 몇 가지 특별한 힘이 있습니다. 혈압을 낮추고, 심장병에 걸릴 위험을 줄입니다. 그리스 사람들은 샐러드에서 빵, 고기에 이르기까지 모든 음식에 올리브 오일을 넣는데요, 이로 인해 그리스 사람들이 건강해졌습니다.

3 어디서 나오는 담화인 것 같은가?

(a) 뉴스   (b) 신문   (c) 소설
(d) 인터넷 블로그   (e) TV 프로그램

4 화자가 무엇을 추천하겠는가?

(a) 그리스에 가는 것   (b) 샐러드와 고기를 더 먹는 것
(c) 다이어트를 하는 것   (d) 올리브 오일을 더 먹는 것
(e) 기름진 음식을 더 먹는 것

5 내용을 가장 잘 요약한 것은 무엇인가?

(a) 그리스인들은 올리브 오일을 많이 먹어서 오래 산다.
(b) 그리스인들은 최상의 올리브 오일을 만들고 그것을 모든 것에 활용한다.

PRACTICE TEST

듣고 문제에 답하시오.

1

M Susan, please come in.
W Thanks. What a great place, Bruce!
M Thank you. Please have a seat while I finish up dinner.
W It smells great.
M Good. I hope you like roast beef.
W It's one of my favorites.
M Can I get you something to drink while you're waiting?
W Sure, do you have any sparkling wine?
M Coming right up.

▶ have a seat 앉다 come up 다가오다, 걸어오다

남 수전, 어서 들어와요.
여 고마워요. 집이 참 멋진데요, 브루스!
남 고마워요. 내가 저녁 준비를 마무리하는 동안 자리에 앉아 있어요.
여 맛있는 냄새가 나네요.
남 잘 됐군요. 당신이 로스트 비프를 좋아하면 좋겠는데.
여 제가 가장 좋아하는 것 중 하나예요.
남 기다리는 동안 뭐 마실 것 좀 갖다 줄까요?
여 네. 혹시 스파클링 와인 있어요?
남 곧 갖고 올게요.

1 화자들은 어디에 있는가?

(a) 브루스의 집에   (b) 식당에   (c) 소풍 장소에
(d) 기내에   (e) 수전의 집에

2

M Hello? Is this Shakin' Chicken? Yes, I'd like to order a 5-piece chicken combo, an order of French fries, a potato salad, a bottle of soda, and… do you have desserts? [...] That sounds good. A small bucket of chocolate ice cream. [...] Yes, that's everything. Oh, and I have a coupon for French fries. [...] Sure, I live at 52 Douglas St. Oh, how long will that be? 30 minutes? Super. Thank you. Bye.

▶ order 주문하다 soda 소다수 bucket 통

남 여보세요? 셰이킹 치킨이죠? 예, 5조각짜리 치킨 콤보 하나랑, 프렌치 프라이 하나, 감자 샐러드 하나, 소다수 한 병에…. 디저트도 있어요? 그거 좋겠네요. 초콜릿 아이스크림 작은 걸로 한 통이요. 예, 그게 다예요. 아, 그리고 프렌치 프라이 쿠폰이 있는데요. 네. 더글러스 가 52번지요. 아, 얼마나 걸릴까요? 30분이요? 아주 좋아요. 고맙습니다. 끊을게요.

2 고객의 주문 내용을 적으시오.

Shakin' Chicken 주문서
주소: ______________________
주문 품목: ______________________
____
____
____
____
총액: $______

3-4

M What a beautiful place for a wedding!

W No kidding!

M And did you see the buffet?

W No, not yet. How does it look?

M It's very nice. Salads, soups, beef, fish, and cake of course.

W Sounds lovely. Good thing I'm pretty hungry.

M You won't be disappointed. There's even a chocolate fountain!

W Are you serious?

M You bet.

W Well, let's go and say hello to the bride and groom so we can start eating. I'm starving.

M Excellent idea.

▶ buffet 뷔페 disappointed 실망한 fountain 분수 You bet. 물론이야.

남 결혼식 올리기 정말 멋진 곳이네요!
여 정말 장난 아닌데요!
남 그리고 뷔페 음식도 봤어요?
여 아뇨, 아직 못 봤어요. 어때 보였나요?
남 진짜 괜찮아요. 샐러드, 수프, 쇠고기, 생선, 물론 케이크도 있고요.
여 정말 괜찮겠네요. 굉장히 배고픈데 잘 됐어요.
남 실망하지 않을 거예요. 초콜릿 분수도 있더라니까요!
여 정말요?
남 그렇다니까요.
여 그럼, 신랑 신부한테 가서 인사하고 먹기 시작하자고요. 나 정말 배고파요.
남 좋은 생각이에요.

3 어떤 종류의 식사가 제공되고 있는가?

(a) 멀티 코스 식사   (b) 뷔페   (c) 3 코스 식사
(d) 영국식 조찬   (e) 브런치

4 화자들은 어떻게 느끼는가?

(a) 실망한다   (b) 화가 나 있다

(c) 심각하다   (d) 감정적이다
(e) 신났다

5

M Last night I cooked dinner for my family. I made pizza. Pizza's a pretty simple dish to make if you're not the best cook. You can put anything you want on it, so I think making pizza is much better than ordering out. Last night, I put on green peppers, onions, olives, pepperoni, and lots of cheese. Everyone loved it. Next time, I'd like to try making seafood pizza.

▶ simple 간단한 green pepper 피망

남 어젯밤에 식구들을 위해서 저녁을 요리했어요. 피자를 만들었죠. 요리를 아주 잘하지 않더라도 피자는 간단히 만들 수 있는 요리예요. 위에 원하는 것을 다 얹을 수 있어서 전 배달해 먹는 것보다 피자를 만들어 먹는 게 훨씬 더 좋은 것 같아요. 어젯밤에는 피망, 양파, 올리브, 페페로니랑 치즈를 듬뿍 올렸죠. 모두가 좋아했어요. 다음에는 해산물 피자를 만들어보고 싶어요.

5 화자가 피자 위에 올리지 않은 것은?

(a) 올리브   (b) 치즈   (c) 버섯
(d) 피망   (e) 페페로니

6

W When you travel, be prepared to try many new types of food. For example, in France, you can eat snails and frog legs. In China, you can eat shark's fin soup. In Peru, it's common to eat guinea pigs. In many parts of Asia, bugs are considered a good and healthy snack. Of course, you don't have to try everything on the menu, but food is a great way to experience other cultures.

▶ prepare 준비하다 snail 달팽이 fin 지느러미 common 보통의, 흔한 bug 벌레 consider ~라고 여기다 experience 경험하다

여 여행할 때 새로운 종류의 음식을 많이 먹어보겠다는 마음의 준비를 하세요. 예를 들어, 프랑스에서는 달팽이 요리와 개구리 다리 요리를 먹을 수 있고요, 중국에서는 상어 지느러미 수프를 먹을 수 있어요. 페루에서는 기니 피그를 먹는 게 보통이랍니다. 아시아의 많은 지역에서는 벌레를 맛있고 건강에 좋은 간식으로 여깁니다. 물론 메뉴에 있는 걸 다 먹어볼 필요는 없지만, 음식은 다른 문화를 경험할 수 있는 멋진 방법이랍니다.

6 무엇에 관한 내용인가?

(a) 세계의 문화
(b) 건강과 여행
(c) 전세계의 유명한 식당들
(d) 여행 중에 새로운 음식을 먹어보는 것
(e) 새로운 종류의 음식

7-8

M What's your favorite type of food, Sharon?

W I'm a big fan of Indian food.

M Oh yeah?

W Yes, I took a cooking course while traveling in India, and I really enjoyed it.

M Do you cook it at home?

W Yes, quite often.

M Isn't it difficult to find the right <u>ingredients</u> here in Canada?

W Nope. There's a big international food store downtown that <u>carries</u> all the spices.

M Cool! I had no idea.

W Well, how about <u>coming over</u> some time for some curry and naan bread?

M ____________________________________

▶ ingredient 재료 Nope. (구어) 아니. international 국제적인 carry (물품을) 가게에 놓다, 팔다 spice 양념, 향신료 come over (지나가는 길에) 들르다 yummy 맛있는

남 섀론, 어떤 종류의 음식을 가장 좋아해?
여 난 인도 요리 팬이야.
남 아, 그래?
여 응. 인도 여행하는 동안 요리 강좌를 수강했는데, 정말 즐겁게 들었어.
남 집에서 인도 요리하니?

여 응, 자주 해.
남 여기 캐나다에서 맞는 재료를 찾는 게 어렵지 않아?
여 아니. 시내에 큰 해외 음식 상점이 하나 있는데, 모든 종류의 양념을 다 팔아.
남 멋진데! 몰랐어.
여 음, 카레랑 난 먹으러 언제 한번 들를래?
남 ____________________________________

7 섀론은 어디서 향신료를 구입하는가?

(a) 인도에서   (b) 해외 음식 상점에서

(c) 인터넷으로   (d) 식료품점에서

(e) 인도인 이웃에게게서

8 남자가 다음에 뭐라고 말하겠는가?

(a) 맛있는데.

(b) 전에 인도에 가 본 적이 있어.

(c) 그래, 넌 그렇게 할 수 있어.

(d) 미안해. 난 내일 바빠.

(e) 물론이지. 맛있겠는데.

Unit **5** # High School Is Tough Sometimes

Answers

GET READY p. 56~57

Key Words & Expressions

1 field trip	2 piece of cake	3 school dance
4 jocks	5 tutoring	6 yearbook
7 school uniforms	8 kicked out of	9 member
10 bunch of		

Questions & Responses

1 c   2 e   3 f   4 a   5 b   6 d

BASIC DRILL p. 58~59

Step 1 • business / yearbook committee and junior band

Q (d)

■ high school, youngest, classes, taking, clubs, middle school, yearbook

Step 2 representative / basketball / English, science / music

1 (b)   2 (1) T   (2) T   (3) F

Plus⁺ Question 1 (c)   2 (d)

EXERCISE p. 60~61

Step 1 1 (c)   2 (a)   3 (b)   4 (d)

Step 2 1

Name	Job
Nicole	the head of the yearbook committee
Krista	head photographer
Charles	secretary
Lee	designer

2 (1) T   (2) F   (3) T   (4) F   (5) T   3 (b)   4 (e)

5 (b)

PRACTICE TEST p. 64~65

1 (a)

2 ✔ English   ✔ math
   ✔ French   ☐ art
   ☐ Spanish   ✔ music
   ✔ science   ☐ drama
   ✔ history   ✔ business
   ☐ geography   ☐ creative writing

3 (e)   4 (b)   5 (e)   6 (b)   7 (b)   8 (c)

* Dictation 1, 2의 정답은 각 Script의 밑줄친 부분임.

GET READY

Key Words & Expressions

다음 문장을 듣고 보기 박스에서 알맞은 단어를 골라 빈칸을 채우시오.

1 우린 이번 주 목요일에 역사 현장학습을 갈 거야.

2 난 공부를 많이 했기 때문에 그 시험이 식은 죽 먹기라고 생각했어.

3 칼라한테 나랑 학교 댄스 파티에 같이 가자고 하고 싶어.

4 '스포츠맨'들은 보통 떼로 몰려 다니면서 체육관 문 밖이나 자기네 라커 주위를 어슬렁거려.

5 션은 여가 시간에 급우들에게 과외 교습을 해.

6 졸업 앨범 준비 위원회에서는 학교 행사 때 사진을 찍을 신입 사진작가를 늘 찾고 있습니다.

7 말레이시아의 학생들 대부분은 교복을 입어야 합니다.

8 어제 닉이 베낀 에세이를 제출했다가 교실 밖으로 쫓겨났어.

9 난 우리 학교 연극 동아리 회원이야.

10 넌 원하는 수업을 선택할 수 있고, 동아리에도 많이 가입할 수 있어.

Questions & Responses

질문에 어울리는 대답과 연결하시오.

1 중학교에 다니니?

2 몇 학년이야?

3 얘, 너 나랑 같은 경제학 수업 듣지 않니?

4 동아리에 가입했어?

5 지금까지 학교 생활은 어때?

6 교복을 입니?

ⓒ 아니요, 전 고등학교에 다녀요.

ⓔ 10학년이에요.

ⓕ 응, 그런 것 같아. 너 두 번째 줄에 앉지?

ⓐ 응, 연극 동아리에 가입했어.

ⓑ 아직까진 나쁘지 않아.

ⓓ 응, 입어. 회색 바지에 파란색 카디건이야.

듣고 정답을 확인하시오.

친구와 함께 연습하시오.

Basic Drill　**Step 1**

다음을 듣고 메모하시오.

W I just started high school this year. Yep, grade nine! Although it's kind of tough being the youngest at school again, I really like high school. I like that I got to choose some of my classes, and there are many types of classes. For example, I'm taking business now. There are also a lot more clubs to join than in middle school. I joined the yearbook committee and the junior band. I think the next four years are going to fly by.

▶ **yearbook** 연감, 연보; 졸업 앨범　**committee** 위원회　**fly by** 시간이 쏜살같이 지나가다

여　난 올해 막 고등학교 생활을 시작했어. 그래, 9학년이지! 또다시 학교에서 가장 아래 학년이라는 게 조금 힘들지만, 고등학교 생활이 진짜 맘에 들어. 수업을 몇 가지 선택한다는 게 좋은데, 수업 종류가 참 많아. 예를 들어, 난 지금 비즈니스 과목을 듣고 있어. 또 중학교 때보다 가입할 수 있는 동아리도 훨씬 많아. 난 학교 연감 위원회와 하급생 밴드에 가입했어. 다음 4년이 금방 휙 지나갈 것 같아.

메모를 바탕으로 다음 문제에 답하시오.

Q 다음 중 사실인 것은?

(a) 화자는 10학년이다.

(b) 화자는 이제 막 고등학교를 졸업했다.

(c) 화자는 밴드에 가입하지 않기로 결심했다.

(d) 화자는 고등학교 생활을 기대하고 있다.

■ 다시 듣고 빈칸을 채우시오.

Basic Drill　**Step 2**

다음을 듣고 메모하시오.

M My name's Ryan, and I'm in the 11th grade at Winchester High School. I really like my school, so I joined the student government. I'm the grade 11 representative at school meetings.

I'm also on the basketball team. My school has a pretty good team. Last year, we made it to the state finals. We got to take a trip to Los Angeles for the final game. We won the championship. That was a great year.

I do peer tutoring as well. That means I use some of my spare time to meet with other students and to help them with their classes. I tutor English and science. I like helping the other kids.

I am also in the drama club. We put on a play for our community twice a year. Actually, I'm not an actor. I help out backstage with the lighting and music. The last play we did was called *Oklahoma*.

▶ **representative** 대표자　**final** 결승전　**championship** 선수권, 우승　**peer** 동료　**tutor** 개인지도 하다　**put on** ~을 상연하다　**community** 지역 사회(사람들)　**backstage** 무대 뒤에서, 분장실[막후]에서　**lighting** 조명

남　내 이름은 라이언이고, 윈체스터 고등학교 11학년이야. 난 우리 학교가 정말 좋아서 학생회에 가입했어. 현재 학교 회의에서 11학년 대표를 맡고 있지.

난 농구팀에도 들었어. 우리 학교 농구팀은 정말 잘해. 작년에 주(州) 대항 결승전에 진출해서 결승 경기를 하러 로스앤젤레스로 가야 했어. 우리가 우승했지. 정말 근사한 한 해였어.

난 급우 과외 교습도 해. 이건 내 여가 시간을 이용해서 다른 학생들을 만나 수업을 따라가도록 도와주는 거야. 난 영어랑 과학을 지도해. 난 다른 애들을 도와주는 게 좋아.

또 연극 동아리에도 들었어. 우리는 1년에 두 번 우리 지역 주민들을 위해 연극을 올리거든. 사실 난 배우는 아니고, 무대 뒤에서 조명이랑 음악을 담당해. 우리가 했던 마지막 연극은 〈오클라호마〉였어.

메모를 바탕으로 다음 문제에 답하시오.

1 라이언은 주로 무엇에 관해 이야기하고 있는가?

(a) 자기가 하는 스포츠

(b) 자기가 하는 학교 활동

(c) 학교에 대한 사랑

(d) 농구 우승

2 맞으면 T, 틀리면 F를 쓰시오.

　(1) 라이언은 자기 학교를 좋아한다.

　(2) 라이언은 학생들이 수업을 따라가도록 돕는다.

　(3) 라이언은 배우다.

다시 듣고 정답을 확인하시오.

Plus⁺ Question

1 작년 농구 결승전은 어디서 했는가?

　(a) 윈체스터　　　　(b) 라이언네 고등학교

　(c) 로스앤젤레스　　(d) 오클라호마

2 라이언은 급우들에게 무엇을 과외 교습하는가?

　(a) 조명과 음악을 담당한다.

　(b) 농구를 지도한다.

　(c) 영어와 수학을 가르친다.

　(d) 영어와 과학을 도와준다.

EXERCISE　Step 1

듣고 문제에 답하시오.

M　Hey, how's it going?

W　Not bad. You?

M　Can't complain. Let's eat.

W　Sure.

M　Where should we sit?

W　How about over there?

M　Are you kidding? That's where all the jocks sit.

W　Jocks?

M　Yeah, the guys who only do sports and always hang out near the gym.

W　Oh, I see. Yeah, I wouldn't want to sit with them. They're so loud.

M　You've got that right. And don't forget that they're annoying, too.

▶ jock 운동선수, 특정 스포츠에 열광하여 대부분의 시간을 그 스포츠를 하는 데 쓰는 젊은이　hang out 서성거리나　annoying 싱가신

남　어이, 어떻게 지내?

여　나쁘지 않아. 넌?

남　괜찮아. 먹자.

여　응.

남　우리 어디 앉을까?

여　저기 저 자리는 어때?

남　농담이지? 저기는 스포츠맨들이 항상 앉는 자리야.

여　스포츠맨?

남　응, 운동만 하면서 항상 체육관 주변을 어슬렁거리는 애들.

여　오, 알겠다. 그래, 나도 쟤네들이랑 같이 앉기 싫어. 너무 시끄러워.

남　바로 맞혔어. 게다가 엄청 성가신 애들이라는 사실을 잊지 마.

1　Jocks는 어디를 돌아다니는가?

(a) 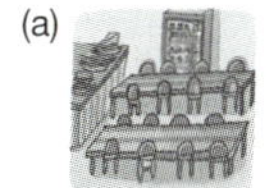　(b) 　(c) 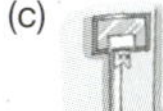　(d) 

W　Hey, Marcel. What are all these papers?

M　Oh, it's information from colleges I'm interested in.

W　Already? You have not even finished high school.

M　I know, but I want to do some research so that I make the right choice.

W　So, what's your top choice?

M　Well, in a perfect world, I'd like to go to Harvard.

W　Yeah, but you'll need a plan B just in case.

M　Right. I'm thinking about NYU. It's a good school and is not too far from home.

W　For sure. And don't you have relatives in New York?

M　Yes, I've got some cousins there. Maybe I'll go and check it out.

▶ paper 종이; 신문　research 조사　top 최고의, 주요한　just in case 만일에 대비하여　in a perfect world '이상적인[완벽한] 세상에서는', 즉 모든 조건이 완벽하다면, 이상적으로는　relative 친척

여　야, 마르셀! 이 종이들 다 뭐야?

남　어, 내가 관심 있는 대학 관련 정보이야.

여　벌써? 아직 고등학교 과정도 다 안 끝냈잖아.

남　알아. 하지만 올바른 선택을 할 수 있게 몇 가지 조사를 하고 싶어서.

여　그래, 네가 가장 염두에 두고 있는 선택은 뭔데?

남　글쎄, 이상적으론 하버드 대학에 가고 싶어.

여　그렇구나. 하지만 만일의 경우를 생각해서 제2안도 필요하잖아.

남　맞아. 그래서 뉴욕대학교(NYU)를 생각하고 있어. 학교도 좋고, 집과도 너무 멀리 떨어져 있지 않으니까.

여　그렇지. 그리고 너 뉴욕에 친척 있지 않아?

남　응. 거기에 사촌들이 몇 명 있어. 한 번 가서 확인해봐야겠어.

2　다음 중 사실이 아닌 것은?

　(a) 뉴욕대학교가 마르셀이 최우선으로 생각하는 곳이다.

　(b) 마르셀은 대학교들을 알아보고 있다.

　(c) 마르셀은 고등학교에 다닌다.

　(d) 마르셀은 하버드 대학에 가고 싶어한다.

3-4

W　Paul, where are you going?

M　I'm just going to hang out at Kenny's place.

W　Don't you have exams next week?

M　Yeah, I do.

W　Well, shouldn't you be studying instead of hanging out at Kenny's?

M　Don't worry, Mom. I'm going to study this weekend.

W　I don't think that's good enough. Your grades have been pretty low. You call Kenny and tell him you're not going there.

M　But Mom!

W　Don't give me any "buts"! You can hang out with Kenny when your exams are over.

M　Fine…

▶ instead of ~대신에

여　폴, 어디 가니?

남 케니네 집에서 놀려고요.

여 너 다음 주에 시험 있지 않아?

남 네, 있어요.

여 그럼 케니네서 노는 대신 공부해야 하지 않을까?

남 걱정 마세요, 엄마. 이번 주말에 공부할 거예요.

여 그것 가지고는 안 될 것 같은데. 너 성적이 상당히 많이 떨어졌잖니. 케니한테 전화해서 걔네 집에 안 갈 거라고 얘기하렴.

남 그렇지만, 엄마!

여 엄마한테 '그렇지만' 이란 말 하지마! 시험이 끝나고 케니랑 놀아도 되잖아.

남 알았어요….

3 폴의 엄마는 _______________.

(a) 마음이 느긋하다

(b) 화가 났다

(c) 만족해한다

(d) 자랑스럽게 느낀다

4 왜 폴은 공부를 해야 하는가?

(a) 성적이 케니보다 낫다.

(b) 아빠가 공부하라고 한다.

(c) 케니를 도와주어야 한다.

(d) 다음 주에 시험이 있다.

Exercise **Step 2**

듣고 문제에 답하시오.

W Hi, everyone, and welcome to our first <u>yearbook</u> <u>committee</u> meeting. I'm Nicole, the head of the committee. Thank you all <u>for joining</u>. I'd like to <u>introduce</u> our senior members. This is Krista, our head photographer. This is Charles, our <u>secretary</u>. And this is Lee, our designer. We have lots of work for you to do. We'll need lots of photographers and reporters for school events. If anyone <u>wants to volunteer</u> for a certain event, please let me know.

▶ **head** 수석, 회장 **secretary** (회의) 간사; 비서 **volunteer** 자진하여 하다

여 여러분, 안녕하세요. 첫 번째 학교 연감 위원회 회의에 오신 걸 환영합니다. 저는 위원장을 맡고 있는 니콜이에요. 모두 와주셔서 감사합니다. 저희 선배 회원들을 소개할게요. 이쪽은 수석 사진작가인 크리스타, 이쪽은 간사를 맡고 있는 찰스, 그리고 이쪽은 디자이너인 리예요. 여러분께서 해주실 일이 무척 많습니다. 학교 행사 때 일할 사진작가와 기자가 많이 필요하게 될 텐데, 특정 행사에 자원하고 싶으신 분이 계시면 제게 알려주세요.

1 선배 회원들이 맡고 있는 일은 무엇인가?

이름	직무
니콜	
크리스타	
찰스	
리	

2

W Hello, everyone. Welcome to English 201. <u>What a big</u> <u>class</u>! My name is Mrs. Cook, and I'm a new teacher at this school. I hope we have a <u>great semester</u> together. I'm a pretty easygoing teacher, but I do have a few rules. First of all, <u>no cell phones</u> or gadgets in the classroom. Two, please <u>respect</u> each other. Three, let's <u>have fun</u>. We're going to read some great stuff, like Shakespeare and Conrad, so <u>get ready</u>!

▶ **semester** 학기 **easygoing** 성격이 수더분한 **gadget** (기계) 장치 **stuff** (문학 등의) 작품

여 안녕하세요, 여러분. 중급 영어(English 201) 수업에 잘 오셨어요. 정말 대규모의 수업이군요. 전 이 학교에 새로 부임한 쿡입니다. 함께 멋진 한 학기를 보낼 수 있으면 좋겠습니다. 전 수더분한 선생님입니다. 하지만 제게도 몇 가지 규칙이 있어요. 첫째, 교실에서는 휴대폰이나 기타 기계장치 같은 건 절대 안 돼요. 둘째, 서로서로 존중합시다. 셋째, 즐겁게 지냅시다. 셰익스피어나 콘래드 같은 명작을 읽을 거예요. 그러니 준비하세요!

2 맞으면 T, 틀리면 F에 체크하시오.

(1) 쿡 선생님은 영어 선생님이다.

(2) 쿡 선생님은 엄격한 선생님이다.

(3) 중급 영어(English 201)를 듣는 학생들은 셰익스피어를 읽는다.

(4) 쿡 선생님은 자기 수업 시간에 휴대폰을 허용한다.

(5) 중급 영어(English 201)는 대규모 수업이다.

3-5

M Dear fellow students. Here we are <u>at the end of</u> this chapter of our lives. Remember our first day here, when the hallways seemed so <u>big and scary</u>? We've certainly come a long way. We're older and hopefully wiser. Although we do not know what lies <u>ahead for us</u>, the experiences and friendships we had here at Elmwood High School will help us as we begin our <u>next journey</u>. Treasure the memories we made here.

▶ **chapter** (인생, 역사 등의) 한 장 **hallway** 복도 **hopefully** 바라건대 **ahead** 앞에 **treasure** 소중히 하다; 보물

남 친애하는 학생 동기 여러분. 우리는 지금 우리 인생에서 학창시절이라는 장의 마지막에 와 있습니다. 여기 처음 온 날, 복도가 굉장히 크고 무서워 보였던 그날을 기억하세요? 우리는 분명 먼 길을 왔습니다. 나이도 들고, 바라건대 더 현명해졌죠. 비록 우리 앞에 무엇이 놓여 있는지 알 수 없지만 이곳 엘름우드 고등학교에서 겪은 경험과 함께 나눈 우정은 우리가 다음 여정을 시작할 때 도움이 될 것입니다. 여기서 우리가 만든 추억을 소중히 간직해주십시오.

3 어떤 종류의 담화인가?

(a) 학교 첫날 행하는 연설

(b) 졸업 연설

(c) 학생회 회의 연설

(d) 여행 동아리 모임 연설

(e) 새로 부임한 선생님을 환영하는 연설

4 화자는 다음에 뭐라고 할 것 같은가?

(a) 내년에 봅시다.

(b) 문에 있는 연감을 집으세요.

(c) 여행 즐겁게 하세요.

(d) 여러분 모두 만나서 반가워요.

(e) 행운을 빌며 축하합니다.

PRACTICE TEST

듣고 문제에 답하시오.

W　School uniforms are a hot topic in many American towns. While some countries, like Britain, for example, have always had their students wear uniforms, America hasn't adopted this tradition. Some schools do, but some don't. People who are pro-uniform say that uniforms help students get along better since they are not competing in a "fashion show" at school. People who are against uniforms say they are too expensive and old-fashioned. It looks like this debate will continue for some time.

▶ adopt 채택하다　tradition 전통　pro ~을 찬성하여　compete 경쟁하다　against ~에 반대하여　old-fashioned 구식의　debate 논쟁

여　미국 내 많은 도시에서 교복이 뜨거운 화제입니다. 몇몇 국가, 예를 들어, 영국 같은 나라는 항상 학생들에게 교복을 입혔습니다. 하지만 미국은 이런 전통을 받아들이지 않았죠. 어떤 학교에서는 받아들이지만 또 어떤 학교에서는 받아들이지 않습니다. 교복 찬성론자들은 교복을 입으면 학생들이 잘 지내는 데 도움이 될 거라고 말합니다. 학교 '패션쇼'에서 서로 경쟁하지 않아도 되기 때문입니다. 교복 반대론자들은 교복이 너무 비싸고 구식이라고 말합니다. 한동안 이 논쟁은 계속될 것 같군요.

1 무엇에 관한 내용인가?

(a) 미국의 교복　　　　　(b) 패션쇼

(c) 영국 학교들　　　　　(d) 미국 학교 대 영국 학교

(e) 학교 전통

M　Today I had to go to school to register and choose my 7 classes. Some classes are mandatory, which means I have to take them. I have to take English, science, math, and a social science. I chose history as my social science. That left me three classes to choose. It was tough making a decision. I wanted to take both music and drama, but I was only allowed to choose one art. I ended up choosing French, music, and business. I hope I made the right choices!

▶ register 등록하다　mandatory 필수의　make a decision 결정하다　end up ~ing 결국 ~하게 되다

남　전 오늘, 일곱 과목을 수강 신청하고 선택하러 학교에 가야 했어요. 그 중 몇몇 과목들은 꼭 들어야 하는 필수과목이에요. 전 영어, 과학, 수학, 그리고 사회 한 과목을 들어야 해요. 사회과목으로 역사를 선택했어요. 그러고 나니 골라야 할 과목이 세 개가 남더라고요. 결정하는 게 참 힘들었어요. 음악과 연극 둘 다 듣고 싶었지만 예술과목은 하나만 신청하도록 되어 있었거든요. 결국은 프랑스어, 음악, 비즈니스를 선택했어요. 제대로 잘 고른 것이었으면 좋겠어요!

Level up

2 화자가 고른 과목에 체크하시오.

□ 영어　　　　　　□ 수학

□ 프랑스어　　　　□ 미술

□ 스페인어　　　　□ 음악

□ 과학　　　　　　□ 연극

□ 역사　　　　　　□ 비즈니스

□ 지리　　　　　　□ 창작 글쓰기

3~4

W　Hey, Jules. The big dance is coming up, huh?

M　Yeah, I suppose so, Amy. Who are you going with?

W　Well, I was thinking of asking someone, but I'm nervous.

M　Nervous? Why?

W　Well, I don't know if this guy really likes me.

M　But you don't know for sure. Just ask him.

W　You think I should?

M　Sure! Why not?

W　All right. Jules, will you go to the dance with me?

M　What?

W　Will you go to the dance with me?

M　Uh… Um… I didn't know you meant me!

W　Well, what do you say?

M　Oh, all right!

▶ come up 다가오다　nervous 불안한　What do you say? 어떻게 할래?

여　야, 줄스. 성대한 댄스 파티가 다가오고 있네?

남　그래, 그렇구나, 에이미. 넌 누구랑 갈 거야?

여　글쎄, 어떤 사람한테 가자고 물어볼 생각이었는데, 좀 불안해.

남　불안해? 왜?

여　글쎄, 그 애가 날 정말 좋아하는지 아닌지 모르거든.

남　하지만 너도 확실히 모르잖아. 그냥 그 애한테 물어봐.

여　내가 정말 그래야 할 것 같아?

남　물론이지! 왜 안 돼?

여　좋아. 줄스, 나랑 같이 댄스 파티 가줄래?

남　뭐?

여　나랑 댄스 파티 같이 갈래?

남　어, 음…. 네가 날 염두에 두고 있었는지 몰랐어!

여　그래, 어떻게 할래?

남　아, 좋지!

3 줄스와 에이미는 어떤 행사에 대해 이야기하고 있는가?

(a) 학교 회의

(b) 스포츠 데이(운동회)

(c) 파티

(d) 결혼식

(e) 학교에서 열리는 댄스 파티

4 줄스는 마지막에 어떻게 느끼는가?

(a) 지루했다　　　　　(b) 놀랐다

(c) 흥분했다　　　　　(d) 화가 났다

(e) 실망했다

5

M Hey, Jan!

W Hey, Will. What's up?

M I've got to ask you for a huge favor.

W Sure, what is it?

M I didn't do my history essay, and it's due today. You have a different teacher… Can I copy one of your essays?

W No way!

M Why not? No one will find out!

W You want to bet? If my teacher finds out, I'll fail the class.

M Well then, what do I do?

W Just go and see your teacher and ask to hand it in late.

M Do you think so?

W Yeah. He might take off some points, but at least you won't be cheating!

▶ **favor** 부탁 **copy** 베끼다, 복사하다 **No way!** 싫어! 안돼! **bet** 내기를 걸다 **hand in** 제출하다 **take off** (값 따위를) 깎다 **at least** 적어도 **cheat** 속이다

남 안녕, 잰!
여 어, 윌. 무슨 일이야?
남 나 너한테 뭐 하나 크게 부탁할 일이 있어.
여 그래. 뭔데?
남 역사 에세이 숙제를 못했는데 오늘이 제출일이야. 너랑 나랑 선생님이 다르니까, 네 에세이 중 하나를 베껴도 될까?
여 안 돼!
남 왜? 아무도 모를 거야!
여 내기 할래? 우리 선생님이 아시는 날엔, 난 그 과목 낙제한단 말이야.
남 그럼 나 어떻게 해야 돼?
여 가서 선생님 뵙고 늦게 제출할 수 있게 해달라고 부탁 드려.
남 그래야 할까?
여 그래. 선생님께서 점수는 좀 깎으시겠지만, 적어도 네가 속이는 건 아니잖아!

5 잰은 윌에게 __________ 말라고 말한다.
(a) 리포트를 늦게 제출하지   (b) 자기를 괴롭히지
(c) 수업에 낙제하지   (d) 선생님께 이야기하지
(e) 속이지

6

M Okay, everyone. Here's a breakdown of our senior band trip to Cleveland. We'll be leaving on Monday, March 10. We'll arrive in Cleveland at around 2:00. We will go directly to the band festival, where we'll perform at 4:30. After that, you'll have some free time in the evening. The next day, Tuesday, we'll be visiting the Rock and Roll Hall of Fame and Cedar Point Amusement Park. We'll head home Wednesday morning. Please fill out the permission slip and have a parent sign it by next Friday. Hope everyone can come.

▶ **breakdown** 내역(서), 설명 **senior** 선임의, 선배의, 최고 학년의 **perform** 연주하다 **head** 향하다, 나아가다 **fill out** ~에 기입하다, 작성하다 **permission slip** 승인서, 허가증

남 자, 여러분. 여기 클리블랜드로 떠나는 우리 상급 학년 밴드 투어의 세부 일정이 있습니다. 3월 10일 월요일에 출발하여 클리블랜드에는 2시경에 도착할 거예요. 곧장 밴드 페스티벌에 가서 4시 30분에 공연할 겁니다. 공연이 끝난 후, 저녁에 자유시간이 좀 주어질 겁니다. 다음날인 화요일에는 로큰롤 명예의 전당과 세다 포인트 놀이동산에 갈 거예요. 수요일 아침에 집으로 향할 것이고요. 여기 승인서를 작성하고 다음 주 금요일까지 부모님 사인을 받아오세요. 모두 갈 수 있기를 바랍니다.

6 화요일의 가장 중요한 일정은 무엇인가?
(a) 명예의 전당과 밴드 페스티벌
(b) 명예의 전당과 놀이동산
(c) 로큰롤 콘서트와 놀이동산
(d) 밴드 페스티벌과 놀이동산
(e) 자유시간과 명예의 전당

7~8

M Hey, Jane. Wow, I'm glad that's over! How do you think you did on that science exam?

W It was a piece of cake. I aced it.

M Really? How can you be so sure?

W I just found it really easy.

M What about the plant cell diagram question? That was pretty tough.

W Nah, simple stuff. Justin, science is easy for me.

M Hmm. Well, I hope you're right and that you did well. But don't get too excited because you never know.

▶ **a piece of cake** 식은 죽 먹기, 아주 쉬운 일 **cell** 세포 **ace it** (구어) 완벽하게 해내다 **diagram** 도해, 도식 **Nah.** 아니. **do well** 잘하다, (성적이) 좋다

남 안녕, 제인. 와, 시험 끝나서 진짜 좋다! 넌 과학 시험 어떻게 본 것 같아?
여 누워서 떡 먹기던데. 완벽하게 해냈지.
남 정말? 어떻게 그렇게 자신해?
여 그냥 너무 쉬웠으니까.
남 식물 세포 도표 문제 어땠어? 그건 꽤 어려웠는데.
여 아니, 간단한 문제였어. 저스틴, 나한테 과학은 쉬워.
남 흠. 어쨌든, 네 말이 맞아서 네가 시험을 잘 본 거였으면 좋겠다. 하지만 사람 일은 모르는 거니까 너무 그렇게 흥분하지는 마.

7 제인과 저스틴의 대화는 언제 일어나고 있는가?
(a) 과학 시험 보기 전에
(b) 과학 시험 끝나고
(c) 과학 수업 중에
(d) 과학 시험 보는 중에
(e) 점심 시간에

8 저스틴이 제인에게 하는 충고는 무엇인가?
(a) 빙빙 돌려서 말하지 마라. (요점만 말해라.)
(b) 유유상종이다.
(c) 떡 줄 사람은 생각도 안 하는데 김칫국부터 마시지 마라.
(d) 말하는 대로 실천하라.
(e) 행운을 빌어.

Action Movies Rule

Answers

GET READY p. 68~69

Key Words & Expressions

1 plot	**2** hog	**3** theater
4 horror movies	**5** released	**6** actors
7 Reality shows	**8** starred	**9** on the edge of
10 sold out		

Questions & Responses

1 d **2** e **3** f **4** a **5** c **6** b

BASIC DRILL p. 70~71

Step 1 ● what will happen at the end. / horror movies / They're too predictable.

Q (b)

■ thriller, popcorn, mystery, suspense, action, horror, predictable

Step 2 A romance **B** action / car chase

C make you think, life **D** musicals / Broadway

1 (b) **2** (1) F (2) T (3) T

Plus⁺ Question **1** (d)

EXERCISE p. 72~73

Step 1 **1**

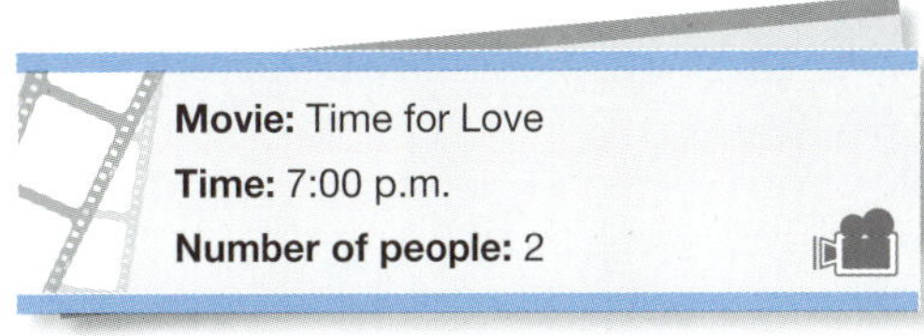

2 (1) F (2) T (3) T (4) T **3** (d) **4** (c)

Step 2 **1** (a) **2** (1) F (2) T (3) T (4) F (5) F **3** (b)

4 (b) **5** (a)

PRACTICE TEST p. 76~77

1 (a)

2

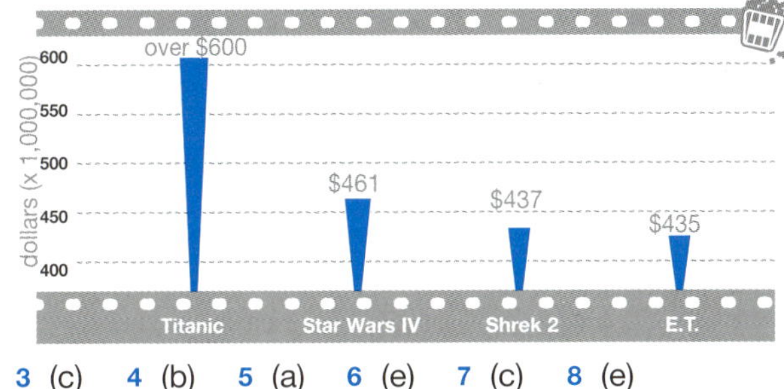

3 (c) **4** (b) **5** (a) **6** (e) **7** (c) **8** (e)

* Dictation 1, 2의 정답은 각 Script의 밑줄친 부분임.

Scripts and Translations

GET READY

Key Words & Expressions

다음 문장을 듣고 보기 박스에서 알맞은 단어를 골라 빈칸을 채우시오.

1 난 서스펜스가 넘치고 줄거리가 탄탄한 영화가 좋아요.

2 내 남동생은 리모컨 욕심쟁이예요. 절대 내가 뭘 보게 하질 않아요.

3 난 극장에서 버터를 바른 팝콘을 먹는 것을 정말 좋아해요.

4 남자친구는 공포영화만 좋아하는데, 전 공포영화는 못 참겠어요.

5 톰 크루즈의 새 액션 영화가 이번 주 토요일에 개봉한대. 보러 가자!

6 동물 배우들도 사람 배우들만큼 힘들게 일해요.

7 리얼리티 쇼는 미국에서 최고로 인기 있어요.

8 크리스티는 학교 뮤지컬에서 주연을 맡았어요.

9 액션 영화가 최고예요. 가슴 졸이게 만들잖아요.

10 오, 저 영화 매진됐어. 다른 걸 봐야겠는걸.

Questions & Responses

질문에 어울리는 대답과 연결하시오.

1 어떤 종류의 영화를 가장 좋아해요?

2 가장 좋아하는 영화는 뭐예요?

3 극장에는 얼마나 자주 가요?

4 가장 좋아하는 배우는 누구예요?

5 피하는 영화 종류가 있다면 뭔가요?

6 영화 볼 때 간식으로 뭘 먹나요?

ⓓ 공상 과학 영화를 좋아해요.

ⓔ 〈세계의 전쟁〉이 말할 필요도 없이 최고죠.

ⓕ 한 달에 한 번 정도 가요.

ⓐ 조디 포스터가 최고의 여배우인 것 같아요.

ⓒ 전 로맨틱 코미디는 못 참겠더라고요.

ⓑ 전 나초랑 치즈라면 사족을 못 써요.

듣고 정답을 확인하시오.

친구와 함께 연습하시오.

Basic Drill **Step 1**

다음을 듣고 메모하시오.

W I've always been a big fan of thriller movies. There's nothing better than sitting down to a thriller with a big bowl of popcorn while the lights are off. I think murder mystery thrillers are the best, but I'll watch anything full of suspense and action. The best movies are the ones where you don't know what will happen at the end. That's why I don't like horror movies. They're too predictable.

▶ thriller 스릴러   predictable 예상할 수 있는

여 전 늘 스릴러 영화의 열렬한 팬이었어요. 불이 꺼져 있는 동안 큰 팝콘 그릇을 들고 앉아 스릴러 영화를 보는 것보다 더 좋은 게 없더라고요. 살인 미스터리 스릴러가 최고라고 생각해요. 하지만 서스펜스와 액션이 많은 영화라면 뭐든 볼 거예요. 막판에 무슨 일이 벌어질지 전혀 감을 잡을 수 없는 영화가 최고의 영화죠. 그래서 전 공포영화를 싫어해요. 너무 뻔하잖아요.

메모를 바탕으로 다음 문제에 답하시오.

Q 주로 무엇에 관한 내용인가?
- (a) 스릴러가 드라마보다 더 나은 이유
- (b) 화자가 스릴러를 좋아하는 이유
- (c) 화자가 공포영화를 좋아하지 않는 이유
- (d) 화자가 영화를 볼 때 먹는 것

■ 다시 듣고 빈칸을 채우시오.

Basic Drill **Step 2**

다음을 듣고 메모하시오.

W1 My name's Patricia, and I absolutely love romance movies. My favorite movie of all time is *Gone with the Wind*. I've watched it at least 10 times. Sometimes my family gets annoyed because I watch it too much, but I can't help it. I love it!

M1 I'm Trevor, and I think action movies rule, especially if Arnold Schwarzenegger's in them. I love car chases when the cars crash and blow up at the end. I want to be a stuntman some day.

W2 I'm Olivia, and I only enjoy watching dramas. I love dramas that make you think about life. That's why I loved *Forrest Gump*. It was an interesting movie that anybody could enjoy.

M2 I'm Victor, and I love musicals. I think I love musicals so much because I'm really into music class at school. I loved the movie *Grease* so much that I went to see it on Broadway. It was awesome!

▶ get annoyed 귀찮아하다, 성내다   rule 최고이다: 지배하다   car chase 자동차 추격   blow up 폭발하다   be into ~에 관심을 가지다, 빠지다   awesome 굉장한, 아주 멋진

여1 내 이름은 패트리샤야. 난 정말 로맨스 영화를 좋아해. 고금을 막론하고 내가 제일 좋아하는 영화는 〈바람과 함께 사라지다〉야. 적어도 열 번은 봤어. 때때로 우리 가족은 내가 그걸 너무 많이 봐서 짜증을 내기도 하지만, 그래도 어쩔 수 없어. 난 그 영화가 너무 좋거든!

남1 난 트레버야. 내 생각엔 액션 영화, 그 중에서도 특히 아놀드 슈왈제네거가

나오는 영화가 지존인 것 같아. 차들이 충돌해서 마침내 폭발해버리는 자동차 추격 장면이 너무 좋아. 언젠가는 스턴트맨이 되고 싶어.

여2 난 올리비아고, 드라마 영화만 즐겨 봐. 인생에 대해 생각해보게 하는 드라마가 난 정말 좋아. 그래서 〈포레스트 검프〉를 좋아했지. 누구나 즐겁게 볼 수 있는 재미있는 영화였어.

남2 난 빅터라고 해. 뮤지컬을 무척 좋아하지. 내가 학교 음악 수업에 푹 빠져 있어서 뮤지컬을 굉장히 좋아하는 것 같아. 영화 〈그리스〉를 너무 좋아해서 그 뮤지컬을 보러 브로드웨이까지 갔었다니까. 정말 끝내줬지!

메모를 바탕으로 다음 문제에 답하시오.

1 화자들은 주로 무엇에 관해 이야기하고 있는가?
- (a) 가장 좋아하는 영화
- (b) 가장 좋아하는 영화 종류
- (c) 고전 영화
- (d) 영화 보러 가기

2 맞으면 T, 틀리면 F를 쓰시오.
- (1) 패트리샤의 가족은 〈바람과 함께 사라지다〉를 보는 것을 좋아한다.
- (2) 트레버는 영화에 나오는 자동차 추격 장면을 좋아한다.
- (3) 빅터는 브로드웨이에서 〈그리스〉를 보았다.

다시 듣고 정답을 확인하시오.

Plus⁺ Question

1 왜 빅터는 브로드웨이에서 〈그리스〉를 보았는가?
- (a) 음악 수업에서 그것을 보러 갔기 때문에
- (b) 음악을 좋아해서
- (c) 브로드웨이 근처에 살아서
- (d) 그 영화를 좋아해서

EXERCISE **Step 1**

듣고 문제에 답하시오.

M Okay, let's see. There are four movies playing at the theater. Which one do you want to see?

W What are the choices?

M Well, there's *Robot Island*, *Time for Love*, *Ghost Girl*, and *Henry VIII*.

W Hmm. How about *Ghost Girl*? I heard that's good.

M Oh, no, sorry… That one's sold out.

W Sold out? I don't know then. What would you like to see?

M Well, I like science fiction, but I know you hate it. So, how about a romance?

W Sure. Let's get some popcorn.

▶ sold out 매진된

남 좋아, 어디 보자. 영화관에서 지금 네 편의 영화가 상영 중인데, 뭘 보고 싶어?
여 뭘 고를 수 있는데?
남 음, 〈로봇 아일랜드〉, 〈타임 포 러브〉, 〈고스트 걸〉, 〈헨리 8세〉가 있네.
여 흠, 〈고스트 걸〉 어때? 괜찮다고 들었어.
남 오, 이런. 미안. 저 영화는 매진됐네.
여 매진됐다고? 그럼, 모르겠다. 넌 뭐 보고 싶어?
남 글쎄, 난 공상 과학 영화가 좋은데, 네가 싫어하잖아. 그러니, 로맨스 영화 어때?
여 좋아. 팝콘 좀 사자.

1 그들은 어떤 영화를 볼 것 같은가? 표에 관련 정보를 써 넣으시오.

2

M Hey, Tammy. Are you going to Ron's Academy Awards party?

W He invited me, but I don't know if I'm going.

M Why not?

W I'm not really into awards shows, John. Plus, I don't have anything to wear.

M What do you mean?

W Didn't you read the invitation?

M No, not yet.

W Everyone has to wear their best clothes.

M Oh, I didn't know that. But, oh well, it'll be fun. Please come.

W Oh, all right.

▶ plus 게다가

남 이봐, 태미. 론이 주최하는 아카데미 시상식 파티에 갈 거니?
여 론이 오라고 초대했는데, 갈지 안 갈지 잘 모르겠어.
남 왜?
여 시상식 쇼 같은 걸 좋아하지 않아서 말이야, 존. 게다가 입고 갈 것도 없고.
남 무슨 말이야?
여 초대장 안 읽어봤어?
남 아니, 아직.
여 모두 자기 옷 중에 제일 좋은 옷으로 차려 입어야 해.
남 어, 그건 몰랐네. 하지만, 뭐, 재미있을 거야. 꼭 와.
여 아, 알았어.

2 맞으면 T, 틀리면 F에 체크하시오.

(1) 존이 파티를 열 것이다.
(2) 태미는 시상식 쇼를 좋아하지 않는다.
(3) 손님들은 좋은 옷을 입고 파티에 와야 한다.
(4) 존은 태미가 파티에 오기를 바란다.

3-4

M Turn the channel.

W No.

M Then give me the remote control.

W Why should I? All you do is channel surf. You never watch anything.

M Well, that's better than watching this silly drama!

W It's not silly. I watch it every Monday night.

M Go watch it in your bedroom.

W I like this TV better.

M You're such a TV hog.

W You're such a whiner.

M I get the remote control after this dumb show is over.

W Fine.

▶ channel surf (리모컨으로) 채널을 자주 바꾸기   hog 욕심쟁이   whiner 우는 소리하는 사람, 불평하는 사람

남 채널 바꿔.
여 싫어.
남 그럼 나한테 리모컨 줘.
여 왜 그래야 하는데? 네가 하는 거라곤 채널만 여기저기 돌리는 거잖아. 아무 것도 제대로 안 보면서.
남 글쎄, 저 바보 같은 드라마 보는 것보다는 그게 더 나아!
여 바보 같은 드라마 아냐. 난 월요일 밤마다 저걸 본단 말이야.
남 네 방에 가서 봐.
여 난 여기 텔레비전이 더 좋아.
남 이 TV 귀신 같으니라고.
여 넌 칭얼칭얼 투덜이야.
남 저 멍청한 프로 끝나면 내가 리모컨 갖는다.
여 맘대로 해.

3 남자의 기분은 어떠한가?

(a) 슬프다　　　　　　(b) 무섭다
(c) 피곤하다　　　　　(d) 짜증난다

4 남자는 여자를 어떻게 짜증나게 하는가?

(a) 여자의 침실에서 TV를 본다.
(b) 멍청한 쇼를 본다.
(c) 채널을 이리저리 돌린다.
(d) 드라마를 본다.

Exercise **Step 2**

들고 문제에 답하시오.

1

M Angela… What are you doing here? I thought you were dead.

W Everyone thought so, Evan. Even myself.

M But where have you been all this time?

W It doesn't matter. I'm here, and that's all that matters.

M But… but… everything is different now.

W Is it? There's still you and me.

M No, there isn't! You're dead!

W I'm not, Evan. I'm right here in front of you.

M No. I must be dreaming. What will I tell Lisa?

W Lisa? You…

M Angela, wait…

▶ dead 죽은   matter 문제가 되다, 중요하다

남 안젤라, 당신이 여기 웬일이야? 난 당신이 죽은 줄 알았는데.
여 모두가 그렇게 생각했죠, 에반. 나 자신도요.
남 대체 그동안 당신 어디에 있었던 거야?
여 그건 중요하지 않아요. 난 여기 있고, 그것만이 중요한 거죠.
남 하지만, 하지만, 지금은 모든 게 달라졌어.
여 그런가요? 여전히 당신과 내가 있잖아요.
남 아냐, 그렇지 않아! 당신은 죽었어!
여 난 죽지 않았어요, 에반. 이렇게 당신 앞에 있잖아요.

남 아니야. 내가 지금 꿈을 꾸는 거야. 리사한테 뭐라고 말하지?
여 리사? 당신….
남 안젤라, 잠깐….

1 남자의 기분은 어떠한가?
(a) 혼란스럽다 (b) 겁먹었다 (c) 지루하다
(d) 안도했다 (e) 신이 났다

2

M After all the excitement leading up to the release of *New York Minute*, I thought I was in for a great movie. But, sadly, I was let down. This movie has an incredible cast of actors, but none of them gave their best performance in this movie. The plot was predictable and boring. The only good thing about it was the beautiful setting of New York in the fall. If you're thinking of seeing this in theaters, don't. Just save your money.

▶ **lead up to** 차츰 ~에 이르다, ~으로 이야기를 몰고 가다 **let down** 실망시키다 **cast** 배역 **plot** 줄거리 **performance** 연기 **setting** 배경

남 〈뉴욕 미니트〉 개봉까지 계속 흥분 상태였던 저는 굉장한 영화를 볼 수 있을 거라 생각했어요. 하지만 슬프게도, 실망했답니다. 이 영화의 캐스팅은 믿을 수 없을 정도로 화려하지만 그들 중 아무도 영화에서 최고의 연기를 보여주지 않았어요. 줄거리는 어떻게 전개될지 예측 가능했고 지루했죠. 영화에서 유일하게 좋았던 건 뉴욕의 가을이 보여주는 아름다운 배경이었어요. 극장에서 이 영화를 볼 생각이라면 그러지 마세요. 그냥 돈을 절약하세요.

2 맞으면 T, 틀리면 F에 체크하시오.
(1) 화자는 영화를 재미있게 보았다.
(2) 뉴욕은 가을에 아름답다.
(3) 그 영화에는 멋진 배우들이 나온다.
(4) 영화는 재미있었다.
(5) 화자는 그 영화를 보라고 권한다.

3–5

W Since the year 2000, both American and international TV viewers have been watching reality shows. *Survivor* was the first successful reality show, and since then, reality shows of all types have popped up. But how real are they? In truth, the makers of these shows often tell the contestants what to say and how to act. It's a mystery how much action on a reality show is real. But one thing is real: TV viewers can't get enough.

▶ **viewer** 시청자 **pop up** 불쑥 나타나다 **contestant** 경쟁자

여 2000년 이후로, 미국과 해외 TV 시청자들이 리얼리티 쇼를 시청하고 있습니다. 〈서바이버〉는 성공을 거둔 최초의 리얼리티 쇼였죠. 그 이후, 각양각색의 리얼리티 쇼들이 등장했는데요, 그 쇼들의 어디까지가 진짜일까요? 사실, 이런 쇼를 제작하는 사람들은 종종 출연자들에게 무엇을 얘기하고 어떻게 행동해야 할지를 말해줍니다. 리얼리티 쇼에서 보이는 행동 중 얼마가 진짜인지는 미스터리입니다. 하지만 한 가지는 진짜입니다. TV 시청자들이 볼 수 있는 '진짜'는 충분치 않다는 거지요.

3 무엇에 관한 내용인가?
(a) 리얼리티 쇼 〈서바이버〉

(b) 리얼리티 쇼 뒤에 숨겨진 진실
(c) 리얼리티 쇼의 창작자들
(d) 미국 리얼리티 쇼 시청자들
(e) 다양한 종류의 리얼리티 쇼

4 담화에 따르면 누가 리얼리티 쇼를 즐겨 보는가?
(a) 생존자들 (b) 전 세계 시청자들
(c) 경쟁자들 (d) 프로듀서들
(e) 액션 팬들

5 내용을 가장 잘 요약한 것은 무엇인가?
(a) 2000년 이후부터 TV 시청자들은 리얼리티 쇼의 많은 부분이 진짜가 아닌데도 리얼리티 쇼를 좋아했다.
(b) 사실은, TV 시청자들은 쇼의 많은 부분이 진짜가 아니라서 리얼리티 쇼를 좋아하지 않는다.

PRACTICE TEST

듣고 문제에 답하시오.

M Everybody, please welcome… Stella Avery!
W Hi!
M Welcome, Stella.
W Thanks, Frank.
M It's been a while, hasn't it? You look great, as always.
W Thanks. I do what I can.
M So, you've got a big movie coming out. Isn't that right?
W Yes, Frank. It's being released this Friday. It's going to be great.
M How was the shooting?
W Just fantastic. The cast was so great to work with, and I just had a blast.
M That's lovely, Stella. So, everyone, Stella's new movie, *Starlight Romance*, comes out this Friday. Go check it out.

▶ **as always** 여느 때처럼 **release** 개봉하다 **shooting** 촬영 **blast** 아주 즐거운 한때

남 자, 여러분, 환영해주십시오. 스텔라 애버리입니다!
여 안녕하세요!
남 어서 와요, 스텔라.
여 고마워요, 프랭크.
남 꽤 오랜만이네요, 그렇죠? 언제나처럼 멋지십니다.
여 감사합니다. 제가 할 수 있는 일을 하는 거죠.
남 출연하신 엄청난 영화가 곧 나온다던데, 맞죠?
여 네, 프랭크. 이번 주 금요일에 개봉해요. 굉장할 거예요.
남 촬영은 어땠어요?
여 환상적이었죠. 출연배우들도 같이 일하기 좋았고요, 진짜 즐거웠어요.
남 좋았겠군요, 스텔라. 자, 여러분, 스텔라의 새 영화 〈스타라이트 로맨스〉가 이번 주 금요일에 개봉합니다. 가서 꼭 보십시오.

1 어떤 종류의 TV 프로그램인가?
(a) 토크쇼 (b) 리얼리티 쇼
(c) 영화 (d) 연속극
(e) 시상식 쇼

❷

W There's no doubt that movies are big money. But how big? Well, on top of the world… um… list, is *Titanic*, which made over $600 million. The second-highest-grossing film was made 30 years earlier, in 1977. *Star Wars Episode 4* made an out-of-this-world $461 million. Another big money-maker was the big mean ogre Shrek in *Shrek 2*, which pulled in $437 million. Yet another strange creature made big bucks. He was E.T., and he went home with $435 million.

▶ **no doubt** 의심할 바 없이 **gross** ~의 총수익을 올리다 **out-of-this-world** 현실에서 동떨어진, 매우 훌륭한 **money-maker** 돈벌이가 되는 일, 재물을 축적하는 사람 **mean** 심술궂은: 의미하다 **ogre** 야만인, 괴물 **pull in** (구어) 돈을 벌다 **creature** 생물, 피조물

여 영화가 큰 돈이 된다는 건 의심할 여지가 없습니다. 하지만 얼마나 큰 돈벌이가 될까요? 글쎄요, 세계 톱 리스트에 〈타이타닉〉이 있는데요, 6억 달러 이상을 벌어들였습니다. 두 번째로 수익이 높은 영화는 30여 년 전인 1977년에 제작된 영화로, 〈스타워즈 에피소드 4〉는 4억 6천 1백만 달러라는 믿기지 않는 액수를 벌어들였습니다. 엄청난 돈을 벌어들인 또 다른 것은 〈슈렉 2〉에 나온 덩치가 크며 심술궂은 괴물 슈렉으로, 4억 3천 7백만 달러를 벌었죠. 게다가 다른 이상한 생물체도 큰 돈을 벌었죠. 바로 E.T였고요, 그는 4억 3천 5백만 달러를 벌어서 고향으로 돌아갔습니다.

Level up

2 그래프를 완성하시오.

3-4

M What do you usually watch on TV, June?

W Honestly, I don't watch a lot of TV. There's nothing very good on.

M Really? You don't watch TV?

W Well, once in a while I'll watch the news or a documentary.

M Wow. I wish I were more like you. I watch about 3 hours of TV a day. I need my game shows, sitcoms, and reality shows.

W That's too much, Tim. You'd better cut back.

M Yeah, I know, but it's tough.

▶ **once in a while** 때때로, 이따금 **cut back** 줄이다

남 준, TV에서 보통 뭘 봐요?
여 솔직히, 전 TV를 많이 안 봐요. 그다지 괜찮은 것을 안 하더라고요.
남 정말요? TV 안 봐요?
여 뭐, 가끔 뉴스나 다큐멘터리는 볼 수 있겠죠.
남 우와, 나도 당신 같았으면 좋겠어요. 전 하루에 세 시간 정도 TV를 봐요. 게임 쇼에 시트콤, 게다가 리얼리티 쇼도 봐야 하거든요.
여 너무 많은데요, 팀. 좀 줄여야겠어요.
남 예, 알아요. 그런데 그게 참 힘드네요.

3 준은 TV에서 무엇을 보는가?
(a) 리얼리티 쇼　　　　(b) 아무것도 안 본다
(c) 뉴스와 다큐멘터리　(d) 게임 쇼
(e) 뉴스와 리얼리티 쇼

4 팀의 문제는 무엇인가?
(a) TV가 고장났다.
(b) TV를 너무 많이 본다.
(c) 절대 TV를 보지 않는다.
(d) 온라인 게임에 중독되었다.
(e) 너무 바빠 TV를 볼 수 없다.

❺

W Often, the most memorable actors from TV programs and movies are not even human. Animal actors play a big role in bringing light-hearted comedy as well as action to viewers. Eddie, the dog on the hit show *Frasier*, got tons of fan mail every week as did the killer whale from *Free Willy*. Animal lovers everywhere were saddened when Bart the bear, who starred in several films, passed away recently. These animals lit up the screen and made viewing movies more enjoyable.

▶ **memorable** 인상적인 **play a role** 역할을 하다 **light-hearted** 쾌활한, 명랑한: 근심 걱정 없는 **killer whale** 범고래 **sadden** 슬프게 하다 **several** 몇몇의 **pass away** 죽다 **lit up** 명랑하게 하다: 밝게 하다 **enjoyable** 즐거운

여 종종 TV 프로그램과 영화에 나오는 가장 인상적인 배우가 사람이 아닐 때도 있습니다. 동물 배우들은 관객들에게 액션뿐 아니라 명랑한 코미디 물을 선사하는 데서도 큰 역할을 하지요. 인기 쇼 〈프레이저〉에 나왔던 개, 에디는 〈프리 윌리〉에 나왔던 범고래가 그랬던 것처럼 매주 엄청난 양의 팬 레터를 받았습니다. 또 도처에 있는 동물 애호가들은 몇몇 영화에서 주연을 했던 곰, 바트가 최근 숨지자 슬픔에 잠기기도 했지요. 이 동물들은 스크린을 밝게 만들고 영화를 더 즐겁게 관람할 수 있게 해주었습니다.

5 무엇에 관한 내용인가?
(a) 동물 배우　　　　(b) 인기를 끈 TV쇼
(c) 팬 레터　　　　　(d) 동물 코미디언
(e) TV를 보는 동물들

❻

M Oh, my goodness! I certainly didn't expect to be on this stage tonight. Thank you so much! It is an honor! First, I want to thank my family for their support. I also want to thank the director and the producer and everyone who worked so hard on this film. Finally, I'd like to thank my fellow cast members, who helped me and taught me so much. I couldn't have won this without everyone's help. Thanks so much!

▶ **expect** 예상하다 **stage** 무대 **honor** 영광 **support** 지지, 원조 **fellow** 동료의

남 오, 이런 세상에! 오늘밤 제가 이 자리에 서게 되리라고는 정말 상상도 못했어요. 정말 감사합니다! 너무 영광이예요! 우선, 절 지지해준 가족들에게 감사하고 싶어요. 또, 감독님과 제작자님, 그리고 이 영화를 위해 열심히 일해 주신 모든 분들께도 감사 드리고 싶어요. 마지막으로, 절 도와주고 너무나

많이 가르쳐준, 저와 함께 출연한 동료 배우분들에게도 감사를 전하고 싶습니다. 모든 분들의 도움이 없었다면 이 상을 탈 수 없었을 거예요. 진심으로 감사드립니다!

6 어떤 종류의 담화인가?

(a) 고별사   (b) 상업광고
(c) 영화배우의 대사   (d) 결혼식 주례
(e) 수상 소감 발표

7~8

M   Hey, Jamie. Get down here! Mom and Dad left, and it's about to start!
W   Oh, great. I can't miss the season finale!
M   I hope Gary wins it all.
W   No way! I hope Gale gets the $1,000,000.
M   Whatever! She hardly helped out at all on the island. Gary did all the work!
W   Yeah, but she's smarter. She won most of the challenges.
M   Okay, if Gary wins, you have to do my chores this week.
W   Sure, and if Gale wins, you do my homework this week.
M   Deal.

▶ get down 내려오다   be about to 막 ~하려고 하다   finale 대단원, 마지막   No way. 안 돼.   hardly 거의 ~않다   challenge 도전   chore 집안일: 허드렛일   Deal. 좋아, 알았다: 그것으로 결정짓자.

남   야, 제이미. 이리 내려와! 엄마랑 아빠 출발하셨어. 이제 곧 시작할 거야!
여   아, 다행이다. 시즌 마지막을 놓칠 수 없지!
남   난 게리가 돈을 다 따면 좋겠어.
여   절대 안 돼! 난 게일이 100만 달러를 따면 좋겠어.
남   어쨌거나! 게일은 섬에서 거의 아무 도움도 못 됐잖아. 게리가 일은 다 했다고!
여   맞아, 그래도 게일이 더 똑똑해. 거의 모든 도전 과제에서 다 이겼어.
남   알았어, 만약에 게리가 이기면 네가 이번 주 내 집안일 해주기다.
여   좋아. 대신 게일이 이기면 오빠가 이번 주에 내 숙제를 하는 거야.
남   좋아, 그렇게 하자.

7 화자들의 관계는 무엇인가?

(a) 이성 친구   (b) 부부
(c) 남매   (d) 친구
(e) 학급 친구

8 그들은 어떤 종류의 쇼를 보고 있는 것 같은가?

(a) 스릴러   (b) 드라마
(c) 코미디   (d) 다큐멘터리
(e) 리얼리티 쇼

Unit 7   Spring Is the Nicest Season

Answers

GET READY   p. 80~81

Key Words & Expressions

1 refreshing   **2** sunlight   **3** Hurricanes
4 supposed   **5** Global warming   **6** scorching
7 fog   **8** harsh   **9** drought
10 forecast

Questions & Responses

1 b   **2** d   **3** c   **4** f   **5** a   **6** e

BASIC DRILL   p. 82~83

Step 1   ● unpredictable / freezing / hot but not scorching
   Q (d)
   ■ coast, windy, beautiful, unpredictable, freezing, scorching, breeze

Step 2   **A** mild   **B** Greece
          C Alaska / winter   **D** hot, humid

1 (a)   **2** (1) F (2) T (3) T

Plus⁺ Question   **1** (c)   **2** (b)

EXERCISE   p. 84~85

Step 1   **1** (d)   **2** (d)   **3** (c)   **4** (b)
Step 2   **1** (b)   **2** (e)   **3** (e)   **4** (c)   **5** (a)

PRACTICE TEST   p. 88~89

1 (a)
2 Vancouver: 18 degrees
   Calgary: 11 degrees
   Winnipeg: 8 degrees
   Toronto: 12 degrees
   Quebec: 5 degrees
3 (b)   **4** (c)   **5** (c)   **6** (e)   **7** (c)   **8** (b)

* Dictation 1, 2의 정답은 각 Script의 밑줄친 부분임.

GET READY

Key Words & Expressions

다음 문장을 듣고 보기 박스에서 알맞은 단어를 골라 빈칸을 채우시오.

1 가을은 내가 제일 좋아하는 계절이야. 날씨도 상쾌하고 나뭇잎도 아름답잖아.

2 햇볕을 충분히 쐬는 것은 즐겁게 지내는 데 도움이 됩니다.

3 허리케인은 한 도시에 수십억 달러의 피해를 입힐 수 있죠.

4 이봐, 우산 갖고 가는 거 잊지 마! TV에서 비가 올 거라고 들었어.

5 지구 온난화는 지구에 영향을 끼치는 주요한 문제입니다.

6 내일, 라스베이거스는 섭씨 40도에 이르는 불볕더위가 찾아오겠습니다.

7 내 생각엔 영국 날씨가 제일 안 좋은 것 같아. 영국의 비와 안개는 끔찍하지.

8 아주 덥거나 추운 곳에서는 동식물이 그런 혹독한 기온에 적응하여 살아갑니다.

9 가뭄은 어떤 지역에 오랫동안 비가 전혀 내리지 않을 때 발생합니다.

10 일기예보에서 뭐래? 스웨터를 입어야 돼, 아니면 그냥 얇은 재킷을 입어야 돼?

Questions & Responses

질문에 어울리는 대답과 연결하시오.

1 네가 사는 곳 날씨는 어때?

2 거기는 눈이 내리니?

3 거기는 어느 계절이 제일 아름다워?

4 그곳에 자연재해가 발생했던 적 있니?

5 혹시 내일 일기예보 들었니?

6 우산을 가져가야 할까?

ⓑ 1년 내내 따뜻해.

ⓓ 보통 1년에 눈이 조금 내리는 편이야.

ⓒ 가을이 제일 아름다운 계절이야.

ⓕ 응. 작년에 허리케인을 겪었어.

ⓐ 응, 흐리고 시원할 거래.

ⓔ 아니. 맑은 것 같아.

듣고 정답을 확인하시오.

친구와 함께 연습하시오.

Basic Drill Step 1

다음을 듣고 메모하시오.

M Weather's a crazy thing where I live on the east coast of Canada. One minute it can be cold, windy, and rainy, and the next minute it's a beautiful spring day. It's pretty unpredictable. The winters are pretty cold. Actually, they're freezing, but it's all worth it when summer arrives. It can get hot, but not scorching. There's always a nice breeze off the ocean.

▶ coast 해안 unpredictable 예측할 수 없는 freezing 몹시 추운; 어는, 얼어 붙는 worth it ~할 보람이 있는, 시간과 노력을 들일 만한 scorching 매우 뜨거운, 불볕의 breeze 미풍, 산들바람

남 제가 사는 캐나다 동부 해안의 날씨는 완전 정신이 없어요. 어느 순간에는 춥고, 바람이 불고, 비가 왔다가 다음 순간에는 아름다운 봄날씨가 되거든요. 정말 예측할 수가 없어요. 겨울은 상당히 춥답니다. 사실 꽁꽁 얼 정도로 몹시 춥지만 여름이 오면 그 추위를 견뎌낸 보람이 있지요. 여름에는 더워지기도 하지만 불볕더위는 아니에요. 해안에서 늘 기분 좋은 미풍이 불어오지요.

메모를 바탕으로 다음 문제에 답하시오.

Q 다음 중 사실인 것은?

   (a) 캐나다는 봄에 눈 내리는 날이 많다.

   (b) 캐나다에는 비가 자주 오지 않는다.

   (c) 캐나다의 겨울은 너무 춥지는 않다.

   (d) 캐나다의 날씨는 자주 바뀐다.

■ 다시 듣고 빈칸을 채우시오.

Basic Drill Step 2

다음을 듣고 메모하시오.

M1 I'm James, and I'm from Australia. I love Australian weather. Our winters don't get too cold like in other places, and the summers are gorgeous, especially near the water. We have great beach weather!

W1 I'm Kate, and I'm from Greece. The Greek climate is great. That's why so many tourists come to the islands. It's extremely hot and dry in the summer, so spring is by far the nicest season.

W2 I'm Sandra from Alaska. I love living here despite the weather. I just take advantage of it by playing lots of winter sports. The summers are great too! I love fishing.

M2 I'm Randy, and I live in Dubai in the United Arab Emirates. It gets so hot and humid here that at times businesses have to shut down. On the really hot days, the streets are empty because people are indoors in the air conditioning.

▶ gorgeous 멋진, 찬란한 be from ~출신이다 climate 기후 extremely 매우 by far 단연, 월등히 despite ~에도 불구하고 take advantage of ~을 활용하다 humid 습기 있는 at times 이따금, 때때로 business 상점, 회사; 사업 shut down 닫다, 유입하다 empty 인적이 없는; 빈

남1 난 제임스고, 호주 출신이야. 난 호주의 날씨가 참 좋아. 호주의 겨울은 다른 곳처럼 그렇게 춥지 않아. 여름은 정말 근사하지. 특히 물가는 더 그래. 해변 날씨는 정말 끝내줘!

여1 난 케이트야. 그리스 출신이지. 그리스의 기후는 정말 좋아. 그러니 그렇게 많은 관광객들이 섬에 오는 거겠지. 여름은 무척 덥고 건조해서 봄이 단연 제일 좋은 계절이야.

여2 난 알래스카에서 사는 샌드라야. 날씨는 좀 그렇지만 여기 사는 게 좋아. 겨울 스포츠를 많이 함으로써 이 곳의 날씨를 잘 활용하지. 여름도 정말 좋아! 낚시하는 걸 참 좋아해.

남2 난 랜디야. 아랍에미리트 연합의 두바이에 살고 있어. 여기는 너무 덥고 습해져서 때때로 상점들이 문을 닫아야 할 지경이야. 진짜 더운 날에는 사람들이 에어컨을 튼 실내에 있어서 거리가 텅 빈다니까.

메모를 바탕으로 다음 문제에 답하시오.

1 화자들은 주로 무엇에 관해 이야기하고 있는가?

   (a) 자기네 나라의 기후   (b) 최고의 계절

   (c) 다른 나라로 여행하기   (d) 극한의 날씨

2 맞으면 T, 틀리면 F를 쓰시오.

(1) 호주의 겨울은 매우 춥다.

(2) 샌드라는 알래스카의 여름을 좋아한다.

(3) 두바이는 매우 덥고 습해지기도 한다.

다시 듣고 정답을 확인하시오.

Plus⁺ Question

1 그리스의 여름은 __________.

(a) 서늘하고 바람이 분다　(b) 그렇게 덥지 않다

(c) 덥고 건조하다　(d) 덥고 습하다

2 두바이에서는 더운 날 사람들이 어디에 가는가?

(a) 해변에　(b) 실내에

(c) 섬에　(d) 산에

EXERCISE　Step 1

듣고 문제에 답하시오.

M　What's it like out today, Mom?

W　It's a nice day.

M　What do you mean? I want to know what to wear.

W　It's not too hot and not too cold.

M　So, a light jacket will be fine?

W　Yeah, I think so.

M　Well, I'll see you after school.

W　Sure. Oh, wait!

M　What?

W　Bring your umbrella just in case. The clouds are a little dark out there.

M　Thanks.

▶ after school 방과 후에　just in case 만일을 위해서

남　엄마, 오늘 바깥 날씨 어때요?

여　날씨가 좋구나.

남　무슨 뜻이에요? 뭘 입어야 할지 알고 싶어요.

여　너무 덥지도 춥지도 않아.

남　그럼 얇은 재킷을 입어도 괜찮겠네요?

여　응, 괜찮을 것 같네.

남　그럼, 학교 끝나고 봬요.

여　그래. 아, 잠깐만!

남　네?

여　혹시 모르니까 우산 가지고 가렴. 밖에 먹구름이 조금 끼었더라.

남　고마워요.

1 소년의 모습을 가장 잘 묘사한 그림은 무엇인가?

(a) 　(b) 　(c) 　(d) 

M　What do you think the worst climate is, Sophie?

W　Probably a really cold place like Russia.

M　Yeah, I heard their winters are pretty harsh.

W　You can say that again. What about you, Scott?

M　I heard the climate in England is pretty bad.

W　Really?

M　Yeah, it rains a lot, and it's often cool and foggy.

W　Actually, I love that kind of weather. It reminds me of a murder mystery novel.

M　You're strange!

▶ harsh 혹독한　You can say that again. 맞아.　remind A of B A에게 B를 생각나게 하다

남　소피, 넌 어떤 기후가 최악인 것 같아?

여　아마도 러시아처럼 정말 추운 곳이겠지.

남　그래, 거기 겨울이 정말 혹독하다고 하더라.

여　그러게 말이야. 스콧, 넌 어때?

남　난 영국의 기후가 상당히 안 좋다고 들었어.

여　정말?

남　응. 비가 많이 오고, 종종 서늘한 데다가 안개도 자주 낀대.

여　사실, 난 그런 날씨를 정말 좋아해. 살인 미스터리 소설을 생각나게 하잖아.

남　너 진짜 이상하구나!

2 다음 중 사실인 것은?

(a) 러시아의 겨울은 서늘하고 안개가 낀다.

(b) 스콧은 추운 날씨를 좋아한다.

(c) 영국 날씨는 매우 따뜻하다.

(d) 소피는 영국 날씨를 좋아한다.

3-4

M　So, tell us about your vacation, Georgia. Where did you go?

W　I took my family to Death Valley National Park in California.

M　You took them to a place called Death Valley?

W　Yeah, it's actually very beautiful. It gets some of the hottest temperatures on Earth, and it's very dry.

M　Then why did you go there?

W　There's great hiking, scenery, and lots of history. And even though it's so hot, there are lots of plants and animals to see.

M　Really?

W　Yeah, the life there has adapted to the extreme temperatures. I saw some of the greatest sunsets on Earth!

▶ temperature 온도　scenery 풍경　adapt 적응하다　extreme 극도의 temperature 온도: 체온; 열　sunset 일몰

남　그래, 조지아, 네 휴가 얘기 좀 해줘. 어디 갔었어?

여　식구들을 데리고 캘리포니아 데스 밸리 국립공원에 갔어.

남　데스 밸리라는 곳에 식구들을 데려갔다고?

여　응. 거기는 정말 아주 아름다운 곳이야. 지상에서 가장 더운 곳이고, 매우 건조해.

남　그럼 왜 거길 간 거야?

여　하이킹 하기에도 좋고, 경치도 근사하고, 유서 깊은 곳이거든. 게다가 그렇게 더운 지역인데도, 볼 만한 동식물들이 많아.

남　정말?

여　응, 그곳의 생물이 극한의 온도에 적응을 한 거지. 지상에서 가장 멋진 일몰도 봤다니까!

3 조지아는 누구와 데스 밸리에 갔는가?

(a) 혼자서   (b) 하이킹 동아리와

(c) 자기 가족과   (d) 여행 그룹과

4 데스 밸리에 대한 내용 중 사실이 <u>아닌</u> 것은?

(a) 좋은 하이킹 코스가 있다.

(b) 멋진 해변이 있다.

(c) 일몰이 멋지다.

(d) 유서가 있다.

Exercise   Step 2

듣고 문제에 답하시오.

M   Okay, Anna! <u>Hurry up</u> and get in the van!

W   I'm coming!

M   <u>According</u> to my tracker, it's heading northeast at 100 km/hour.

W   Here we go!

M   Wait, there's a tree in the road up ahead. We'll have to turn around!

W   <u>Hold on tight</u>. I'll turn around and take another road.

M   Hurry, we're going to lose it!

W   I'm <u>trying my best</u>. There it is!

M   Keep going, but be careful.

W   No kidding! Are you <u>taping</u> this?

▶ **get in** (차를) 타다: (안으로) 들어가다   **tracker** 추적기, 추적자: 수색자   **Here we go.** (구어) 시작합시다. 자, 시작이다.   **up ahead** (그) 앞쪽에   **hold on** 매달리다   **tight** 단단히   **try one's best** 최선을 다하다   **keep -ing** 계속 ~하다   **tape** 테이프에 녹음하다

남   좋아, 애나! 서둘러서 밴에 타!

여   가고 있어!

남   내 추적기에 따르면 그것이 지금 시속 100킬로미터로 북동쪽으로 향하고 있어.

여   자, 시작하자!

남   잠깐만. 도로 앞쪽에 나무가 있어. 차를 돌려야 될 것 같아!

여   꽉 잡아. 차를 돌려서 다른 길로 갈 테니까.

남   서둘러. 이러다 놓치겠어!

여   나도 최선을 다하고 있어. 저기 있다!

남   계속 가. 하지만 조심해.

여   농담 하지 마! 이거 녹음하고 있는 거지?

1 화자들의 직업은 무엇인가?

(a) 기상예보관   (b) 토네이도 추적자

(c) 벌목공   (d) 택시 운전사

(e) 트럭 운전사

2

M   How do you feel on a warm, sunny day <u>as opposed to</u> a cold, cloudy day? If you feel worse on the colder day, you're not alone. Scientific studies have shown that our moods are very much <u>affected by the weather</u>. When in sunlight, our bodies produce <u>certain chemicals</u> that <u>make us happier</u> and more alert. So if you're in darkness too long, you could find yourself getting sad. For some people, the emotional problems are more serious than for others, but there's no doubt that a sunny day <u>brings a smile</u> to most people's faces.

▶ **as opposed to** ~와는 대조적으로   **mood** 기분   **affect** 영향을 미치다   **produce** 생산하다, 만들어내다   **chemical** 화학물질: 화학의   **alert** 민첩한, 기민한   **no doubt** 의심할 바 없이: 물론

남   춥고 구름 낀 날씨와 반대로 따뜻하고 해가 쨍쨍 나는 날에는 기분이 어떠십니까? 만약 추운 날 기분이 더 안 좋다면 당신만 그런 것이 아니랍니다. 과학적 조사에 따르면 우리의 기분은 날씨의 영향을 굉장히 많이 받는다고 합니다. 햇볕을 쬘 때 우리 몸에서는 기분을 더 좋게 하고, 더 민첩하게 만드는 어떤 화학물질들이 생성됩니다. 그래서 어두운 곳에 너무 오래 있으면 슬픈 감정을 느끼는 자기 자신을 발견하게 될 수도 있는 것이지요. 어떤 사람들에게는 감정적인 문제가 다른 사람들보다 훨씬 더 심각합니다. 하지만 해가 쨍쨍한 맑은 날씨일 때 대다수 사람들의 얼굴에 미소가 나타난다는 건 의심할 나위가 없습니다.

2 다음 중 사실이 <u>아닌</u> 것은?

(a) 사람들은 날씨가 맑은 날 더 기분이 좋다.

(b) 어떤 사람들은 날씨 때문에 심각한 문제를 겪기도 한다.

(c) 햇볕을 쬐면 우리 몸에서 화학물질들이 생성된다.

(d) 햇볕을 충분히 쬐지 못하면 슬퍼질 수도 있다.

(e) 어두운 곳에 있는 것이 때로는 좋을 수도 있다.

3~5

M   A hurricane <u>swept through</u> Fort Meyers, Florida, yesterday, leaving damaged homes and businesses <u>in its path</u>. The winds reached 160 km/hour, which made it a category 2 hurricane. There are now millions of dollars worth of repairs to be done to the many buildings that were damaged. Roofs <u>were ripped off</u> of houses, and cars <u>were overturned</u>. Luckily, no one was killed during the hurricane, and there were only a few serious injuries.

▶ **sweep through** ~을 휩쓸고 지나가다   **path** 진로, 궤도   **repair** 수리: 수리하다   **damage** 피해를 입히다: 피해, 손해   **rip off** 벗겨내다, 뜯어내다   **overturn** 전복시키다   **injury** 부상(자)

남   이제 허리케인이 플로리다 주 포트 마이어스를 휩쓸고 지나가, 그 진로에 있던 가옥과 상점에 피해를 입혔습니다. 바람은 시속 160킬로미터에 달해 2등급에 해당하는 허리케인이었습니다. 이제 수 백만 달러를 들여 피해를 입은 많은 건물들을 수리할 일이 남았습니다. 집의 지붕은 뜯겨 나갔고, 자동차는 전복됐습니다. 다행히, 허리케인이 지나가는 동안 사망자는 없었고, 심각한 부상자는 몇 명뿐이었습니다.

3 무엇에 관한 내용인가?

(a) 세찬 바람

(b) 허리케인 등급

(c) 허리케인 때문에 다친 사람들

(d) 미국에서 발생하는 허리케인

(e) 플로리다를 강타한 허리케인

4 허리케인의 등급을 결정하는 것은 무엇인가?

(a) 부상자 수   (b) 발생한 피해

(c) 풍속   (d) 위치

(e) 계절

5 내용을 가장 잘 요약한 것은 무엇인가?

(a) 어제 2등급 허리케인이 플로리다 주 포트 마이어스에 많은 피해를 입혔다.

(b) 2등급 허리케인이 지나간 후 플로리다 주 포트 마이어스가 입은 피해를 복구하는 데 사업체들이 수백만 달러를 내놓고 있다.

PRACTICE TEST

듣고 문제에 답하시오.

W I remember it like it was yesterday. I'm talking about that long, long drought in the 1930s. Being from Saskatchewan, I'm used to hot, dry weather, but this was different. The ground dried up until nothing would grow. The land is all we had to make a living in those hard times, but it wouldn't produce anything. We didn't get a drop of rain for years. I don't know how we got through it, but we did.

▶ drought 가뭄 Saskatchewan 서스캐처원(캐나다 남서부의 주) dry up 바짝 마르다, 말라붙다 make a living 생계를 유지하다 hard times 궁핍한 시기, 불경기 get through 타개해 나가다, 극복하다

여 전 그 일을 어제 일처럼 생생히 기억해요. 1930년대에 정말 오래도록 지속되었던 가뭄에 대해 이야기하는 거랍니다. 전 서스캐처원 출신이라서 덥고 건조한 날씨에는 익숙하지만 그 가뭄은 달랐어요. 땅은 아무것도 자랄 수 없게 될 정도로 완전히 말라버렸죠. 그 곤궁한 시기에는 생계수단이라곤 땅뿐이었는데, 땅에서는 아무것도 자라지 않았죠. 몇 년 동안 비 한 방울 내리지 않았어요. 그 어려움을 어떻게 극복했는지는 모르겠지만 어쨌든 이겨냈어요.

1 여자의 이야기를 묘사하는 사진은 무엇인가?

(a) 　(b) 　(c) 

(d) 　(e) 

2

W Good morning, Canada. I'm Janet Smith, and here's your weather forecast for today. It's a comfortable spring day in Vancouver today with temperatures reaching about 18 degrees. It seems winter still has a hold on Calgary, where it's a chilly 11 degrees. Winnipeg is the same, except colder. It's only 8 degrees there. Toronto will be 12 degrees and rainy today. Quebec is not doing too well. It's only 5 degrees there.

▶ weather forecast 일기 예보 comfortable 기분 좋은, 편안한 reach ~에 이르다 have a hold on ~에 위력을 가지다 chilly 쌀쌀한

여 안녕하세요, 캐나다 국민 여러분. 재닛 스미스입니다. 오늘의 일기예보입니다. 오늘 밴쿠버는 기온이 18도에 이르는 기분 좋은 봄날씨입니다. 겨울이 아직 캘거리에서 위력을 떨치고 있는 듯이 보이는데요, 11도의 쌀쌀한 날씨가 되겠습니다. 위니펙 또한 마찬가지이지만, 캘거리보다 더 춥고 기온은 8도가 되겠습니다. 토론토의 오늘 기온은 12도이고 비가 내리겠습니다. 퀘벡의 날

씨도 그다지 좋지 않은데요, 기온은 겨우 5도가 되겠습니다.

Level up

2 각 지역의 기온을 써넣으시오.

밴쿠버: ______ 도

캘거리: ______ 도

위니펙: ______ 도

토론토: ______ 도

퀘 벡: ______ 도

3~4

M What's your favorite season, Terry?

W I love weather just like this, so summer suits me fine.

M Why is that? I find it too hot. I'm sweating!

W No way. It's great. I love rollerblading by the sea and surfing.

M I can't stand the heat.

W Well then, what about you, Ron?

M Winter is the best season. The snow is beautiful, and the weather is refreshing.

W Refreshing? I don't think sub-zero temperatures are refreshing.

M You've just got to dress for the weather. That's all.

W I suppose ________________________________.

▶ suit ~에게 맞다; ~의 마음에 들다 sweat 땀을 흘리다 stand 참다, 견디다 heat 더위; 열 refreshing 상쾌한 sub-zero temperature 영하의 기온

남 테리, 어느 계절을 가장 좋아해?
여 난 딱 이런 날씨가 좋아. 그래서 나한테는 여름이 맞아.
남 그건 왜? 난 너무 더워. 땀까지 나고 있다고!
여 아니, 좋잖아. 바닷가에서 롤러블레이드도 타고 서핑하는 게 너무 좋아.
남 난 더위는 못 참아.
여 그래, 그럼 넌 어느 계절이 가장 좋아, 론?
남 겨울이 가장 좋은 계절이지. 눈은 아름답고, 날씨도 상쾌하잖아.
여 상쾌하다고? 영하의 기온이 상쾌한 것 같지는 않은데.
남 날씨에 맞춰서 옷을 잘 갖춰 입기만 하면 돼. 그게 다야.
여 ________________________________

3 지금은 어떤 계절인가?

(a) 겨울　　　　　　　(b) 여름

(c) 가을　　　　　　　(d) 봄

(e) 알 수 없다.

4 테리는 다음에 뭐라고 말할 것 같은가?

(a) 지는 게 이기는 거지.

(b) 제한은 없어. (하려고만 하면 무엇이든 할 수 있다.)

(c) 의견 차이는 할 수 없는 거지.

(d) 로마에 가면 로마법을 따라야지.

(e) 네가 알아서 처리해. (너의 결정이 남았어.)

5

W This is a special alert. Weather France warns all citizens to stay indoors whenever possible, preferably in an air-conditioned room. Drink lots of water and do not engage in exercise. Cases of heatstroke are rising. Elderly people are advised not to go outside at all. Check on your elderly neighbors from time to time. This heat wave is likely to be over in the next week, so take precautions until then.

▶ alert 경계 태세 preferably 가급적 engage in ~에 참가하다 case 환자; 사례 heatstroke 열사병 advise 권하다, 충고하다 elderly 나이가 지긋한 from time to time 때때로, 이따금 heat wave 장기간의 혹서 take precautions ~을 조심하다

여 특별 경보입니다. 프랑스 기상청은 모든 시민들에게 가급적 냉방기기가 가동되는 실내 공간에 계시라는 경고 말씀을 드립니다. 물을 많이 드시고, 운동을 하지 마십시오. 열사병에 걸리는 환자의 수가 증가하고 있습니다. 나이 드신 분들은 외출을 절대 삼가해 주시고, 이따금 이웃 어르신들을 들여다 봐 주십시오. 이번 혹서는 다음 주가 돼야 끝날 것 같사오니 그때까지 조심해주시기 바랍니다.

5 사람들이 하지 말아야 할 것은 무엇인가?

 (a) 실내에 있는다
 (b) 물을 마신다
 (c) 운동을 한다
 (d) 냉방이 되는 곳에 있는다
 (e) 나이 드신 이웃들의 상태를 확인한다

6

M Do you hate getting into a freezing cold car in the winter? Who doesn't? Now you can warm up your life for only $29.99! Quick De-icer is the cure for your wintertime blues. You just have to have the Quick De-icer installed by your local mechanic, and then you'll be all set. 10 minutes before you leave your home, simply press "quick de-ice" on the handy remote control from inside your home! When you open your car door, you'll be greeted by a warm and toasty interior! Order Quick De-icer today!

▶ warm up 데우다, 따뜻해지다 cure 치료, 해결책 blues (구어) 우울한 기분 install 설치하다 mechanic 기계공 be all set 준비가 되어있다 handy 바로 곁에 있는, 편리한 press 누르다 greet 맞이하다, 인사하다 toasty (방 등이) 따뜻하고 쾌적한 interior 내부, 실내

남 겨울에 꽁꽁 언 추운 차 안으로 들어가는 것을 싫어하십니까? 하긴 누가 안 그렇겠습니까? 이제 단돈 29달러 99센트로 여러분의 생활을 따뜻하게 만들 수 있습니다! 퀵 디아이서는 겨울철 우울한 기분의 치료책입니다. 여러분이 사시는 지역의 기술자에게 퀵 디아이서를 설치하게 하시면 모든 준비가 끝납니다. 집에서 나오시기 10분 전, 집안에서 리모콘에 있는 '퀵 디아이스' 버튼만 눌러주세요! 자동차 문을 열면 따뜻하고 쾌적한 실내가 여러분을 맞이할 겁니다! 오늘 퀵 디아이서를 주문하세요!

6 어떤 종류의 담화인가?

 (a) 전자레인지 사용설명서
 (b) 자동차 논평

 (c) 일기예보
 (d) 눈보라 경보
 (e) 상품 광고

7~8

M What are your views on global warming, Rita?

W I think it's something that has to be stopped before it's too late.

M But seriously, nothing really bad is going to happen in our lifetimes. The temperatures are rising very slowly.

W That may be true, but what if everyone says that? Plus, what about the damage to the environment now? Many glaciers are almost gone, and animal species are disappearing, too. What about you, Jimmy? You don't agree?

M Well, I agree that it's a problem, but there's very little I can do about it as one person, so I choose not to worry about it.

▶ view 의견 global warming 지구 온난화 lifetime 평생, 일생 What if ~? ~하면 어떻게 될까? environment 환경 glacier 빙하 species (생물의) 종 disappear 사라지다, 멸종되다 chose ~하기로 결정하다, ~하는 쪽을 택하다

남 리타, 지구 온난화에 대한 네 의견은 뭐야?
여 너무 늦기 전에 멈춰야 하는 것이라고 생각해.
남 하지만 진지하게 얘기해서, 진짜로 안 좋은 일은 우리가 사는 동안에는 일어나지 않을 거야. 기온은 아주 더디게 올라가고 있거든.
여 그 말이 맞을 수도 있어. 하지만 모든 사람들이 다 그렇게 말한다면 어떻게 될까? 게다가 지금 환경이 입고 있는 피해는 어떻고? 많은 빙하들이 거의 없어졌고, 동물 종들도 사라지고 있어. 너는 어떻게 생각해, 지미? 넌 그렇게 생각 안 해?
남 글쎄, 나도 그게 문제라는 의견에는 동의해. 하지만 한 개인으로서 내가 할 수 있는 일은 거의 없잖아. 그래서 난 그 문제에 관해 걱정하지 않기로 했어.

7 화자들은 무엇을 하고 있는가?

 (a) 농담하고 있다
 (b) 계획을 세우고 있다
 (c) 논쟁하고 있다
 (d) 브레인스토밍하고 있다
 (e) 싸우고 있다

8 지미의 의견은 무엇인가?

 (a) 뭔가를 해야 한다.
 (b) 지구 온난화에 대해 걱정하지 마라.
 (c) 환경은 중요하지 않다.
 (d) 지구 온난화는 사실이 아니다.
 (e) 지구 온난화는 문제가 아니다.

Answers

GET READY   p. 92~93

Key Words & Expressions

1 activities   2 enjoyed   3 trendy
4 unique   5 collecting   6 careers
7 involved in   8 Cooking   9 take up
10 into

Questions & Responses

1 c   2 e   3 b   4 a   5 d   6 f

BASIC DRILL   p. 94~95

Step 1 • reading, blogging / coins, postcards

Q (b)

■ hobbies, collection, coin, learned, into, blogging, collecting

Step 2 A martial arts, martial arts

B crafts, painting, ceramics

C horror movie / old

D fashion / fashion designer

1 (a)   2 (1) T (2) F (3) F

<u>Plus⁺ Question</u>   1 (c)   2 (a)

EXERCISE   p. 96~97

Step 1   1 (a)   2 (1) T (2) F (3) T (4) F   3 (d)   4 (b)

Step 2   1 (a)   2 (c)   3 (d)   4 (a)   5 (a)

PRACTICE TEST   p. 100~101

1 (e)

2

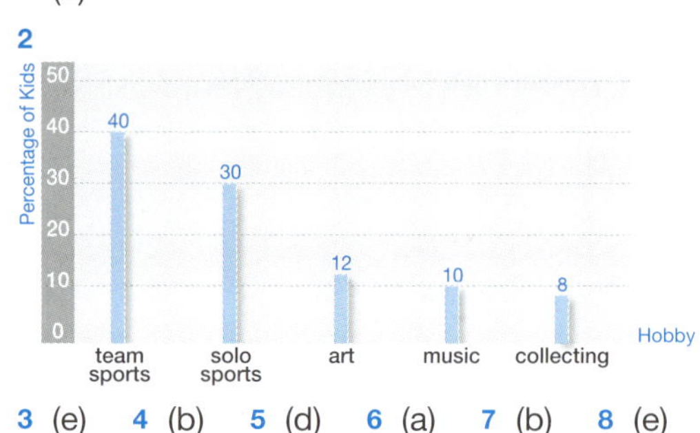

3 (e)   4 (b)   5 (d)   6 (a)   7 (b)   8 (e)

* Dictation 1, 2의 정답은 각 Script의 밑줄친 부분임.

Scripts and Translations

GET READY

Key Words & Expressions

다음 문장을 듣고 보기 박스에서 알맞은 단어를 골라 빈칸을 채우시오.

1 전 하이킹, 산악자전거 타기 같은 활동을 좋아해요.

2 게일은 어렸을 때부터 늘 요리하는 것을 좋아했어요.

3 요가는 젊은이들 사이에서 유행하는 취미랍니다.

4 때로는 껌 포장지나 펜 뚜껑처럼 아무도 수집하지 않는 독특한 것을 모으는 게 훨씬 더 재미있죠.

5 제겐 영화 포스터나 동전 수집 같은 것은 정말 지루한 일이에요.

6 몇몇 사람들의 성공한 직업은 어린 시절의 단순한 취미에서 비롯되었더라고요.

7 많은 아이들이 운동을 하고 미술, 음악, 물건 수집을 합니다.

8 요리나 제빵은 결과물을 먹을 수 있기 때문에 인기 있는 취미랍니다.

9 전 취미로 사진을 해보고 싶어요.

10 전 정말 음악이 좋아요. 피아노를 치고 노래도 작곡이죠.

Questions & Responses

질문에 어울리는 대답과 연결하시오.

1 취미가 뭐야?   ⓒ 그림 그리는 거랑 조류 관찰하는 걸 좋아해.

2 뭐 수집하는 거 있니?   ⓔ 소금이랑 후추 뿌리는 병을 모아.

3 실내에 있는 걸 좋아해, 실외에 있는 걸 좋아해?   ⓑ 난 정말 실외 활동하는 걸 좋아하는 사람이야.

4 취미가 당신의 직업이랑 연관이 있어요?   ⓐ 예. 제 취미가 영화제작인데, 그게 바로 제 직업이죠!

5 친구나 가족들이랑 취미를 공유하나요?   ⓓ 예, 우리 뜨개질 모임은 한 달에 두 번 만나요.

6 취미에 돈이 많이 드나요?   ⓕ 네, 유감스럽게도 그러네요.

들고 정답을 확인하시오.

친구와 함께 연습하시오.

Basic Drill   Step 1

다음을 듣고 메모하시오.

W   I've always had too many hobbies. I especially love collecting things. So far, I have a sticker collection, a coin collection, and a postcard collection. It was easy to start my collections because people sometimes gave me things like stickers or coins. Then I learned more about them, so I got more into them. I also like reading and blogging, but my true love is collecting.

▶ so far 지금까지   collection 수집, 수집품   get into (취미 등에) 열중하게 되다

여 전 늘 취미가 너무 많았어요. 특히 물건 수집하는 것을 좋아하죠. 지금까지 스티커와 동전, 엽서를 수집했어요. 때때로 사람들이 내게 스티커나 동전 같은 것들을 주었기 때문에 쉽게 수집을 시작할 수 있었어요. 그 후에 수집한 것들에 대해 더 많이 알게 돼서, 거기에 더 빠져 들었죠. 전 독서와 블로그하는 것도 좋아하지만, 그래도 제가 진짜 좋아하는 건 수집이죠.

메모를 바탕으로 다음 문제에 답하시오.

Q 화자는 주로 무엇에 관해 이야기하고 있는가?

(a) 자신의 우표 수집품

(b) 자신의 다양한 취미

(c) 블로그를 하는 것에 대한 관심

(d) 자신이 물건을 수집하는 이유

■ 다시 듣고 빈칸을 채우시오.

Basic Drill Step 2

다음을 듣고 메모하시오.

M1 Hi, I'm Mark, and I've always been into martial arts. I've done *taegwondo*, judo, karate, and kung fu. When I'm not at the gym training, I'm watching martial arts films.

W1 I'm Hannah, and I love doing any kind of craft, like painting or ceramics. Recently, I made candles and decorated them with dried flowers. They were gorgeous.

M2 I'm Pete. I collect movie posters. I have quite a lot, but I think I have more horror movie posters than any other kind. I even have some old ones from the 1950s and 1960s, which are worth a lot of money.

W2 I'm Brandy, and I'm into fashion. I make sketches of my designs, and I even try to sew some of my own clothes. My friends all love what I make. I hope to be a fashion designer some day.

▶ be into ~에 관심을 가지다 craft 공예 ceramic 도예, 도자기 candle 양초 gorgeous 멋진, 화려한 worth ~의 가치가 있는 sew 바느질하다, 재봉하여 만들다

남1 안녕, 난 마크야. 난 항상 무술에 관심이 있었어. 태권도, 유도, 가라테, 쿵후를 했지. 체육관에서 운동을 하지 않을 때는 무술 영화를 봐.

여1 난 한나야. 그림이나 도예 같은 종류의 공예 작업을 참 좋아해. 최근에는 양초를 만들고 말린 꽃으로 초를 장식했어. 진짜 멋졌지.

남2 난 피트야. 난 영화 포스터를 모으는데, 상당히 많이 가지고 있어. 하지만 다른 영화보다 공포영화 포스터를 더 많이 갖고 있는 것 같아. 돈 가치가 꽤 되는 1950년대와 1960년대 옛날 영화 포스터들도 가지고 있어.

여2 난 브랜디야. 패션에 관심이 있지. 내가 직접 디자인을 스케치하고, 내 옷가지 몇 벌은 직접 재봉하려고 하지. 친구들 모두 내가 만든 걸 아주 좋아해. 언젠가는 패션 디자이너가 되고 싶어.

메모를 바탕으로 다음 문제에 답하시오.

1 화자들은 주로 무엇에 관해 이야기하고 있는가?

(a) 자신의 취미　　　　(b) 자신의 미래

(c) 영화　　　　(d) 학교 동아리

2 맞으면 T, 틀리면 F를 쓰시오.

(1) 한나는 그림을 그리고 도자기를 만들 수 있다.

(2) 마크는 공포영화 보는 것을 좋아한다.

(3) 브랜디는 친구들 옷을 바느질한다.

다시 듣고 정답을 확인하시오.

Plus⁺ Question

1 마크가 하지 않은 무술은?

(a) 유도　　　(b) 쿵후　　　(c) 합기도　　　(d) 태권도

2 피트가 소유한 옛날 영화 포스터의 특별한 점은 무엇인가?

(a) 돈 가치가 상당하다.

(b) 새 것 같다.

(c) 사인을 받은 것들이다.

(d) 피트가 제일 좋아하는 영화들의 포스터이다.

EXERCISE Step 1

듣고 문제에 답하시오.

M You look excited. What's up?

W Oh, I just got a new stamp for my collection.

M You collect stamps? That sounds boring.

W Whatever. It's really interesting. Have you heard of the Inverted Jenny?

M No, what's that?

W It's a very rare stamp. It was printed in 1918 with a picture of an airplane on it.

M So, what's so special about that?

W They printed the airplane upside down. Now those stamps are worth around $300,000 each!

▶ inverted 역의, 반대의, 반전된 rare 희귀한 upside down 위아래가 뒤바뀐, 거꾸로

남 너 신나 보인다. 무슨 일이야?

여 어, 방금 내 수집목록에 넣을 새 우표를 손에 넣었거든.

남 우표 수집해? 재미없을 것 같은데.

여 무슨 소리. 정말 재미있어. 역쇄 제니라고 들어봤니?

남 아니, 그게 뭔데?

여 진짜 희귀한 우표야. 1918년에 인쇄됐는데, 우표에 비행기 그림이 있어.

남 그래서 그게 뭐가 특별한 건데?

여 비행기가 거꾸로 인쇄되었거든. 현재는 그 우표가 한 장에 30만 달러 정도 한다니까!

1 어느 것이 역쇄 제니(Inverted Jenny)인가?

(a) 　(b)  　(c) 　(d) 

M Hey, Alexis. Did you get your new remote-controlled car yet?

W Nope, but I ordered it.

M What kind of car is it? Battery-powered or gas-powered?

W Battery-powered. The gas-powered ones are too expensive.

M Yeah, but they're faster.

W Yeah, I know. I'm saving my money to get one. But don't worry, Jacob. I'll still beat you when we race.

M Yeah, right! Think again!

▶ **remote-controlled** 원격조정의　**gas** 가솔린, 휘발유　**beat** 이기다: 치다, 두드리다

남　이봐, 알렉시스. 새 원격조정 자동차 받았어?
여　아직. 하지만 주문은 했어.
남　차종은 뭐야? 배터리로 가는 거야, 가솔린으로 가는 거야?
여　배터리로 가는 거야. 가솔린으로 가는 건 너무 비싸.
남　맞아. 하지만 더 빠르지.
여　그래, 나도 알아. 그래서 그런 차를 구입하려고 돈을 모으는 중이야. 하지만 걱정하지 마, 제이콥. 경주하게 되면 여전히 내가 널 이길 걸.
남　오호, 그러서? 다시 생각해보시지!

2　맞으면 T, 틀리면 F에 체크하시오.
(1) 알렉시스는 새 차를 주문했다.
(2) 배터리로 가는 차는 가솔린으로 가는 차보다 더 비싸다.
(3) 알렉시스는 돈을 모으고 있다.
(4) 배터리로 가는 차가 가솔린으로 가는 차보다 더 빠르다.

3-4

M　I'm going bird watching this weekend, Deanna. Want to come?
W　Bird watching? I'd rather watch paint dry.
M　Huh? There are so many cool birds around this time of year. Come on!
W　Where exactly?
M　Out to the marsh. There are so many types of birds in the wetlands.
W　What do we do once we're there?
M　Just look for types of birds and try to photograph them.
W　Sorry, Dave. I'll take a rain check.

▶ **I'd rather watch paint dry.** '차라리 물감이 마르는 것을 보겠다', 즉 조류 탐사는 정말 지루하겠다는 의미.　**exactly** 정확히　**marsh** 늪　**wetland** 습지대　**take a rain check** 후일의 초대에 응하다

남　디애나, 나 이번 주말에 조류 탐사 갈 거야. 너도 갈래?
여　조류 탐사? 진짜 지루하겠다.
남　뭐? 지금 이 무렵에 멋진 새들이 얼마나 많은데. 가자!
여　정확히 어딘데?
남　늪지 쪽이야. 습지대에는 정말 많은 종류의 새가 있어.
여　거기 가면 우리 뭐하는 건데?
남　그냥 여러 종류의 새들을 보고 사진 찍는 거지.
여　미안, 데이브. 다음에 갈게.

3　디애나는 조류 탐사에 대해 어떻게 생각하는가?
(a) 스트레스 받는 일이다.　(b) 신나는 일이다.
(c) 멋진 일이다.　(d) 지루한 일이다.

4　"I'll take a rain check"은 대략 ＿＿＿＿＿＿＿라는 뜻이다.
(a) 비가 올 것 같아　(b) 다음에
(c) 날씨를 알아볼게　(d) 너랑 같이 하겠어

Exercise　Step 2

듣고 문제에 답하시오.

M　Wow, Sheryl! These cookies are amazing!
W　I'm glad you like them, Neil.

M　How long have you been baking?
W　Since I was a kid. I just love it. I love making cookies, cakes, brownies. Pretty much any sweet dessert!
M　But you're so thin! How do you make all this delicious food and not get fat?
W　I hardly ever eat what I make. I give it to others.
M　I see. Well, next time you have something to give away, give me a call.

▶ **amazing** 굉장한　**bake** (빵 등을) 굽다　**brownie** 작고 납작한 초콜릿 비스킷[케이크]　**hardly** 거의 ~않다　**give away** 넘겨주다

남　와, 셰릴! 이 쿠키 정말 끝내줘요!
여　맛있다니까 좋네요, 닐.
남　쿠키 구운 지는 얼마나 됐어요?
여　어렸을 때부터요. 그냥 뭘 굽는 걸 참 좋아해요. 쿠키, 케이크, 브라우니 만드는 걸 정말 좋아해요. 달콤한 디저트라면 뭐든지 다요!
남　하지만 이렇게 말랐는데! 어떻게 이 모든 맛있는 음식을 만들고도 살이 찌지 않을 수가 있죠?
여　전 제가 만든 것을 거의 먹지 않아요. 다른 사람들에게 주죠.
남　그렇군요. 그럼 다음에 뭔가 줄 것이 생기면 저한테 전화 주세요.

1　대화에 따르면, 여자는 어떻게 해서 살이 찌지 않는가?
(a) 자기가 구운 것을 남에게 준다.
(b) 운동을 한다.
(c) 저지방 제품을 굽는다.
(d) 조금만 먹는다.
(e) 자기가 구운 것을 닐에게 준다.

M　The newest trend sweeping the country is knitting! Ever since Angelina Jolie and Jennifer Aniston were spotted holding knitting needles, everyone is into it! Knitting is now the new yoga; it is good for the mind and helps you relax. Plus, you can give your friends and family handmade gifts of knitted pieces. A hand-knit sweater is more comfortable than a store-bought one. And, most importantly, knitting will probably cost you far less than other trendy hobbies. Give it a try!

▶ **trend** 트렌드, 유행　**sweep** 휩쓸다　**knitting** 뜨개질　**spot** 발견하다　**handmade** 수제의, 손으로 만든　**trendy** 최신 유행의　**give it a try** 시도하다, 한번 해보다

남　전국을 휩쓸고 있는 최신 트렌드는 뜨개질입니다! 안젤리나 졸리와 제니퍼 애니스톤이 뜨개질 바늘을 들고 있는 모습이 포착된 후로 모든 사람들이 뜨개질에 빠졌습니다. 뜨개질은 이제 새로운 형태의 요가입니다. 정신 건강에 좋고 마음을 편히 하는 데 도움이 됩니다. 게다가 친구들과 식구들에게 손수 짠 뜨개질 선물을 줄 수도 있습니다. 손으로 짠 스웨터는 가게에서 파는 것보다 훨씬 편안합니다. 그리고 가장 중요한 것은, 뜨개질이 다른 유행하는 취미들보다 돈도 훨씬 덜 들 거라는 점입니다. 한번 해보세요!

2　다음 중 사실이 아닌 것은?
(a) 뜨개질은 비싸지 않다.
(b) 뜨개질은 마음을 편안하게 한다.
(c) 뜨개질은 체중을 감량하는 좋은 방법이다.
(d) 몇몇 스타들이 뜨개질을 한다.
(e) 뜨개질이 새로운 트렌드다.

M　Do you find that average hobbies don't get you excited? Why don't you try something a little different? It doesn't have to be expensive. Just use your imagination. For example, collect something that's all around you, but you haven't noticed, like toothpaste caps. Or make a sculpture out of junk lying around the house. Make art from magazine clippings. Remember, doing something unique makes you a unique person!

▶ imagination 상상력　notice 알아차리다　cap 뚜껑　sculpture 조각　junk 폐물, 고물　clipping 잘라낸 것　unique 독특한, 진기한, 유일한

남　일상적인 취미는 재미가 없으십니까? 조금 다른 것을 해보는 건 어떨까요? 꼭 돈을 많이 들일 필요는 없습니다. 그냥 상상력을 이용하세요. 예를 들어, 치약 뚜껑처럼 주변에 있지만 알아채지 못했던 뭔가를 수집하는 겁니다. 아니면 집 주변에 널려 있는 고물들로 조각을 해보는 것입니다. 잡지에서 오려낸 것으로 예술 작품을 만들어보십시오. 뭔가 색다른 것을 하면 독특한 사람이 된다는 사실을 기억하세요!

3　무엇에 관한 내용인가?
(a) 색다른 물건 수집하기　(b) 따분한 취미
(c) 돈이 별로 안 드는 취미　(d) 재미있는 취미 찾기
(e) 고물로 예술 작품 만들기

4　화자는 어떤 종류의 재료를 이용해보라고 제안하는가?
(a) 일상적인 재료　(b) 값비싼 재료
(c) 미술 재료　(d) 희귀한 재료
(e) 쓰레기

5　내용을 가장 잘 요약한 것은 무엇인가?
(a) 지루하다면, 색다르지만 돈이 안 드는 취미를 시작해보라.
(b) 독특한 사람들은 쓰레기로 예술 작품을 만드는 경향이 있다. 그러니 시도해보라.

PRACTICE TEST

듣고 문제에 답하시오.

W　The HandyShot 120 is the perfect camera for people who want to get into photography as a hobby but don't want to spend too much money. It has a 3X zoom and macro lens. There's even a manual mode. Large, complicated cameras make taking photos look scary, but with the HandyShot 120, anyone can be a photographer, even beginners! Happy shooting!

▶ get into 시작하다, (취미 등에) 열중하게 되다　perfect 완벽[완전]한, 더할 나위 없는　macro lens (사진) 매크로 렌즈, 접사용 렌즈　complicated 복잡한　scary 무서운, 두려운　shooting 촬영

여　핸디샷 120은 취미로 사진에 입문하고 싶지만 돈은 많이 들이고 싶지 않은 사람들에게 안성맞춤인 카메라입니다. 3배 줌에 매크로 렌즈를 탑재했습니다. 매뉴얼 모드도 있고요. 크고 복잡한 카메라는 사진 찍는 일을 두렵게 하지만 핸디샷 120만 있으면 누구든, 초보자들도 사진작가가 될 수 있습니다! 즐겁게 찍으세요!

1　어느 것이 핸디샷 120 카메라인가?

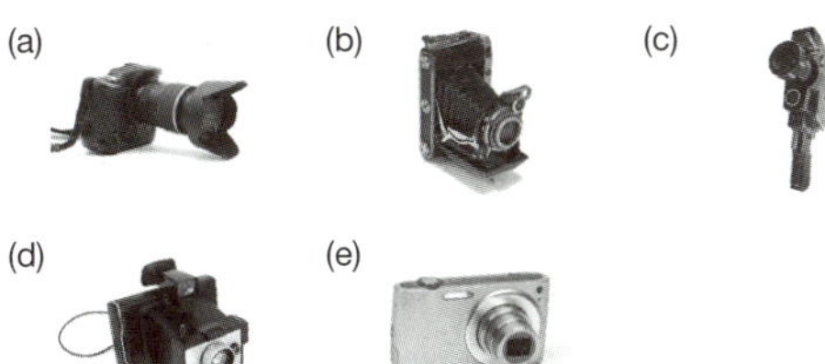

W　What are the most popular hobbies for kids these days? For American kids ages 8 to 15 who were surveyed last summer, here are the results. Sports of any kind ranked the highest, with 40% of kids involved in team sports. Next were solo sports like swimming and cycling. 30% of kids do solo sports. Next came art, with 12% of kids. After that was music, with 10% of kids learning an instrument or singing. Finally, 8% of kids collect something or another. Who said kids are lazy?

▶ survey 조사하다　rank 상위를 차지하다; 자리잡다, 지위를 차지하다　involve in ~에 관계하다　cycling 사이클링, 자전거 타기　instrument 악기

여　요즘 아이들에게 가장 인기 있는 취미는 뭘까요? 작년 여름에 설문 조사를 받은 8세에서 15세 사이의 미국 어린이들에 대한 결과가 여기 있습니다. 종류를 불문하고 스포츠가 가장 높은 비율을 차지했는데요, 40%의 어린이들이 팀을 이뤄 하는 스포츠를 합니다. 그 다음이 수영과 사이클링 같은 개인 스포츠로, 30%의 어린이가 개인 스포츠를 하는군요. 다음이 미술로, 12%의 어린이가 하고 있고요. 그 뒤를 이은 것은 음악이었습니다. 10%의 아이들이 악기를 배우거나 노래를 합니다. 마지막으로, 8%의 아이들이 뭔가를 수집합니다. 누가 어린이들이 게으르다고 했을까요?

Level up

2　그래프를 완성하시오.

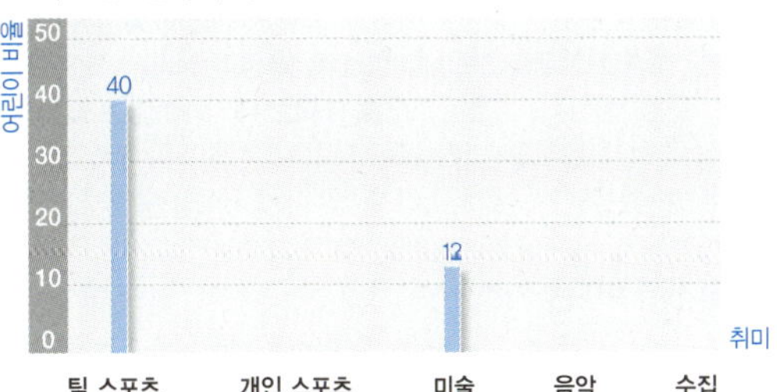

3-4

M　All right. Here's the map. Which trail do you want to take tomorrow?

W　Let's take the easiest one. It's supposed to rain, so it'll be slippery.

M　Yeah, that's a good idea. We'll take the easiest trail.

W　I'll bring the snacks if you bring the water.

M　Sounds good. Bring some rain ponchos, too.

W　For sure. I can't wait to try out my new boots.

M　Yeah, it'll be fun.

W　See you bright and early at 7:30!

► trail 오솔길, 산길   be supposed to ~하기로 되어 있다   slippery 미끄러운   poncho 비옷   try out (신발을) 신어 보다   bright and early 아침 일찍이

남 좋아. 자, 여기 지도. 내일 어느 경로를 타고 싶어?
여 가장 쉬운 길로 가자. 비가 내린다고 하니까 길이 미끄러울 거야.
남 그래, 좋은 생각이야. 가장 쉬운 경로를 타야겠다.
여 네가 물 가져오면 내가 간식 가져갈게.
남 좋아. 비옷도 가져와.
여 물론이지. 빨리 새로 산 부츠 신어보고 싶어.
남 그래, 재미있을 거야.
여 아침 일찍 7시 30분에 보자!

3 이들은 내일 무엇을 할 것인가?
(a) 운동경기   (b) 요리   (c) 뜨개질
(d) 우표 수집   (e) 하이킹

4 이들의 모토는 무엇이겠는가?
(a) 모든 것을 걸자.
(b) 후회하는 것보다 안전한 게 더 낫다.
(c) 연습을 하면 완벽해진다.
(d) 손바닥도 마주쳐야 소리가 난다.
(e) 평지풍파를 일으키지 마라.

❺

W Dear Diary. Today was not a good day. I came home from school and <u>went downstairs</u> to work on my model airplane, but I found it <u>broken</u> into little pieces. I've been working on that airplane for <u>months</u>. It really hurt to see it like that. My brother says he didn't do it, so that only leaves the cat. Who do I believe? There's <u>nothing left</u> to do but start over.

► downstairs 아래층으로   into pieces 산산조각으로   There's nothing left to do but~ 이제는 ~할 수밖에 없다

여 안녕, 일기야. 오늘은 좋지 않은 날이야. 학교에서 집으로 돌아와서 모형 비행기 작업을 하려고 아래층으로 내려갔는데, 글쎄 비행기가 산산조각이 나 있는 거야. 몇 달 동안 그 비행기 작업을 했었는데, 그렇게 된 모습을 보고 있자니 마음이 정말로 아팠어. 남동생은 자기가 한 짓이 아니라고 하니 그럼 고양이밖에 안 남는데, 누구를 믿어야 할까? 다시 시작할 수밖에 없지 뭐.

5 화자의 심정은 어떠한가?
(a) 기쁘다   (b) 질투가 난다   (c) 지루하다
(d) 슬프다   (e) 호기심이 난다

❻

M It's important to take kids' hobbies seriously. Of course, some kids <u>start and quit</u> hobbies very quickly, but other kids do a hobby because of a <u>deep interest</u>. Take film director Steven Spielberg for example. As a child, his hobby was <u>making films</u>. Now, he's one of the <u>most celebrated</u> directors in history. David Beckham is another example of a child who followed his hobby to success. Even if you don't care for a child's hobby, be <u>supportive</u>. It might pay off.

► seriously 진지하게   quit 그만두다   interest 관심   celebrated 유명한   care for ~을 좋아하다, 바라다; 돌보다   supportive 격려하는   pay off 성과를 거두다

남 아이들의 취미를 진지하게 여겨주는 게 중요합니다. 물론 어떤 아이들은 취미활동을 시작했다가 무척 빨리 그만두기도 하지만 다른 아이들은 관심이 아주 많기 때문에 취미활동을 하기도 합니다. 한 예로 영화감독 스티븐 스필버그를 볼까요? 어렸을 때 스필버그의 취미는 영화 만들기였습니다. 오늘날 그는 역사상 가장 유명한 영화감독 가운데 한 명입니다. 데이비드 베컴은 자신의 취미를 쫓아가다 성공하게 된 어린이의 또 다른 예입니다. 아이의 취미가 맘에 들지 않더라도 지지해주십시오. 좋은 성과를 낼 수도 있으니까요.

6 담화의 요지는 무엇인가?
(a) 때때로, 큰 성공은 어린 시절의 취미에서 비롯된다.
(b) 취미활동을 하다가 유명해지는 건 매우 드문 일이다.
(c) 스티븐 스필버그는 역사상 가장 유명한 영화감독 가운데 한 명이다.
(d) 데이비드 베컴은 어린 시절에 축구 선수가 되고 싶었다.
(e) 자신의 꿈을 이루기 어려워 보일지라도 그것을 좇을 만한 가치가 있다.

7~8

M What's all this, Joan?
W Oh, it's my <u>herb garden</u>. It's a bit of a hobby now.
M I didn't know you <u>grew herbs</u>. Are they <u>difficult to grow</u>?
W No, not really, Louis. And they're really useful.
M What do you use them for?
W I use them in cooking, in teas, and in soaps and to make <u>scented oils</u>.
M That's <u>pretty neat</u>. What do I need to start?
W Just some <u>seeds</u> and a place with good sunlight.
M Is that all?

► a bit of a 조금: 작은   useful 유용한   scented 향료가 든   neat (구어) 굉장한, 멋진; 산뜻한, 깔끔한   seed 씨앗

남 조운, 이게 다 뭐야?
여 아, 내 허브 정원이지. 요즘 조촐한 취미로 하는 거야.
남 네가 허브를 키우는 줄 몰랐어. 키우기 힘드니?
여 아니, 안 어려워, 루이스. 또 허브는 무척 유용해.
남 그걸 어디다 쓰는데?
여 요리할 때도 쓰고, 차로도 마시고, 비누에도 쓰고, 향유 만들 때도 쓰지.
남 야, 굉장한데. 시작하려면 뭐가 필요해?
여 그냥 씨앗 몇 개랑 햇볕이 잘 드는 장소만 있으면 돼.
남 그게 다야?

7 조운은 허브를 어디에 이용하지 않는가?
(a) 향유   (b) 약품   (c) 차
(d) 비누   (e) 요리

8 이 대화에서__________을 짐작할 수 있다.
(a) 조운이 오랫동안 식물을 길러왔다는 것
(b) 루이스는 취미가 없다는 것
(c) 허브를 키우는 것이 일반적인 취미라는 것
(d) 조운이 자주 외출하지 않는다는 것
(e) 조운이 이제 막 허브를 키우기 시작했다는 것

I Love the Holidays

Answers

GET READY p. 104~105

Key Words & Expressions

1 send 2 Halloween 3 annual
4 Groundhog Day 5 reunions 6 baby showers
7 treats 8 making toasts 9 jokes
10 celebrate

Questions & Responses

1 b 2 d 3 a 4 f 5 e 6 c

BASIC DRILL p. 106~107

Step 1
● Halloween / (1) Getting dressed up in scary costumes and trying to scare other people (2) Halloween parties

Q (d)

■ Christmas, holiday, dressed up, costumes, parties, haunted, Halloween

Step 2 A pick, buy B Valentine's Day
C egg hunt D Scariest Costume

1 (d) 2 (1) T (2) T (3) F

Plus⁺ Question 1 (a)

EXERCISE p. 108~109

Step 1 1 (d) 2 (d) 3 (a) 4 (b)
Step 2 1 (c) 2 (1) F (2) T (3) T (4) F (5) F
3 (d) 4 (b) 5 (a)

PRACTICE TEST p. 112~113

1 (c)

2

11 November

Sun	Mon	Tue	Wed	Thur	Fri	Sat
1	2	3	4	5	6	7
8	9	10	11	12	13	14
15	16	17	18	19	20	21
22	23	24	25	(26)	27	28
29	30					

3 (d) 4 (a) 5 (e) 6 (e) 7 (a) 8 (d)

* Dictation 1, 2의 정답은 각 Script의 밑줄친 부분임.

Scripts and Translations

GET READY

Key Words & Expressions

다음 문장을 듣고 보기 박스에서 알맞은 단어를 골라 빈칸을 채우시오.

1 사람들은 종종 2월 14일에 서로에게 발렌타인 데이 카드를 보냅니다.

2 핼로윈과 그 상징물들은 아일랜드와 스코틀랜드에서 북미로 왔습니다.

3 파크뷰 몰에서 열리는 부활절 달걀 찾기 연례행사에 오셔서 함께 하세요!

4 성촉절은 마멋이 굴 속에서 나와 봄이 언제 올지 알려주는 재미있는 날이에요.

5 가족들이 함께 모여 시간을 보내게 되면서, 많은 가족들은 일 년에 한 번 가족모임을 갖습니다.

6 미국에서는 여성들이 아기에게 필요한 용품을 예비 엄마가 받을 수 있게 베이비 샤워를 열어줍니다.

7 많은 사람들이 연휴 때 음식을 너무 많이 먹고 있는 자신 발견하게 됩니다.

8 사람들은 대개 뿔피리를 불고 샴페인으로 건배를 하면서 새해를 맞이합니다.

9 만우절 때 사람들은 때때로 서로에게 짓궂은 농담을 하기도 합니다.

10 성 패트릭 축일에는 많은 사람들이 초록색 옷을 입고 아일랜드 음식을 먹으면서 축하합니다.

Questions & Responses

질문에 어울리는 대답과 연결하시오.

1 제일 좋아하는 휴일이 뭐야?　ⓑ 추수감사절을 제일 좋아해.

2 생일날 뭔가 특별한 일을 하니?　ⓓ 응, 보통 식구들이랑 저녁 먹으러 나가.

3 너네 나라에는 어떤 독특한 휴일이 있니?　ⓐ 응, 5월 5일이 어린이 날이야.

4 중요한 휴일은 어디서 축하하니?　ⓕ 보통은 부모님 고향에 가서 조부모님들과 함께 지내.

5 새해맞이를 어떻게 하니?　ⓔ 보통 카운트다운을 하고 새해가 온 것을 축하하며 건배를 해.

6 크리스마스를 축하하니?　ⓒ 아니, 난 불교신자야.

듣고 정답을 확인하시오.

친구와 함께 연습하시오.

다음을 듣고 메모하시오.

M Everyone always says that their favorite holiday is Christmas, but I'm different. Sure, Christmas is great, but to me Halloween is the best holiday. I love getting dressed up in scary costumes and trying to scare other people. Halloween parties are awesome, and, of course, the candy is the best part. Sometimes my dad and I make a haunted house in the garage. Halloween is definitely my favorite time of year.

▶ dress up ~로 가장하다, 차려입다 scary 무서운 costume 복장 scare 깜짝 놀래주다 awesome 굉장한, 아주 멋진 haunted 귀신이 나오는 garage 차고

남 모두들 제일 좋아하는 휴일은 크리스마스라고 늘 말하지만 전 달라요. 물론 크리스마스도 좋지만, 제게는 핼로윈이 최고의 휴일이에요. 무서운 복장으로 차려입고 다른 사람들을 겁나게 하는 게 정말 좋아요. 핼로윈 파티는 정말 굉장해요. 그리고 물론 사탕이 핼로윈에서 최고로 좋아하는 것이죠. 때로는 아빠랑 내가 차고에 귀신 나오는 집을 만들기도 해요. 핼로윈은 일 년 중에서 제가 제일 좋아하는 날이에요.

메모를 바탕으로 다음 문제에 답하시오.

Q 화자에 대한 내용 중 사실인 것은?
   (a) 핼로윈보다 크리스마스를 더 좋아한다.
   (b) 귀신 나오는 집을 두려워한다.
   (c) 때때로 쉽게 겁을 먹는다.
   (d) 핼로윈 파티를 무척 즐긴다.

■ 다시 듣고 빈칸을 채우시오.

Basic Drill Step 2

다음을 듣고 메모하시오.

M1 I'm Kyle, and I have a really big family. It can get expensive buying gifts for everyone at Christmas. So, we pick names from a hat to see who we have to buy a gift for. It's great, and no one gets stressed out.

W1 I'm Ellen, and my girl friends and I hate Valentine's Day. Instead, we have a special "girls' night" on February 14 and don't worry about boys. It's lots of fun!

W2 I'm Emily. On Easter, the families in my neighborhood all get together at the park and have a huge Easter egg hunt. Our parents hide the eggs first, and then we find them. It's the best!

M2 John's my name, and scaring people is my game. On Halloween, I have a party at my place. It's also a "Scariest Costume" contest. I get to judge who has the best costume. It's great to see all the cool costumes!

▶ stressed out 스트레스를 받는 Easter 부활절 hide 숨기다 get together 모이다 judge 심사하다; 재판하다, 판단하다

남1 난 카일이야. 우리 집은 정말 대가족이라서, 크리스마스 때 모든 식구에게 줄 선물을 사려면 돈이 많이 들 수가 있어. 그래서 우리는 각자 누구에게 선물을 사줘야 할지 정하려고 모자에서 이름을 뽑아. 굉장히 재미있기도 하고 아무도 스트레스를 받지 않아.

여1 난 엘렌이야. 내 친구들이랑 난 발렌타인 데이를 싫어해. 대신에 우린 2월 14일에 '소녀들의 밤'이라는 특별한 행사를 갖고 남자애들에 대해선 신경 안

써. 정말 재미있어!

여2 난 에밀리야. 부활절에 우리 동네 사람들은 가족 단위로 모두 공원에 모여서 대규모의 부활절 달걀 찾기 놀이를 해. 부모들이 먼저 달걀을 숨겨 두시면 우리가 그걸 찾는 거야. 그게 제일 좋아!

남2 내 이름은 존이고, 사람들을 깜짝 놀라게 하는 게 내가 즐기는 놀이지. 핼로윈 때 우리 집에서 파티를 해. 그건 또한 '가장 무서운 의상' 경연대회기도 하지. 난 누가 의상을 제일 잘 입었는지 심사하는데, 모든 멋진 의상들을 보는 것도 큰 즐거움이야!

메모를 바탕으로 다음 문제에 답하시오.

1 화자들은 주로 무엇에 관해 이야기하고 있는가?
   (a) 자기들이 싫어하는 휴일
   (b) 자기들이 가장 좋아하는 휴일
   (c) 휴일의 보편적인 전통들
   (d) 휴일을 축하하는 자기들의 독특한 방식

2 맞으면 T, 틀리면 F를 쓰시오.
   (1) 에밀리의 부모님은 부활절 달걀을 숨기신다.
   (2) 존은 핼로윈 때 의상 경연대회를 연다.
   (3) 카일의 가족은 크리스마스 선물을 사지 않는다.

다시 듣고 정답을 확인하시오.

Plus⁺ Question

1 앨렌은 _______을[를] 싫어한다.
   (a) 발렌타인 데이   (b) 크리스마스
   (c) 핼로윈   (d) 설날

EXERCISE Step 1

듣고 문제에 답하시오.

❶

M What are we shopping for, Flora?

W My friend Nikki is having a baby shower on Sunday. I need to pick up a gift.

M Okay, I can help. Hmm… What about this little baby dress?

W Um, no, she's having a boy.

M Well, why not get her something useful like some baby bottles, blankets, or diapers?

W Good idea. I'll get her a few cute bottles. Wait here.

▶ baby shower 출산 파티 baby bottle 젖병 blanket 담요 diaper 기저귀

남 플로라, 우리 뭘 사려는 거야?
여 내 친구 니키가 일요일에 베이비 샤워를 하거든. 선물을 골라야 해.
남 알았어. 도와줄게. 흠, 이 앙증맞은 아기 드레스는 어때?
여 안 돼. 남자애거든.
남 그럼, 젖병이나 담요, 기저귀 같이 실용적인 것을 주면 어때?
여 좋은 생각이야. 니키한테 귀여운 젖병을 좀 사줘야겠다. 여기서 기다려.

1 여자는 무엇을 살 것인가?

(a)    (b)    (c)    (d) 

2

M　Happy Groundhog Day, Wendy!

W　Oh yeah, it's February 2, isn't it? I never remember Groundhog Day.

M　Really? I always do. I can't wait to hear the forecast!

W　How does it work again?

M　If the groundhog comes out, sees his shadow, and goes back to sleep, we'll have six more weeks of winter.

W　And if not?

M　If it's cloudy out or he decides to stay up, we'll have an early spring.

W　And you believe that, Eric?

M　The famous groundhog, Punxsutawney Phil, is hardly ever wrong.

▶ **Groundhog Day** 성촉절　**groundhog** (동물) 마멋　**stay up** 일어나 있다: 그대로 있다　**Punxsutawney** 미국 펜실베니아 주의 한 도시로, 가장 성대한 성촉절 행사가 치러짐　**Punxsutawney Phil** Punxsutawney에서 성촉절에 날씨 예보를 할 때 사용하는 마멋의 이름

남　성촉절 잘 보내, 웬디!
여　아, 맞다. 오늘이 2월 2일이구나, 그렇지? 성촉절을 절대 기억 못한단 말이야.
남　정말? 난 늘 기억하는데. 빨리 일기예보를 듣고 싶어!
여　그게 어떻게 되는 거였더라?
남　이날 마멋이 나왔다가 자기 그림자를 보고 다시 잠자러 들어가면 겨울이 6주가 더 남았다는 거지.
여　그렇지 않으면?
남　날씨가 흐리거나 마멋이 굴로 안 들어가고 그대로 있으면 봄을 일찍 맞게 되는 거야.
여　에릭, 넌 그걸 믿어?
남　유명한 마멋인 펑스타오니 필은 거의 틀리지 않아.

2　다음 중 사실이 아닌 것은?
(a) 2월 2일은 성촉절이다.
(b) 에릭은 성촉절을 좋아한다.
(c) 날씨가 흐리면 봄이 빨리 올 것이다.
(d) 마멋이 자기 그림자를 보면 봄이 일찍 올 것이다.

3~4

W　Hey, Al. What's up?

M　Um… not much. What's up with you?

W　Oh, nothing. Want to grab a burger?

M　Uh, Valerie… Are you forgetting something?

W　I don't think so. Why?

M　Well, it's my birthday.

W　Oh! Oh no! I totally forgot! I'm so sorry! Are you mad?

M　No, but we've been friends for so long, so…

W　I'm sorry, Al. It totally slipped my mind. I'll make it up to you. I promise.

▶ **grab** 간단하게 요기하다; 부여잡다, 움켜쥐다　**mad** 몹시 화난; 미친　**slip one's mind** 잊어버리다　**make up to** ~에게 변상하다, 만회하다

여　안녕, 앨. 잘 지내?
남　음, 뭐 그렇게 잘은 아니고. 넌 별일 없어?
여　어, 없어. 햄버거 먹을래?
남　저기, 발레리. 너 뭐 잊은 거 없어?

여　없는 것 같은데. 왜?
남　음, 오늘 내 생일이야.
여　어머! 이걸 어째! 까맣게 잊고 있었어! 정말 미안해! 화났니?
남　아냐, 하지만 우리는 아주 오랜 친구잖아. 그래서….
여　미안해, 앨. 완전히 잊어버렸어. 내가 제대로 챙겨줄게. 약속해.

3　화자들의 관계는 무엇인가?
(a) 친구　　　　　　　(b) 남매
(c) 부부　　　　　　　(d) 부녀지간

4　소년의 심정은 어떠한가?
(a) 화가 났다　　　　　(b) 실망했다
(c) 겁먹었다　　　　　(d) 지루하다

Exercise　Step 2

듣고 문제에 답하시오.

1

M　Look at this, Beth.

W　What is it?

M　It's a Valentine's Day card.

W　That's nice. Who's it from?

M　It doesn't say.

W　What do you mean?

M　It says "Dear Larry. Be Mine. From your secret admirer." It doesn't have a name.

W　No name?

M　Yeah. Weird, huh?

W　Maybe it was Melanie or Sarah. A lot of people like you, you know.

M　Oh, come on.

W　Well, you should feel good. I didn't get anything for Valentine's Day.

▶ **admirer** 구애자, 흠모자; 찬양자　**weird** 이상한

남　베스, 이것 좀 봐.
여　그게 뭐야?
남　발렌타인 데이 카드야.
여　예쁘다. 누가 보낸 거야?
남　안 쓰여 있네.
여　무슨 뜻이야?
남　여기 '친애하는 래리, 내 사람이 돼줘. 몰래 너를 흠모하는 사람이.'라고 써 있어. 이름은 없고.
여　이름이 없어?
남　응. 이상하지?
여　멜라니나 아니면 새라일지도 몰라. 알다시피 많은 사람들이 널 좋아하잖아.
남　야, 됐어.
여　어쨌든, 기분은 좋겠다. 난 발렌타인 데이 때 아무 것도 못 받았는데.

1　누가 래리에게 카드를 보냈는가?
(a) 래리의 여자친구
(b) 베스
(c) 누가 보냈는지 모른다.
(d) 새라
(e) 멜라니

②

M This Wednesday, March 17, is St. Patrick's Day! As usual, Irish Eyes Restaurant is getting festive. The party starts at 7:00 p.m. The first 3 people at the door will get a free meal, and the next 10 will get 50% off. Speaking of meals, our special is the Irish platter: Irish stew with mashed potatoes and soda bread. Later on, we'll enjoy some traditional Irish songs and dancing. Come and join the fun this Wednesday!

▶ **as usual** 여느 때처럼 **festive** 축제의 **speaking of** ~에 관해 말하자면 **platter** (큰 접시에 담긴) 모듬 요리 **later on** 나중에 **mashed potato** 으깬 감자 요리 **traditional** 전통의

남 3월 17일 이번 주 수요일은 성 패트릭 축일입니다! 여느 때처럼 아이리쉬 아이즈 식당은 축제를 열지요. 파티는 저녁 7시에 시작합니다. 처음 입장하시는 세 분께는 무료 식사를 제공하고, 그 다음 열 분께는 식사 가격의 50%를 할인해 드립니다. 식사에 대해 말씀 드리자면, 저희가 준비한 특별 요리는 으깬 감자를 곁들인 아이리쉬 스튜와 소다 빵이 함께 나오는 아이리쉬 플래터입니다. 나중에 아이리쉬 전통 노래와 춤을 즐기실 수 있고요. 이번 주 수요일에 오셔서 즐거운 시간을 함께 해주세요!

2 맞으면 T, 틀리면 F에 체크하시오.
(1) 아이리쉬 플래터에는 스튜와 감자튀김이 포함된다.
(2) 성 패트릭 축일은 3월 17일이다.
(3) 아이리쉬 아이즈 식당은 보통 성 패트릭 축일을 축하한다.
(4) 처음 입장하는 열 명에게 무료로 식사를 제공한다.
(5) 아이리쉬 플래터는 밤새도록 50% 할인된다.

3~5

M The Christmas holiday can be a very stressful time for some people, especially in North America, where Christmas means gifts. First of all, it's difficult to find the perfect gift for everyone. Second, it's often difficult to pay for all those gifts! Also, many people find getting together with their families a stressful event, especially if some family members don't get along. Add to this all those holiday treats and the thought of gaining weight, and you can see that Christmas isn't such a happy holiday for everyone.

▶ **stressful** 스트레스가 많은 **get along** 사이 좋게 지내다 **add to this** 이에 더하여 **treat** 진수성찬, 대접

남 크리스마스 휴일이 어떤 사람들에게는 굉장히 스트레스를 주는 시간이 될 수 있습니다. 특히 크리스마스가 선물을 뜻하는 북미 사람들에게는 더 그렇죠. 우선, 모든 사람에게 안성맞춤인 선물을 찾기가 어렵습니다. 둘째, 그 모든 선물 비용을 지불하는 것은 힘들 때가 많죠! 또 많은 사람들이 가족들과 함께 모이는 것을 스트레스 받는 일이라고 봅니다. 특히 일부 가족 구성원이 서로 잘 지내지 못하면 더 그렇죠. 여기에 크리스마스 때 먹는 음식과 늘 어나는 몸무게에 대한 생각까지 더하면 크리스마스가 모든 사람에게 그렇게 행복한 휴일은 아님을 알 수 있습니다.

3 무엇에 관한 내용인가?
(a) 북미의 크리스마스
(b) 크리스마스 때 스트레스를 피하는 방법
(c) 크리스마스 때 생기는 가족 간 문제

(d) 크리스마스에서 스트레스가 되는 점
(e) 크리스마스에 선물 사기

4 다음 중 스트레스의 원인으로 언급되지 않은 것은?
(a) 체중 증가
(b) 크리스마스 저녁 식사 만들기
(c) 선물에 쓰는 돈
(d) 안성맞춤인 선물 찾기
(e) 사이가 안 좋은 가족 구성원

5 내용을 가장 잘 요약한 것은 무엇인가?
(a) 어떤 사람들에게 크리스마스는 선물 구입 및 가족들과 보내는 시간, 체중 증가와 같은 여러 가지 이유 때문에 즐겁기보다는 스트레스를 받는 시기이다.
(b) 크리스마스가 선물을 의미하는 북미 지역에 사는 사람들은 크리스마스 선물 구입에 너무 스트레스를 받는다. 왜냐하면 그 모든 선물을 사는 데 돈이 많이 들기 때문이다.

PRACTICE TEST
듣고 문제에 답하시오.

① 

W Back in the 1800s, people from Scotland and Ireland going to North America brought their special days and traditions with them. One of these was Halloween. People in North America quickly made it their own. Now, kids go door to door saying "trick-or-treat" and then receive candy. The colors of Halloween are orange and black, and the symbols of Halloween are usually of these colors. They include, for example, pumpkins, black cats, bats, and witches.

▶ **bring** 가져오다 **tradition** 전통 **door to door** 집집마다 **receive** 받다 **symbol** 상징 **include** 포함하다 **witch** 마녀, 여자 마법사

여 1800년대로 거슬러 올라가 보자면, 스코틀랜드와 아일랜드에서 북미로 간 사람들은 자신들의 특별한 휴일과 전통도 함께 가져갔습니다. 그 중 하나가 핼로윈이었죠. 북미 사람들은 재빨리 그것을 자기네 것으로 만들었습니다. 오늘날, 아이들이 집집마다 다니며 "사탕 안 주면 장난칠 테야"라고 말하면서 사탕을 받습니다. 핼로윈을 대표하는 색깔은 오렌지 색과 검정이고, 핼로윈을 상징하는 것들도 대개 이 두 가지 색입니다. 예를 들어, 호박, 검은 고양이, 박쥐와 마녀가 포함되지요.

1 핼로윈의 상징으로 언급되지 않은 것은?

② 

W Thanksgiving is an important holiday in the U.S. and falls on the fourth Thursday of November. It is only a one-day holiday, but family members often travel from around the country to be together for Thanksgiving dinner. Usually, families eat roast turkey for dinner. It is also important because it marks the beginning of the shopping season for the Christmas holiday.

▶ fall on 해당하다 turkey 칠면조 mark 나타내다

여 미국에서 추수감사절은 중요한 휴일이고, 11월 넷째 주 목요일이 그날이랍니다. 딱 하루 간의 휴일이지만, 추수감사절 저녁식사를 함께 하러 종종 전국 각지에서 가족 구성원들이 이동합니다. 대개 가족들은 저녁식사로 구운 칠면조를 먹습니다. 또한 추수감사절은 크리스마스 휴일을 위한 쇼핑 시즌의 막이 올랐음을 알려주기 때문에 중요하죠.

Level up

2 추수감사절은 언제인가? 날짜에 동그라미 하시오.

11월

일	월	화	수	목	금	토
1	2	3	4	5	6	7
8	9	10	11	12	13	14
15	16	17	18	19	20	21
22	23	24	25	26	27	28
29	30					

3-4

M Hey, Hailey. What's up?

W Not much, Devon. Are you ready for the science test today?

M Science test? It was cancelled. Didn't you hear?

W What? It was cancelled? Oh, wow! That's great!

M Hailey…

W What?

M April Fools!

W Huh? Are you kidding me? So the test is still on?

M Yeah, I was just pulling your leg.

W That was a mean joke, Devon. See you…

▶ cancel 취소하다 April Fools 만우절 on 행하여져; 예정하여 pull one's leg ~을 놀리다, 농담하다 mean 심술궂은, 짓궂은

남 안녕, 헤일리. 어떻게 지내?
여 그저 그렇게 지내, 데본. 오늘 칠 과학 시험 준비는 했어?
남 과학 시험? 그거 취소됐잖아. 너 못 들었어?
여 뭐? 취소됐다고? 와, 잘됐다!
남 헤일리….
여 응?
남 만우절이지롱!
여 뭐? 너 농담한 거야? 그럼 여전히 시험도 보는 거고?
남 응. 그냥 널 놀린 거야.
여 정말 짓궂은 농담이었어, 데본. 너 두고 봐.

3 헤일리와 데본의 관계는 무엇인가?
(a) 직장 동료 　　　(b) 팀원 　　　(c) 남매
(d) 학급 친구 　　　(e) 운동 파트너

4 대화 마지막에 헤일리의 심정은 어떠한가?
(a) 언짢다 　　　(b) 슬프다 　　　(c) 신난다
(d) 두렵다 　　　(e) 혼란스럽다

 **5**

W Do you ever wonder why so many brides wear white? Actually, many modern Western wedding traditions have their roots in England. This is where the tradition of wearing a white dress comes from. Queen Victoria is the one who started the trend in 1840. At the time, many people admired her wedding photo, and now people from many countries, from Spain to China, choose to wear white on their wedding day.

▶ wonder 궁금해 하다 bride 신부 modern 현대의 tradition 전통 root 뿌리, 근원 trend 경향, 유행 admire 감탄하다; 존경하다

여 왜 그렇게 많은 신부들이 흰색 웨딩 드레스를 입는지 궁금해 한 적이 있나요? 사실 여러 현대 서양 결혼식 전통이 영국에 그 뿌리를 두고 있습니다. 흰색 웨딩 드레스를 입는 전통이 유래한 곳이 바로 영국입니다. 빅토리아 여왕이 1840년에 이 유행을 일으켰죠. 그 당시 많은 사람들이 여왕의 결혼 사진을 보고 감탄했지요. 그리고 현재는 스페인에서 중국에 이르기까지 많은 나라의 사람들이 결혼식 날 흰색 드레스를 입습니다.

5 어디서 흰색 웨딩 드레스를 입는 관습이 시작되었는가?
(a) 중국 　　　(b) 스페인 　　　(c) 프랑스
(d) 미국 　　　(e) 영국

6

M This Saturday is New Year's Eve, and you know what that means! The Mandarin Hotel is having its annual New Year's Eve Bash! For only $75 per couple, you can have dinner and enjoy live music as you ring in the New Year. You will also get noisemakers and a glass of champagne to toast the beginning of a brand new year. Come and join us this Saturday and start next year on the right foot!

▶ annual 해마다의 bash 떠들썩한 파티 ring in (새해 등을) 종을 울리서 맞다 noisemaker 뿔피리 toast ~을 위해 축배를 들다, 건배하다 brand new 아주 새로운 on the right foot 출발이 순조로운

남 이번 주 토요일은 섣달 그믐날입니다. 그게 무슨 의미인지 아시죠? 만다린 호텔에서는 연례 행사인 섣달 그믐날 파티를 엽니다! 커플 당 단돈 75달러로 새해를 맞이하며 저녁식사와 생음악을 즐기실 수 있습니다. 또한 뿔피리와 새해의 시작을 축하하며 건배할 샴페인 한 잔도 제공됩니다. 이번 주 토요일에 오셔서 함께 하시고, 내년을 순조롭게 출발하시기 바랍니다!

6 어떤 종류의 담화인가?
(a) 전화 회사 광고
(b) 새해맞이 연설
(c) 새로 개업한 식당 광고
(d) 새해를 어떻게 시작할 것인가에 관한 조언
(e) 새해맞이 파티 광고

M Hey.
W Hey.
M Another family reunion.
W Yep, another one.
M Why does our family keep this up anyway? Every summer it's the same thing.
W I don't know. I guess it's a tradition.
M Not everyone enjoys it though.
W Obviously.
M Did you see Aunt Diane and Uncle Nick?
W Yeah. Fighting as usual.
M What do we do now?
W I don't know. Let's try to find some food.

▶ family reunion 가족 모임   keep up 계속하다   obviously 분명히, 명백히

남 안녕.
여 안녕.
남 또 식구들이 한자리에 모였네.
여 그러게. 또 모였어.

남 왜 우리 가족들은 이걸 계속하지? 매년 여름마다 똑같은 것을.
여 모르겠어. 전통이라서 그런 것 같아.
남 하지만 모두가 좋아하는 것도 아닌데 말이야.
여 맞아.
남 다이앤 숙모랑 닉 삼촌 봤어?
여 응. 평소대로 싸우시던 걸.
남 우리 이제 뭐하지?
여 모르겠어. 음식이나 찾아보자.

7 화자들의 기분은 어떠한가?
   (a) 지루하다
   (b) 행복하다
   (c) 흥분돼 있다
   (d) 화가 났다
   (e) 미심쩍다

8 그들은 얼마나 자주 가족 모임을 갖는가?
   (a) 일년에 두 번
   (b) 생일 때마다
   (c) 크리스마스에
   (d) 일 년에 한 번
   (e) 한 달에 한 번

Unit 10 · I'd Like a One-way Ticket to New York

Answers

GET READY p. 116~117

Key Words & Expressions

1 one-way   2 adventure vacations
3 camped out   4 boarding pass 5 planning a trip
6 travel   7 historical sites 8 landmarks
9 natural sites 10 pack

Questions & Responses

1 c   2 d   3 a   4 e   5 f   6 b

BASIC DRILL p. 118~119

Step 1 • New York / She buys souvenirs.
   Q (c)
   ■ trip, traveling, camera, sightseeing, souvenirs, places, Europe

Step 2 A Australia / surfing   B canoeing / three
   C Rome   D racing
   1 (d)   2 (1) T (2) F (3) T

Plus⁺ Question 1 (c)   2 (a)

EXERCISE p. 120~121

Step 1 1 (b)   2 (1) T (2) F (3) F (4) T   3 (a)   4 (c)
Step 2 1 (c)   2 (b)   3 (d)   4 (c)   5 (b)

PRACTICE TEST p. 124~125

1 (e)   2 (1) Cuzco (2) English   3 (c)   4 (a)   5 (b)
6 (d)   7 (e)   8 (a)

* Dictation 1, 2의 정답은 각 Script의 밑줄친 부분임.

GET READY

Key Words & Expressions

다음 문장을 듣고 보기 박스에서 알맞은 단어를 골라 빈칸을 채우시오.

1 밴쿠버 행 편도 표 두 장 주세요.

2 어떤 사람들은 스릴 넘치는 모험 만점의 휴가를 즐깁니다.

3 우린 카누를 타고, 하이킹을 하고, 캠핑을 했어요.

4 비행기표와 신분증을 보여주시겠어요? 탑승권 여기 있습니다.

5 예산을 세우는 게 여행 계획을 짤 때 해야 할 가장 중요한 일 가운데 하나죠.

6 여행할 때, 여행하는 그 나라의 몇 가지 중요한 표현은 꼭 알아두세요.

7 난 따분한 유적지를 방문하느니 해변에서 휴가를 보내겠어.

8 에펠탑은 세계에서 가장 유명한 역사적 건축물 가운데 하나입니다.

9 그랜드 캐년은 사람들이 가장 많이 찾는 자연 관광지 가운데 하나랍니다.

10 어떤 여행이든 짐은 가볍게 꾸리는 것이 최고예요.

Questions & Responses

질문에 어울리는 대답과 연결하시오.

1 여행하는 거 좋아해? 　ⓒ 응, 1년에 한 번씩 가려고 해.

2 여행에서 제일 힘든 부분이 뭐야? 　ⓓ 언어가 정말 제일 힘든 부분이지.

3 어디를 여행했었니? 　ⓐ 미국이랑 호주에 다녀 왔어.

4 어디를 여행하고 싶어? 　ⓔ 난 남미에 가고 싶어.

5 비행기로 여행하는 거 좋아해? 　ⓕ 좋아하지 않지만 다른 방법이 없잖아. 이 세상은 너무 넓어!

6 안 가고 싶은 곳이 있어? 　ⓑ 난 러시아는 가지 않겠어. 너무 춥잖아.

듣고 정답을 확인하시오.

친구와 함께 연습하시오.

Basic Drill　Step 1

다음을 듣고 메모하시오.

W　Every summer, my family goes on a trip somewhere different. I love traveling, so I really look forward to this time. Last summer, we went to California, and this summer we're going to New York. This summer's trip is going to be great because I just got a new camera. I can't wait to go sightseeing downtown and snap some photos! I also buy souvenirs wherever I go. So far, I have 11 key chains all from different places. My dream is to go to Europe someday, so I'll have to start saving my money now!

▶ **somewhere** 어딘가에　**look forward to** ~을 고대하다　**go sightseeing** 관광하다　**snap** 사진 찍다　**souvenir** 기념품

여　우리 가족은 매년 여름마다 다른 곳으로 여행을 가요. 전 여행하는 걸 무척 좋아해서 이때를 손꼽아 기다리죠. 작년 여름에는 캘리포니아에 갔었고, 올

여름에는 뉴욕에 갈 거예요. 새 카메라를 샀기 때문에 이번 여름 여행은 아주 즐거울 것 같아요. 얼른 시내 곳곳을 관광하며 사진을 찍고 싶어요! 전 또한 여행을 가는 곳마다 기념품을 사요. 지금까지 각각 다른 곳에서 산 열쇠 체인이 11개나 있어요. 제 꿈은 언젠가 유럽에 가는 거예요. 그래서 지금부터 돈을 모아야 해요.

메모를 바탕으로 다음 문제에 답하시오.

Q 다음 중 사실인 것은?

(a) 화자의 가족은 올 여름에 유럽에 갈 것이다.

(b) 화자는 뉴욕에서 사진을 찍었다.

(c) 화자는 다양한 곳에 가는 것을 좋아한다.

(d) 화자는 12개 이상의 열쇠 체인을 가지고 있다.

■ 다시 듣고 빈칸을 채우시오.

Basic Drill　Step 2

다음을 듣고 메모하시오.

M1　I'm Sam. The best trip I ever went on was to Australia last year. I've always wanted to go to Australia, so it was awesome. I saw kangaroos and koalas, went scuba diving, and even tried surfing.

W1　I'm Julia. The best trip I remember was a canoeing trip with my gym class. We canoed for three days on some small, beautiful lakes and camped out on little islands at night. Those were good times.

W2　My name's Jenny, and I've traveled a lot, but I'd have to say my favorite trip was to Rome 2 years ago. There were so many amazing historic sites to see. I loved the Coliseum. I'd like to return to Rome some day.

M2　I'm Taylor, and my favorite trip of all time was to the Daytona Speedway in Florida. I'm a big racing fan, so seeing the track and the cars was pretty cool. My dad and I even watched a race.

▶ **awesome** 굉장한　**canoe** 카누를 젓다, 카누로 가다　**camp out** 야영하다　**historic site** 유적지　**return** 돌아가다　**track** 경주로, 트랙　**race** 경주

남1　난 샘이야. 내가 갔던 최고의 여행은 작년에 호주로 간 거였어. 늘 호주에 가고 싶었는데, 정말 굉장했어. 캥거루랑 코알라를 보고, 스쿠버 다이빙을 하고, 서핑도 해봤다니까.

여1　난 줄리아야. 내가 기억하는 최고의 여행은 함께 체육 수업 듣는 애들이랑 카누 타고 여행한 거야. 3일 동안 조그맣고 아름다운 호수에서 카누를 타고 밤에는 작은 섬에서 캠핑을 했어. 좋은 시간이었지.

여2　내 이름은 제니야. 여행을 많이 다녔지만 내가 제일 좋아했던 여행은 2년 전에 로마에 갔던 거야. 봐야 할 굉장한 유적지가 너무나 많았어. 난 콜로세움이 정말 맘에 들더라고. 언젠가 로마에 다시 가고 싶어.

남2　난 테일러라고 해. 제일 좋았던 여행은 플로리다에 있는 데이토너 고속도로에 갔을 때야. 난 자동차 경주 광팬이어서 경주로와 경주용 차들을 보는 게 정말 좋았어. 아빠랑 난 경주를 보기도 했지.

메모를 바탕으로 다음 문제에 답하시오.

1 화자들은 주로 무엇에 관해 이야기하고 있는가?

(a) 최신 인기 휴양지

(b) 가족 휴가

(c) 자기들이 가장 좋아하는 곳

(d) 자기들이 가장 좋아한 여행

2 맞으면 T, 틀리면 F를 쓰시오.

(1) 샘은 호주에서 서핑을 해보았다.

(2) 줄리아는 4일 동안 카누를 탔다.

(3) 테일러는 자동차 경주 팬이다.

다시 듣고 정답을 확인하시오.

Plus⁺ Question

1 줄리아는 누구와 여행했는가?

(a) 부모님

(b) 친구들

(c) 함께 체육 수업 듣는 급우들

(d) 친척들

2 테일러는 여행에서 무엇을 보는 것을 즐겼는가?

(a) 경주로와 경주용 차들

(b) 콜로세움

(c) 해변

(d) 자신이 제일 좋아하는 레이싱 선수

EXERCISE Step 1

듣고 문제에 답하시오.

M　Bad news. The weather doesn't <u>look</u> <u>so</u> <u>good</u>. It's raining.

W　Oh, no. We came to Thailand to go to the beaches.

M　I know, but this isn't very good beach weather.

W　What does your travel book say we can do around here?

M　Okay, <u>let</u> <u>me</u> <u>check</u>. There are elephant rides, a <u>temple</u>, a market, a tiger zoo. What do you think?

W　I guess if we go to a temple, at least we can <u>stay</u> <u>out</u> <u>of</u> the rain.

M　True. Let's <u>check</u> <u>it</u> <u>out</u> and then grab a nice dinner.

▶ temple 사원　at least 적어도　stay out ~가 끝날 때까지 있다; 밖에 있다　grab 급히 하다

남　안 좋은 소식이야. 날씨가 그다지 좋지 않네. 지금 비 와.

여　오, 안 돼. 해변에 가려고 태국에 온 건데.

남　알아, 하지만 해변에 가기에 좋은 날씨가 아니야.

여　네 여행 책자에 이 근처에서 할 만한 게 뭐가 있다고 나와 있어?

남　좋아, 찾아볼게. 코끼리 타기, 사원, 시장, 호랑이 동물원이 있어. 어때?

여　사원에 가면 적어도 비는 피할 수 있을 것 같아.

남　맞아. 거기 들른 다음에 맛있는 저녁 먹자.

1 그들은 무엇을 할 것인가?

(a) 　(b) 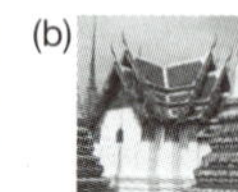　(c) 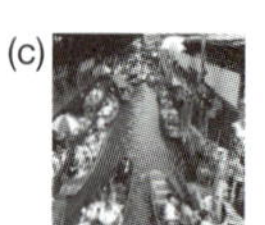　(d) 

2

W　Hello, I'd like a ticket from Calgary to Vancouver.

M　Trains <u>depart</u> at 8:00 a.m. daily. What day would you like to leave?

W　In two weeks <u>if</u> <u>possible</u>, on June 2.

M　Okay. Just yourself traveling, ma'am?

W　Yes.

M　Return or <u>one-way</u>?

W　One-way, please.

M　Would you like a regular seat or a sleeper?

W　A <u>sleeper</u>, please.

M　Okay, that's $350.

W　Can I pay by credit card?

M　Sure.

▶ ticket 표, 승차권　depart 출발하다　if possible 가능하다면　return 왕복표　one-way 편도　sleeper 침대차

여　안녕하세요. 캘거리에서 밴쿠버 가는 표 한 장이요.

남　기차는 매일 오전 8시에 출발합니다. 며칠날에 떠나실 건가요?

여　가능하다면 2주 뒤인, 6월 2일이요.

남　알겠습니다. 혼자 가시는 건가요?

여　네.

남　왕복이요, 편도요?

여　편도로 주세요.

남　일반 좌석을 원하십니까, 침대칸을 원하십니까?

여　침대칸으로 주세요.

남　네, 350달러입니다.

여　신용카드로 해도 되죠?

남　그럼요.

2 맞으면 T, 틀리면 F에 체크하시오.

(1) 여자는 혼자 여행할 것이다.

(2) 여자는 캘거리로 돌아올 것이다.

(3) 6월 2일에 여행하는 것이 불가능하다.

(4) 여자는 기차에서 잠을 자고 싶어한다.

3-4

M　There's just so much to see in Turkey. I think we'll have to choose <u>what</u> <u>we</u> <u>want</u> <u>to</u> <u>see</u> because we can't do it all. So, what's most important to you, Kelly?

W　I really want to see all the mosques and museums in Istanbul. I'd also like to see the <u>ancient</u> <u>city</u> of Ephesus.

M　But I'm more of a beach person. There are supposed to be some gorgeous beaches <u>along</u> <u>the</u> <u>coast</u>.

W　We can go to beaches anywhere. The <u>historical</u> <u>sites</u> are far more interesting.

M　Can't we do both?

W　I don't think we'll have time, Mike.

▶ mosque 모스크(이슬람교 성원)　ancient 고대의　coast 해안　historical site 유적지　far 훨씬

남　터키에는 볼 게 참 많아. 다 볼 수는 없으니까 우리가 보고 싶은 것을 골라야 할 것 같아. 그래, 너한테는 뭐가 제일 중요해, 켈리?

여　난 이스탄불에 있는 모든 모스크랑 박물관에 다 가고 싶어. 고대 도시 에베소도 보고 싶고.

남　하지만 난 해변을 더 좋아하는 편이잖아. 해안을 따라 멋진 해변이 펼쳐져 있을 거라고.

여　해변은 어디서나 갈 수 있잖아. 유적지가 훨씬 더 재미있다고.

남　둘 다 할 수는 없을까?

여　그럴 시간이 없을 것 같아, 마이크.

3 그들은 무엇에 의견 일치가 안 되고 있는가?

  (a) 터키에서 할 일   (b) 찾아갈 해변

  (c) 방문할 유적지   (d) 찾아갈 해안

4 켈리는 ______에 더 관심이 있지만, 마이크는 ______에 더 관심이 있다.

  (a) 대도시, 해안   (b) 터키 문화, 파티

  (c) 유적지, 해변   (d) 모스크와 박물관, 낚시

Exercise **Step 2**

듣고 문제에 답하시오.

M What are you taking?

W Well, I'm trying to pack lightly. Just <u>a</u> <u>few</u> <u>pairs</u> <u>of</u> <u>shorts</u>, <u>shirts</u>, and a bathing suit.

M Are you bringing shampoo?

W Yeah, I've <u>packed</u> <u>it</u> <u>already</u>.

M Okay. Where's my beach towel?

W It's in the <u>closet</u>.

M Do you have the tickets?

W Yes, I've got everything <u>under</u> <u>control</u>.

M What about our passports?

W I've got mine. Where's yours?

M Don't you have it? Oh, no!

W Don't worry. I was just joking. I've <u>got</u> <u>it</u> right here.

▶ **pack** (짐을) 꾸리다 **bathing suit** 수영복 **towel** 타월, 수건 **closet** 옷장 **under control** 통제되는, 지배되는 **passport** 여권

남 뭘 가져갈 거야?

여 음, 가볍게 꾸리려고 해. 반바지와 셔츠 몇 벌, 그리고 수영복 한 벌.

남 샴푸 가져갈 거지?

여 응, 그건 이미 챙겼어.

남 잘했어. 내 비치 타월은 어딨지?

여 옷장 안에 있어.

남 비행기표 가지고 있지?

여 응. 다 챙겼어.

남 우리 여권은?

여 내 것은 있는데. 네 것은 어디 있어?

남 네가 안 가지고 있어? 아, 이런!

여 걱정 마. 농담한 거야. 여기 이렇게 가지고 있어.

1 남자의 심정은 어떠한가?

  (a) 차분하다   (b) 화가 났다

  (c) 안도했다   (d) 부끄럽다

  (e) 무관심하다

M You're tired and <u>stressed</u> and need a vacation, right? <u>Keep</u> <u>in</u> <u>mind</u> that the type of vacation you choose is the most important decision. Sure, the <u>thought</u> <u>of</u> <u>relaxing</u> on a beach with a cold drink and a book is great for some, but others might find that boring. For some, <u>something</u> <u>thrilling</u>, like a trek in the jungle or bungee jumping, might be a better choice. You have to consider how you personally <u>deal</u> <u>with</u> stress so that you will feel relaxed when you return to the "real world."

▶ **keep in mind** 유의하다, 기억해두다 **thrilling** 스릴 만점의 **consider** 고려하다, 숙고하다 **personally** 개인적으로 **deal with** 다루다, 처리하다

남 피곤하고 스트레스를 받아 휴가가 필요하시죠? 어떤 형태의 휴가를 선택하느냐가 가장 중요한 결정이라는 걸 잊지 마세요. 물론 차가운 음료수 한 잔과 책 한 권 들고 해변에서 편안하게 보내겠다는 생각이 어떤 이들에게는 좋을 수도 있지만, 다른 사람에게는 지루할 수도 있습니다. 어떤 사람들에게는 정글 트레킹이나 번지 점프 같은 스릴 넘치는 것이 더 좋은 선택일 수도 있고요. '현실 세계'로 돌아왔을 때 푹 쉬었다고 느끼려면 여러분이 개인적으로 스트레스를 어떻게 처리하는지를 고려해야 합니다.

2 다음 중 사실인 것은?

  (a) 스릴 넘치는 휴가가 최고다.

  (b) 사람들은 각자 다른 종류의 휴가를 즐긴다.

  (c) 휴가가 스트레스를 유발한다.

  (d) 해변에서 푹 쉬는 것이 최고의 휴가다.

  (e) 현실 세계에서 푹 쉬는 것이 최고의 휴가다.

3~5

M Okay, everyone, if you <u>look</u> <u>out</u> on your right, you'll see the world-famous Niagara Falls. This is the Canadian Falls, <u>also</u> <u>known</u> as the Horseshoe Falls. In 2 minutes, we'll be <u>coming</u> <u>up</u> to the American Falls, which includes the Bridal Veil Falls. The first person to <u>go</u> <u>over</u> it was Annie Taylor <u>in</u> <u>1901</u>. She barely survived. Since her stunt, about 15 other people have tried the same thing, but <u>few</u> <u>have</u> survived.

▶ **fall** (보통 복수 취급) 폭포 **horseshoe** 편자 **go over** 건너다, 넘다 **barely** 간신히, 겨우 **survive** 살아남다 **stunt** 묘기, 곡예

남 자, 여러분. 오른쪽을 보시면 세계적으로 유명한 나이아가라 폭포가 보이실 겁니다. 이쪽은 캐나다 폭포고요, 호스슈 폭포라고도 알려져 있습니다. 2분 후에는 미국 폭포에 다다르게 되는데, 이 폭포에 브라이들베일 폭포가 포함되어 있지요. 여기를 최초로 건넌 사람은 애니 테일러로, 그 시기는 1901년이었죠. 그녀는 간신히 살았습니다. 그녀의 곡예 이후로 15명 정도가 같은 일에 도전했지만 살아남은 사람은 거의 없었답니다.

3 화자의 직업은 무엇인가?

  (a) 웨딩 플래너   (b) 식당 주인

  (c) 택시 운전사   (d) 여행 가이드

  (e) 스턴트맨

4 애니 테일러는 언제 폭포를 건넜는가?

  (a) 1920년   (b) 1902년

  (c) 1901년   (d) 19년 전

  (e) 1915년

5 내용을 가장 잘 요약한 것은 무엇인가?

  (a) 남자는 사람들에게 폭포를 건너도록 격려하고 있다.

  (b) 남자는 관광객들에게 나이아가라 폭포를 소개하고 있다.

PRACTICE TEST

들고 문제에 답하시오.

W Built from 1887 to 1889, this is one of the most famous sights in the world. It was designed by Gustave Eiffel for a World Fair and has received over 200 million visitors. It stands 325 meters tall and must be painted every seven years. It is the tallest building in Paris, but not in France. These days, there is a light show every night from its top, and there is an ice rink on the first floor.

▶ **sight** 관광지, 명소 **design** 디자인하다 **World Fair** 만국 박람회

여 1887년에서 1889년 사이에 세워진 이것은 세계에서 가장 유명한 관광 명소 가운데 하나입니다. 만국 박람회를 위해 귀스타브 에펠이 디자인했고, 지금까지 2억 명 이상의 관광객들을 맞이했습니다. 높이는 325미터에 이르고, 7년마다 새로 칠을 해줘야 합니다. 파리에서는 제일 높은 건축물이지만 프랑스에서 제일 높은 건물은 아닙니다. 요즘에는 꼭대기에서 밤마다 라이트 쇼가 펼쳐지고요, 제일 아래층에는 아이스링크가 있습니다.

1 어느 장소인가?

(a)  (b)  (c) 

(d)  (e) 

W On day one of our trip to Peru, after arriving in Lima, we will transfer immediately to the city of Cuzco. We will take a city tour after lunch. On day two, we will take a 6:00 a.m. train to Machu Picchu, an ancient city built by the Incas. We will provide an English-speaking guide for you. Lunch is included in your fee. On day three, we will visit the village of Pisac and see its famous market. On day four, we will return to Lima.

▶ **transfer** 이동하다 **immediately** 즉시, 곧 **ancient** 고대의 **provide** 제공하다
included 포함된 **fee** 요금

여 저희 페루 여행 첫째 날에는 리마에 도착한 후 곧바로 쿠스코 시로 이동할 것입니다. 점심 식사 후에 시내 관광을 할 예정이고요. 둘째 날에는, 잉카족이 건설한 고대 도시 마추픽추로 가는 오전 6시 기차를 탈 것입니다. 여러분의 편의를 위해 영어를 말하는 가이드를 붙여 드리겠습니다. 점심식사는 비용에 포함되어 있습니다. 셋째 날에는 피삭 마을에 들러 그곳의 유명한 시장을 둘러볼 것입니다. 넷째 날에는 리마로 돌아옵니다.

2 올바른 정보를 골라 체크하고 빈칸을 채우시오.

패키지 투어
첫째 날: (1) _________로 이동. 시내 관광. (쿠스코 / 리마)
둘째 날: (2) _________하는 가이드가 따라다니는 마추픽추 관광 (영어 / 스페인어)
셋째 날: 피삭 마을과 시장
넷째 날: 리마로 귀환

3-4

M Can I have your ticket and identification, please?

W Sure.

M How many bags do you have?

W Two.

M Okay, put them up here. Would you like a window or an aisle seat?

W Um, a window seat, please.

M Okay. Here is your boarding pass. Go to Gate 39 by 4:50 p.m. Your flight leaves at 6:00.

W Are there any delays today?

M No, not that I know of.

W Thank you.

▶ **identification** 신분증 **aisle** 복도 **boarding pass** 탑승권 **flight** 항공편
delay 연기

남 비행기표와 신분증을 보여주시겠습니까?
여 네.
남 가방은 몇 개나 있으세요?
여 두 개요.
남 알겠습니다. 여기다 올려놓으세요. 창가 쪽 좌석 드릴까요, 복도 쪽 좌석 드릴까요?
여 음, 창가 쪽으로 주세요.
남 네. 여기 탑승권입니다. 오후 4시 50분까지 39번 게이트로 가세요. 비행기는 6시에 출발합니다.
여 오늘 비행기가 연착된 게 있나요?
남 아뇨, 제가 아는 한 없습니다.
여 감사합니다.

3 화자들은 어디에 있는가?
(a) 기차역에
(b) 기내에
(c) 공항에
(d) 버스터미널에
(e) 식당에

4 여자는 남자에게 무엇을 제시해야 하는가?
(a) 비행기표와 신분증
(b) 탑승권
(c) 가방
(d) 돈
(e) 좌석번호

W Budgeting your money is an important part of every vacation. While we'd all like to stay at luxury hotels, eat at the best restaurants, and buy expensive souvenirs, for most of us, that's impossible. The easiest way to take the stress out of traveling is to budget your money. Figure out how much money you have, and divide it by the number of days you'll be traveling. That will give you a rough idea of how much money you can spend per day.

▶ budget 예산을 세우다 luxury 고급의 souvenir 기념품 figure out 계산하다 divide 나누다 rough 대강의, 대충의

여 예산을 세우는 것은 모든 휴가에서 중요한 부분입니다. 우리 모두 고급 호텔에서 묵고, 최고급 식당에서 먹고, 값비싼 기념품을 구입하고 싶어하지만 대부분의 사람들에게는 불가능한 일입니다. 여행 중 발생하는 스트레스에서 벗어나는 가장 쉬운 방법은 예산을 짜는 것입니다. 지금 돈이 얼마나 있는지 계산한 다음 여행할 날짜 수로 나누세요. 그럼 하루에 돈을 얼마나 써야 할지 대충 감이 올 겁니다.

5 유럽으로 5일 동안 여행갈 예정이고 현재 550달러가 있다. 가장 적당한 하루 예산은 무엇인가?

(a) 15달러

(b) 110 달러

(c) 50 달러

(d) 55 달러

(e) 150 달러

6

M Language is always something to consider when traveling. If the place you're traveling to does not have English as an official language, consider learning some basic phrases before you go. Phrases like "Please" and "Thank you" make you appear more polite to local people. Phrases like "Where's the bathroom?" can help you out in a tough situation. If you don't have time to study the language, bring a phrasebook with you just in case.

▶ consider 고려하다, 숙고하다 official language 공용어 phrase 표현, 말 polite 공손한, 예의 바른 tough 곤란한, 힘든 situation 상황 just in case 만약을 위해서 phrasebook 관용구집, 기본 회화 표현집

남 여행할 때 언어는 늘 고려해야 할 대상입니다. 여러분이 여행하려는 곳이 영어를 공용어로 쓰지 않는다면 가기 전에 기본 표현 정도는 배우는 쪽으로 생각해보세요. "부탁 드립니다", "고맙습니다" 같은 표현을 하면 현지인들에게 더 예의 바르게 보일 것입니다. "화장실은 어디 있어요?" 같은 표현은 곤란한 상황에서 도움이 될 것입니다. 그 나라 언어를 배울 시간이 없다면 만약을 대비해 기본 표현집을 들고 가세요.

6 무엇에 관한 내용인가?

(a) 새로운 언어 배우기

(b) 예의 바르게 행동하기

(c) 좋은 기본 표현집 찾기

(d) 여행에 필요한 표현들 배우기

(e) 여행할 때 처하게 되는 곤란한 상황들

7~8

M How's your trip planning going, Dawn?

W Oh, okay I guess, Sid.

M What do you mean?

W Well, I haven't found a good travel partner yet.

M Really? What about Whitney?

W She's busy then.

M Paula?

W She never wants to try new foods.

M Jessica?

W She doesn't want to go to the same places that I do.

M Did you try looking online? There are some sites that will match you with travel partners.

W Go with a stranger?

M Well, it's better than not going at all!

▶ match 맞추다, 짝지우다 stranger 모르는 사람, 낯선 사람

남 던, 여행 계획은 잘 돼가?

여 어, 뭐 잘 되어가겠지, 시드.

남 무슨 말이야?

여 그게, 아직까지 괜찮은 여행 파트너를 못 찾았어.

남 정말? 휘트니는 어때?

여 그땐 걔가 바쁘대.

남 폴라는?

여 걔는 절대 새로운 음식을 먹어보려 하지 않아.

남 제시카는?

여 내가 가려는 곳을 가고 싶어하지 않아.

남 온라인에서 찾아봤니? 여행 파트너를 이어주는 사이트가 몇 개 있어.

여 모르는 사람과 가라고?

남 뭐, 아예 안 가는 것보다는 낫잖아!

7 여자의 문제는 무엇인가?

(a) 돈이 충분하지 않다.

(b) 인터넷에서 여행 사이트를 찾을 수가 없다.

(c) 어디로 가야 할지 모른다.

(d) 새로운 음식을 먹는 걸 좋아하지 않는다.

(e) 여행 파트너를 찾을 수가 없다.

8 남자의 마지막 충고와 가장 잘 맞는 표현은 무엇인가?

(a) 찬 밥 더운 밥 가릴 때가 아니야.

(b) 헛다리를 짚었네.

(c) 떡 줄 사람 생각도 안 하는데 김칫국부터 마시지 마.

(d) 전화위복이지.

(e) 천리 길도 한 걸음부터야.

Dogs Are My Favorite Animals

Answers

GET READY p. 128~129

Key Words & Expressions

1 smart	2 reduce	3 loyal
4 Vets	5 pet	6 breeds
7 personalities	8 goof	9 lizard
10 take care of		

Questions & Responses

1 c 2 d 3 e 4 f 5 a 6 b

BASIC DRILL p. 130~131

Step 1
- dogs, cats, fish, hamsters, turtles / to be a veterinarian

  Q (c)

- animals, hamsters, turtles, taking care, loyal, affectionate, veterinarian

Step 2 **A** wolves / gentle

B scary, beautiful / magnificent

C snakes

D monkeys

1 (b) 2 (1) T (2) F (3) T

Plus⁺ Question 1 (c) 2 (a)

EXERCISE p. 132~133

Step 1 1 (a), (c) 2 (d) 3 (a) 4 (d)

Step 2 1 (d) 2 (1) T (2) F (3) T (4) F (5) T

3 (c) 4 (e) 5 (a)

PRACTICE TEST p. 136~137

1 (a)

2

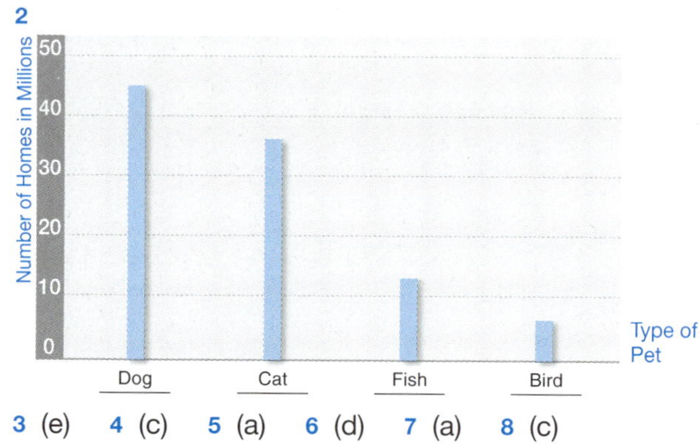

3 (e) 4 (c) 5 (a) 6 (d) 7 (a) 8 (c)

* Dictation 1, 2의 정답은 각 Script의 밑줄친 부분임.

Scripts and Translations

GET READY

Key Words & Expressions

다음 문장을 듣고 보기 박스에서 알맞은 단어를 골라 빈칸을 채우시오.

1 고양이는 똑똑하고 우아해서 내가 제일 좋아하는 동물이에요.

2 애완동물이 있으면 스트레스와 질병이 줄어들 수 있대요.

3 대부분의 개 애호가들은 개들이 충성심이 강하고 믿을 수 있기 때문에 개를 더 좋아하지요.

4 수의사는 여러 종류의 동물들에 대해서 배워야 합니다.

5 고양이 애호가와 개 애호가는 어느 쪽이 더 좋은 애완동물인가에 대해서 의견 일치를 절대로 못 볼 것 같아요.

6 어떤 개나 고양이의 품종은 가격이 수 천 달러가 되기도 합니다.

7 난 정말 동물을 좋아해요. 너무 귀엽고, 사람들처럼 모두 자기만의 개성이 있거든요.

8 아이들 대부분이 동물원에 가서 원숭이들이 빈둥거리며 노는 걸 보기 좋아하지요.

9 난 사람들이 이구아나 같은 도마뱀을 어떻게 키울 수 있는지 모르겠어요. 소름이 쫙 끼치는데!

10 아이는 애완동물을 보살필 정도로 책임감이 충분할 때에만 애완동물을 키워야 합니다.

Questions & Responses

질문에 어울리는 대답과 연결하시오.

1 동물 좋아해?

2 제일 좋아하는 동물은 뭐야?

3 애완동물을 많이 키워봤니?

4 애완동물에 알레르기 있어?

5 애완동물 키우는 데 가장 힘든 점이 뭐야?

6 아이들에게 애완동물이 있어야 할까?

ⓒ 응. 고양이를 특히 좋아하지.

ⓓ 물고기. 개네들을 보고 있으면 정말로 마음이 편안해지는 것 같아.

ⓔ 자라면서 개 한 마리만 키워봤어.

ⓕ 아니, 다행히도 아무 알레르기도 없어.

ⓖ 쫓아다니면서 치워줘야 하는 게 제일 힘든 점이야.

ⓑ 책임질 수만 있다면, 그렇지.

들고 정답을 확인하시오.

친구와 함께 연습하시오.

Basic Drill Step 1

다음을 듣고 메모하시오.

M A lot of kids love animals, but I really love animals. In my life, I've had two dogs, three cats, six fish, two hamsters, and two turtles. I love taking care of them and getting to know their different personalities. Dogs are my favorite animals because they're so loyal and affectionate. I'm going to be a veterinarian when I grow up, so I can work with animals all the time. That's my dream.

▶ take care of ~을 돌보다 personality 성격, 성질, 개성 loyal 충성스러운 affectionate 애정이 깊은, 상냥한 veterinarian 수의사

남 많은 아이들이 동물을 좋아하지만 난 정말로 동물을 사랑해. 살면서 개 두 마리, 고양이 세 마리, 물고기 여섯 마리, 햄스터 두 마리랑 거북이 두 마리를 키웠어. 걔네들을 돌보면서 서로 다른 성격들을 알게 되는 게 참 좋아. 개는 굉장히 충성심이 강하고 애정이 많아서 내가 가장 좋아하는 동물이야. 난 커서 수의사가 될 거야. 그럼 늘 동물과 함께 일할 수 있으니까. 그게 내 꿈이야.

메모를 바탕으로 다음 문제에 답하시오.

Q 화자가 수의사가 되려는 주요 원인은 무엇인가?
   (a) 돈을 많이 벌고 싶기 때문에
   (b) 그의 애완동물을 보살피고 싶기 때문에
   (c) 동물들과 함께 일하고 싶기 때문에
   (d) 동물들의 성격을 이해하고 싶기 때문에

■ 다시 듣고 빈칸을 채우시오.

Basic Drill Step 2

다음을 듣고 메모하시오.

M1 I'm Isaac, and my favorite animal is the wolf. I think wolves are mysterious and beautiful animals. Many people are afraid of wolves, but they are really gentle creatures.

W1 I'm Maria, and I love lions. Lions are cool because they can be both scary and beautiful. Male lions look so proud. I think they're magnificent. And there's nothing cuter than a little lion cub!

W2 My name's Hannah, and snakes are definitely the coolest animals on Earth. The patterns on their bodies are so pretty. I love the sound rattlesnakes make. I wouldn't want to hear it while I'm out walking though!

M2 I'm Eric, and I love monkeys. At the zoo, I go straight to the monkey cages, so I can watch them play and goof off. They're so funny and cute! My dream is to have my own pet monkey.

▶ mysterious 신비한 gentle (동물이) 온순한; 상냥한, 부드러운 male 수컷의, 남자의 magnificent 숭고한, 웅장한, 장엄한 cub 동물의 새끼 pattern 무늬 rattlesnake 방울뱀 cage 우리, 새장 goof off 게으름 피우다

남1 난 아이작이야. 내가 제일 좋아하는 동물은 늑대지. 늑대는 참 신비롭고 아름다운 동물인 것 같아. 많은 사람들이 늑대를 무서워하지만 사실은 참 온순한 동물이지.

여1 난 마리아야. 사자를 참 좋아해. 사자는 무서우면서도 아름다워서 참 멋있어. 수사자는 정말 당당해 보여. 위엄 있어 보이기도 하고. 그리고 새끼 사자보

다 더 귀여운 것은 없어!

여2 내 이름은 한나야. 확실히 지상에서 뱀이 가장 멋진 동물이지. 몸에 있는 무늬가 정말 예쁘잖아. 난 방울뱀이 내는 소리가 참 좋아. 물론 밖에서 산책할 때 그 소리를 듣고 싶지는 않지만 말이야!

남2 난 에릭이고, 원숭이를 좋아해. 동물원에 가면 난 곧장 원숭이 우리로 가. 원숭이들이 놀고 빈둥거리는 모습을 볼 수 있게 말이야. 걔네들은 참 웃기면서도 귀여워! 내 꿈은 애완용 원숭이를 갖는 거야.

메모를 바탕으로 다음 문제에 답하시오.

1 화자들은 주로 무엇에 관해 이야기하고 있는가?
   (a) 동물원에 있는 동물들   (b) 자기들이 가장 좋아하는 동물
   (c) 아름다운 동물들   (d) 자기들이 꿈꾸는 애완동물

2 맞으면 T, 틀리면 F를 쓰시오.
   (1) 아이작은 늑대가 온순하다고 생각한다.
   (2) 마리아는 수사자가 귀엽다고 생각한다.
   (3) 에릭은 동물원에 있는 원숭이를 좋아한다.

다시 듣고 정답을 확인하시오.

Plus⁺ Question

1 한나는 뱀의 어떤 점이 마음에 드는가?
   (a) 새끼
   (b) 충성심
   (c) 몸에 있는 무늬
   (d) 신비함

2 에릭의 꿈은 무엇인가?
   (a) 애완용 원숭이를 갖는 것
   (b) 동물원 사육사가 되는 것
   (c) 동물원에 가는 것
   (d) 원숭이들과 일하는 것

EXERCISE Step 1

듣고 문제에 답하시오.

1 

M So, Jane, do you have any pets?

W Yeah, I have two iguanas. They're great.

M Iguanas? That's creepy!

W Why? They're harmless but beautiful to watch.

M What do you feed them?

W Just small insects and sometimes some fruits and vegetables.

M No mice?

W No, you're thinking of snakes.

M Are they affectionate?

W Well, in their own way, I guess. They're good around me, but they snap at my brother.

▶ pet 애완동물 creepy 소름 끼치는 harmless 해롭지 않은 feed 먹이를 주다, 먹이다 insect 곤충, 벌레 snap 덥석 물다, 콱 물다

남 그래, 제인. 너 애완동물 있니?
여 응. 이구아나 두 마리 있어. 진짜 멋져.
남 이구아나? 소름 끼친다!
여 왜? 해롭지도 않고 보기에도 예쁜데.

57

남 걔네들한테 뭐 먹여?
여 조그만 곤충들이랑 가끔씩 과일이랑 채소도 먹여.
남 쥐는 안 먹여?
여 아니, 네가 생각하는 건 뱀이야.
남 애교 있게 굴어?
여 음, 자기네 방식으로는 그런 것 같아. 내 주위에 있을 때는 괜찮은데, 내 동생은 콱 물거든.

1 이구아나는 무엇을 먹는가? 그림 두 개를 고르시오.

(a) 　(b) 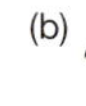　(c) 　(d) 

②

W Hey, Dad. Do you think I can get a dog?

M Well, Louise, I don't know about that. Taking <u>care</u> <u>of</u> a pet is a lot of work!

W Yeah, I know, but I can <u>handle</u> it.

M Do you think so?

W Yeah, I'll <u>feed</u> it every day.

M There's more to do than just feeding it. It'll need to be walked every day, and you'll have to <u>bathe</u> it and train it.

W Yes, I know, Dad. I think I can do it.

M All right. I guess you're <u>old</u> <u>enough</u>. Let's talk more about it later.

W Okay.

▶ handle 다루다　bathe 목욕시키다　train 훈련하다

여 아빠, 저 개 한 마리 길러도 돼요?
남 글쎄, 루이즈. 그건 잘 모르겠다. 동물을 보살피는 건 손이 많이 가는 일이거든!
여 예, 알아요. 하지만 제가 다 할 수 있어요.
남 그렇게 생각하니?
여 예. 제가 매일 먹이 줄게요.
남 단순히 먹이만 주는 것 말고도 할 일이 더 많아. 매일 산책도 시켜줘야 하고 목욕도 시키고 훈련도 시켜야 돼.
여 예, 알아요, 아빠. 저 할 수 있을 것 같아요.
남 좋아. 그만큼 큰 것 같기도 하구나. 나중에 좀 더 얘기해보자.
여 좋아요.

2 다음 중 사실이 <u>아닌</u> 것은?

(a) 루이즈는 개를 목욕시키고 훈련시켜야 할 것이다.
(b) 루이즈는 자기가 개를 돌볼 수 있을 거라고 생각한다.
(c) 개를 돌보는 것은 힘들다.
(d) 루이즈의 아빠는 루이즈가 개를 키우기에는 너무 어리다고 생각한다.

3-4

M What do you <u>like</u> <u>better</u> Darla, cats or dogs?

W Dogs, definitely. They're loyal, <u>affectionate</u>, dependable, cute, active…

M Dog lovers always say the same things.

W Oh really, Rudy? Well, I can tell you don't <u>feel</u> <u>the</u> <u>same</u> <u>way</u>, so why are cats so special?

M It's simple. They're smarter.

W Whatever!

M They are! They're smarter, more <u>sophisticated</u>, and so much cuter.

W Let's end <u>this</u> <u>conversation</u>. I don't think the <u>dogs</u> <u>versus</u> <u>cats</u> <u>issue</u> <u>will</u> <u>ever</u> <u>be</u> <u>resolved</u>.

▶ dependable 의존할 수 있는, 신뢰할 수 있는　active 활동적인　sophisticated 세련된, 약아빠진; 정교한　versus ~대(vs.)　resolve 해결하다

남 달라, 고양이랑 개 중에서 어느 쪽이 더 좋아?
여 당연히 개지. 충성심 강하고 애정 있게 굴고, 믿을 수 있고, 귀엽고, 활동적이고….
남 개 좋아하는 사람들은 늘 똑같이 말하더라.
여 어, 정말이야, 루디? 글쎄, 너는 그렇게 안 느끼는 것 같네. 그럼 고양이는 어디가 그렇게 특별한 건데?
남 간단해. 더 똑똑하잖아.
여 무슨!
남 정말 그렇다니까! 고양이들이 더 똑똑하고, 더 세련되고, 훨씬 더 귀여워.
여 이제 그만 얘기하자. 내 생각에는 개가 좋으냐, 고양이가 좋으냐 하는 문제는 영원히 해결이 안 날 것 같아.

3 대화에 따르면 왜 루디는 고양이를 좋아하는가?

(a) 똑똑하다.　　　　　(b) 활동적이다.
(c) 깨끗하다.　　　　　(d) 조용하다.

4 달라는 왜 대화를 끝내고 싶어하는가?

(a) 이제 그만 가야 한다.
(b) 고양이를 싫어한다.
(c) 루디 때문에 화가 난다.
(d) 절대 의견 일치가 안 될 것이다.

Exercise　Step 2

듣고 문제에 답하시오.

①

M Come on! Come on! Look at the monkeys!

W I'm coming. I'm coming.

M Oh, wow. They're adorable!

W Yeah, the baby is really cute!

M Oh, look at that one! He's <u>sticking</u> <u>out</u> his tongue at us!

W Oh, my gosh. He is!

M Maybe he wants some food. Do you have anything?

W Yeah, here. <u>Throw</u> <u>this</u> <u>to</u> <u>him</u>.

▶ adorable 귀여운　stick out one's tongue 혀를 내밀다　throw 던지다

남 빨리, 빨리! 저 원숭이들 좀 봐!
여 가고 있어. 가고 있다고.
남 와, 쟤네들 진짜 귀엽다!
여 그러게. 새끼 원숭이가 진짜 귀엽네!
남 어, 저기 쟤 좀 봐! 우리한테 혀를 내밀고 있어!
여 어허, 진짜 그렇네!
남 음식을 먹고 싶은가 봐. 너 뭐 좀 가지고 있어?
여 응, 여기. 이거 쟤한테 던져줘.

1 원숭이는 무엇을 하고 있는가?

(a) 　(b) 　(c) 

(d) 　(e) 

2

W　Are you thinking of getting a dog or a cat? You probably haven't thought of the cost of getting one in the first place. Depending on the pet you want, it could cost you thousands of dollars. Dog and cat breeders sell top-quality animals, and they aren't cheap. For example, the popular breed called the Labradoodle, a mix between a Labrador retriever and a poodle, sells for about $2,500. Before going to the pet store, do some research, or, better yet, go to the animal shelter and adopt a homeless pet for free.

▶ cost 비용; 비용이 들다　in the first place 애당초, 처음부터; 첫째로　depend on ~에 달렸다　breeder 사육자　breed (동물의) 품종　research 조사　animal shelter 동물 보호소　adopt 입양하다

여　개나 고양이를 키워볼까 생각 중이십니까? 처음에는 구입 비용을 생각하지 않으셨을지도 모릅니다. 원하는 애완동물에 따라서 수 천 달러가 들 수도 있습니다. 개와 고양이 사육업자들은 최고 등급의 동물을 판매하기 때문에 저렴하지 않습니다. 예를 들어, 인기 종인 래브라두들은 래브라도 리트리버와 푸들의 교배종인데 약 2,500달러에 판매됩니다. 애완동물 가게에 가기 전에 조사를 해보세요. 아니면 더 좋은 방법으로, 동물 보호소에 가서서 집 없는 애완동물을 무료로 입양하세요.

2 맞으면 T, 틀리면 F에 체크하시오.

(1) 어떤 애완동물은 가격이 수 천 달러에 이른다.
(2) 래브라두들의 가격은 대개 약 1,500달러 정도 된다.
(3) 집 없는 애완동물을 무료로 입양할 수 있다.
(4) 래브라두들은 래브라도 리트리버의 다른 이름이다.
(5) 개와 고양이 사육업자들은 자기들이 기운 동물을 판매한다.

3-5

M　This is just in! Two tigers have escaped from their enclosure at the San Diego Zoo and are terrorizing the city. So far, they only injured two people as they escaped from the zoo, but the police are worried they could do more damage. Police tried to fire shots at the tigers, but there were too many people in the area. The tigers were last seen heading into a forest behind the zoo's parking lots. Police and animal experts are doing their best to capture the animals.

▶ escape 탈출하다　enclosure 울타리　terrorize 무서워하게 하다　fire 발사하다　shot 탄환; 발포, 발사　expert 전문가　capture 포획하다, 생포하다

남　방금 들어온 소식입니다! 호랑이 두 마리가 샌디에이고 동물원 울타리 밖으로 탈출하여 도시를 공포로 몰아넣고 있습니다. 호랑이들은 동물원을 탈출

하면서 지금까지 두 명에게 부상을 입혔지만 경찰은 더 많은 피해가 발생할까 봐 염려하고 있습니다. 경찰은 호랑이에게 총을 발사하려 했지만 그 지역에 사람들이 너무 많았습니다. 호랑이들이 동물원 주차장 뒤쪽의 숲으로 향하는 것이 마지막으로 목격되었습니다. 경찰과 동물 전문가들은 호랑이들을 생포하기 위해 최선을 다하고 있습니다.

3 어떤 종류의 담화인가?

(a) 영화 광고　　　　(b) 강의　　　　(c) 뉴스 보도
(d) 동물원 광고　　　(e) 연설

4 왜 경찰은 호랑이들에게 총을 발사할 수 없었는가?

(a) 일부 동물 전문가들이 경찰을 막았다.
(b) 호랑이들이 경찰관을 공격했다.
(c) 호랑이들이 숲에 있었다.
(d) 호랑이들이 너무 빨랐다.
(e) 주변에 사람들이 너무 많았다.

5 내용을 가장 잘 요약한 것은 무엇인가?

(a) 호랑이 두 마리가 샌디에이고 동물원을 탈출해서 동물원 근처 숲으로 들어갔다.
(b) 호랑이 두 마리가 샌디에이고 동물원을 탈출해서 사람들을 공격하며 죽이고 있다.

PRACTICE TEST

들고 문제에 답하시오.

1 

W　What do you want to be when you grow up, Mitch?

M　I really want to be a vet.

W　Oh, yeah? That sounds like a lot of work though.

M　Yeah, I'll have to study for years.

W　I think being a vet would be more difficult than being a doctor. There are so many types of animals to learn about!

M　That's a good point, Alice. It won't be easy, but I just love animals. I'll do whatever it takes.

▶ grow up 성장하다　vet(= veterinarian) 수의사

여　미치, 넌 커서 뭐가 되고 싶어?
남　난 정말로 수의사가 되고 싶어.
여　어, 그래? 그렇지만 공부를 많이 해야 할 것 같은데.
남　응. 여러 해 동안 공부해야 돼.
여　내 생각에는 의사가 되는 것보다 수의사가 되는 게 훨씬 어려울 것 같아. 공부해야 할 동물의 종류가 무척 많잖아!
남　좋은 지적이야, 앨리스. 쉽지는 않겠지. 하지만 난 동물을 사랑해. 무슨 일이 있어도 하고 말겠어.

1 수의사의 일은 의사의 일에 비해 어떻게 다른가?

(a) 수의사는 여러 종류의 동물들에 대해 배워야 한다.
(b) 수의사는 몇 년 간 공부해야 한다.
(c) 수의사는 일을 많이 해야 한다.
(d) 수의사가 의사보다 돈을 더 많이 번다.
(e) 수의사는 병원에서 근무하지 않는다.

W Everyone knows that Americans love their pets. And it seems that every year, they love them more and more as the number of pet owners is on the rise. But what are the most popular pets? Well, you should be able to guess. Here they are: 45 million homes have a dog. 38 million homes have a cat. 14 million have a fish, and 6.5 million have a bird. It seems that dog is still man's best friend, but cats are close behind!

▶ owner 소유자   on the rise 올라, 오름세에   close 가까운, 바짝 다가서

여 미국인들이 애완동물을 좋아한다는 것은 모두가 아는 일입니다. 애완동물 주인의 숫자가 올라가고 있는 것을 보니 해마다 동물을 더욱더 좋아하는 것 같네요. 하지만 가장 인기 있는 애완동물은 뭘까요? 글쎄요, 여러분들도 아마 추측하실 수 있을 겁니다. 여기 자료가 있네요. 4,500만 가정에서 개를 키웁니다. 3,800만 가정에서 고양이를 키우고요. 1,400만 가정에서는 물고기를, 650만 가정에서는 새를 키웁니다. 개가 여전히 인간의 가장 친한 동물인 것 같네요. 하지만 고양이들이 그 뒤를 바짝 쫓고 있습니다!

Level up

2 동물을 써서 그래프를 완성하시오.

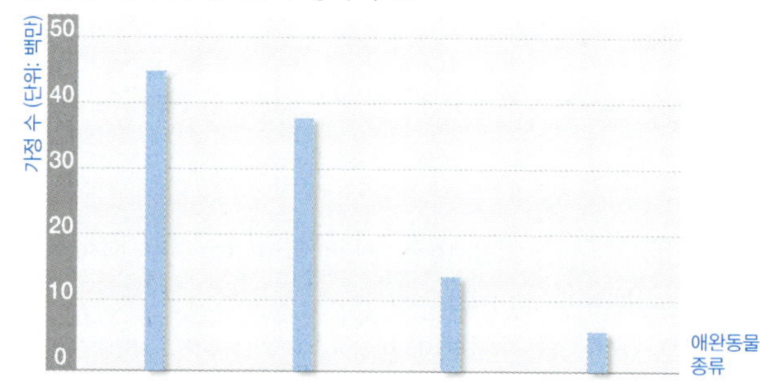

M Hey, Yolanda. Do you want to shoot some baskets tomorrow?

W Sorry, Rick, but I can't. I'm busy.

M How about just lunch then?

W Sorry, I have an RSA meeting tomorrow.

M RSA? What's that?

W The Rat Society of America.

M You like rats?

W Yes. In fact, I have three.

M That's just weird. So, what do you do at your rat meetings?

W We just talk about ways to make the world love and accept rats. Do you want to come? You can meet my rats.

M I think I'll pass.

▶ shoot 공을 던지다   rat 쥐   society 모임, 회; 사회   weird 이상한   accept 받아들이다   pass (카드 놀이에서) 패스하다, 기권하여 다음 사람에게 넘기다

남 이봐, 욜란다. 내일 농구 게임 하러 갈래?
여 미안해, 릭. 나 못 가. 바쁘거든.
남 그럼 점심이나 먹는 건 어때?

여 미안해. 내일 나 RSA 모임이 있어.
남 RSA? 그게 뭔데?
여 미국 생쥐 협회야.
남 너 생쥐 좋아해?
여 응. 사실 나 세 마리 키워.
남 그거 특이하다. 그래, 생쥐 모임에선 뭘 하니?
여 그냥 세상 사람들이 생쥐를 사랑하고 받아들일 수 있게 하는 방법에 대해 이야기하지. 너도 갈래? 가면 내 생쥐들을 볼 수 있어.
남 난 빠질래.

3 릭은 내일 무엇을 하고 싶어하는가?
(a) 저녁 식사
(b) 욜란다의 생쥐 보기
(c) RSA 모임에 가기
(d) 바구니 만들기
(e) 농구하기

4 RSA의 슬로건은 무엇일 것 같은가?
(a) 생쥐는 세상에서 가장 무서운 애완동물입니다.
(b) 생쥐는 소름 끼치지만, 좋은 애완동물입니다.
(c) 단번에 생쥐의 이미지 개선시키기
(d) 생쥐들이 세상을 접수하게 도와줍시다!
(e) 생쥐―수 세기 동안 인간이 가장 좋아한 애완동물

W Did you know that owning a pet can actually be good for you? Recently, there has been a lot of research into the benefits of owning pets, and the results are surprising. People who own pets go to the doctor less often. Sick people who own pets live longer. Researchers say that part of the reason is that pets are always affectionate and loyal and do not judge us. If you were considering getting a pet, it's probably a good idea.

▶ actually 실제로   benefit 이익, 이점   research 연구   judge 판단하다

여 애완동물이 있으면 실제로 유익할 수 있다는 사실을 알고 계셨습니까? 최근에 애완동물을 키우는 이점에 대해서 많은 연구가 행해졌는데요, 결과가 아주 놀랍습니다. 애완동물이 있는 사람들은 의사를 덜 찾아갑니다. 애완동물이 있는 환자들은 더 오래 삽니다. 연구자들은 이러한 원인의 일부를 애완동물이 언제나 애정 표현을 하고 충성심이 강하며 사람을 판단하지 않기 때문이라고 말합니다. 애완동물을 키워볼까 생각 중이시라면 좋은 생각인 것 같습니다.

5 무엇에 관한 내용인가?
(a) 애완동물을 키우는 것의 장점
(b) 애완동물이 필요한 사람들
(c) 애완동물을 키우는 것의 단점
(d) 쉽게 병에 걸리는 사람들의 유형
(e) 애완동물의 다양한 특징들

M Today on *Strange News*, we bring you the story of a man who was killed by his own pet. This wasn't any average pet; it was a 4-meter-long boa constrictor. Neighbors say that the man, Mr. Cruz, had raised the snake since it was a baby. He would <u>take it out</u> to play from time to time, but he always seemed to have <u>control of it</u>. No one was present <u>during the attack</u>, so it is unknown what <u>went wrong</u>. "It's sad," said a neighbor. "He loved that snake."

▶ **average** 보통의　**boa constrictor** 왕뱀, 보아구렁이　**raise** 기르다　**have control of** ~을 관리[제어]하고 있다　**present** 참석한, 있는　**attack** 공격　**unknown** 알려지지 않은　**go wrong** 잘못되다

남　오늘 〈기묘한 뉴스〉에서는 자신이 키우던 애완동물에게 살해당한 남자 이야기를 전해드립니다. 이 동물은 평범한 애완동물이 아니었습니다. 길이가 4미터나 되는 보아뱀이었죠. 이웃사람들은 주인인 크루즈 씨가 이 뱀을 새끼였을 때부터 길렀다고 말합니다. 때때로 뱀을 바깥으로 데리고 나와 놀기도 했지만 크루즈 씨는 늘 뱀을 잘 다루는 것 같았다고 합니다. 뱀이 크루즈 씨를 공격했을 때 현장에는 아무도 없었기 때문에 무엇이 잘못 됐는지는 알려지지 않았습니다. 한 이웃이 이렇게 말했습니다. "슬픈 일이에요. 그 사람은 그 뱀을 정말 사랑했거든요."

6　이 뉴스 보도의 제목은 무엇이겠는가?

(a) 죽은 남자를 발견한 이웃

(b) 애완뱀을 사랑한 남자

(c) 죽은 뱀을 발견한 남자

(d) 애완뱀에게 살해된 남자

(e) 길이가 4미터에 달하는 뱀

7~8

M　<u>Did you hear</u> the news from Russia, Jeannie?

W　No, Will. What news?

M　They found a <u>baby mammoth frozen</u> in the ice.

W　Really? How old is it?

M　They think it's 37,000 years old.

W　Wow, that's <u>incredible</u>! What are they doing with it?

M　I think scientists are <u>keeping it really cold</u> so it doesn't go bad. And they're studying it of course. Wouldn't it be awesome if they could <u>clone</u> a mammoth?

W　For sure. That's so interesting, especially since elephants are my favorite animals. Mammoths must have been so cool.

▶ **frozen** 언　**incredible** 놀라운, 믿어지지 않는　**go bad** 썩다　**clone** 복제하다

남　지니, 러시아에서 들어온 뉴스 들었어?

여　아니, 윌. 무슨 뉴스인데?

남　얼음 속에 얼어 있던 새끼 맘모스를 찾아냈대.

여　정말? 얼마나 된 거야?

남　37,000년 정도 됐다고 생각하나 봐.

여　와, 진짜 놀랍다! 그걸로 뭘 하고 있대?

남　상하지 않게 과학자들이 그걸 아주 차갑게 보관하고 있는 것 같아. 물론 그것에 대해 연구도 하고 있겠지. 맘모스를 복제해낼 수 있다면 정말 대단하지 않겠어?

여　그렇고말고. 내가 특히 코끼리를 제일 좋아하다 보니 진짜 흥미진진하다. 맘모스는 틀림없이 정말 멋졌을 거야.

7　다음 중 사실이 아닌 것은?

(a) 맘모스는 아이슬란드에서 발견되었다.

(b) 맘모스는 37,000년 된 것이다.

(c) 과학자들은 맘모스를 차갑게 보관하고 있다.

(d) 화자들은 맘모스를 복제하면 멋질 거라고 생각한다.

(e) 여자가 제일 좋아하는 동물은 코끼리다.

8　왜 지니는 그 뉴스가 흥미롭다고 생각하는가?

(a) 역사를 좋아하기 때문에

(b) 맘모스를 연구하기 때문에

(c) 동물을 좋아하기 때문에

(d) 믿을 수 없을 정도로 놀라운 일이기 때문에

(e) 맘모스가 복제될 것이기 때문에

Answers

GET READY   p. 140~141

Key Words & Expressions

1 position   2 try out   3 soccer
4 athletes   5 match   6 competitive
7 were held   8 batting   9 goalie
10 championship

Questions & Responses

1 b   2 f   3 e   4 c   5 a   6 d

BASIC DRILL   p. 142~143

Step 1 • baseball / it takes some thought and strategy

  Q (a)

  ■ involved in, baseball, soccer, team, physical, strategy, position

Step 2 A favorite, goalie   B strength, balance
   C forward   D last summer

1 (b)   2 (1) F (2) T (3) F

Plus⁺ Question   1 (d)   2 (b)

EXERCISE   p. 144~145

Step 1 1 (c)   2 (1) T (2) F (3) T (4) T   3 (b)   4 (d)

Step 2 1 (a)   2 (d)   3 (d)   4 (a)   5 (a)

PRACTICE TEST   p. 148~149

1 (b)

2

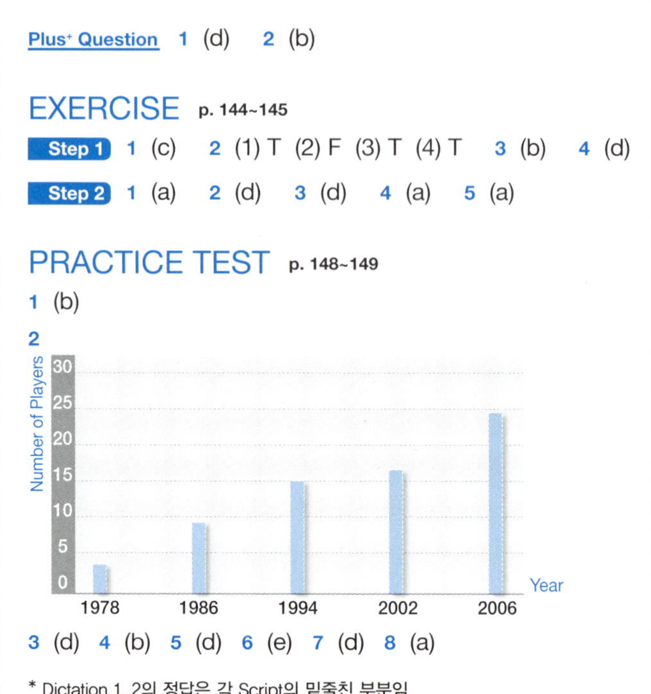

3 (d)   4 (b)   5 (d)   6 (e)   7 (d)   8 (a)

* Dictation 1, 2의 정답은 각 Script의 밑줄친 부분임.

Scripts and Translations

GET READY

Key Words & Expressions

다음 문장을 듣고 보기 박스에서 알맞은 단어를 골라 빈칸을 채우시오.

1 축구할 때 내 포지션은 수비야.
2 학교 스포츠팀에 들어가기 위한 시험 치는 걸 두려워하지 마.
3 영국의 풋볼은 미국의 사커와 같은 거야.
4 때때로 운동선수들은 스트레스를 받으면 나쁘게 반응을 해. 지난 월드컵 대회에서 28명의 선수가 레드 카드를 받았잖아.
5 어제 월드컵 경기에서 브라질이 코스타리카를 5:2로 이겼어.
6 많이 먹기 대회 챔피언들은 대개 몸집이 작은 사람들이야.
7 올림픽 경기는 고대 그리스에서 4년마다 열렸어.
8 야구에서 배트를 휘두를 때 가장 중요한 것은 공에서 눈을 떼지 않는 거야.
9 난 겨울에 아이스 하키를 해. 골키퍼를 맡고 있지.
10 야구 챔피언 결정전을 월드 시리즈라고 해.

Questions & Responses

질문에 어울리는 대답과 연결하시오.

1 팀 스포츠를 즐겨, 개인 스포츠를 즐겨?   ⓑ 난 팀 스포츠를 더 좋아해.

2 가장 좋아하는 스포츠는 뭐야?   ⓕ 미식축구가 제일 좋아하는 스포츠야.

3 여러 가지 스포츠를 해봤니?   ⓔ 응, 여러 운동 팀에 있었어.

4 스포츠 뉴스를 보니?   ⓒ 그럼, 매일 스포츠면을 읽는 걸.

5 제일 좋아하는 운동선수는 누구야?   ⓐ 배리 본즈가 최고야.

6 텔레비전에서 스포츠 중계 보니?   ⓓ 가끔 보는데, 골프는 안 봐. 너무 지루해서 볼 수가 없어.

듣고 정답을 확인하시오.

친구와 함께 연습하시오.

Basic Drill   **Step 1**

다음을 듣고 메모하시오.

M I think I've always liked sports because, as a kid, I was always involved in them. I played everything from baseball to tennis to soccer. Some I was better at than others, but I always enjoyed being part of a team. After trying a lot of sports, the one I enjoyed the most and the one I was the best at was baseball. I like it because it's both physical and it takes some thought and strategy. I've hit 5 homeruns so far, and my position is shortstop.

▶ involve in ~에 참여하다 physical 신체의 strategy 전략 shortstop 유격수

남 난 어렸을 때 늘 운동을 했기 때문에 지금도 운동을 좋아하는 것 같아. 야구, 테니스부터 축구까지 모든 것을 다 했어. 어떤 스포츠는 다른 것들보다 잘했지만 난 늘 팀의 일원으로 있는 걸 좋아했어. 많은 스포츠를 해보고 나서 내가 가장 좋아하고 가장 잘하게 된 것은 야구였어. 몸을 쓰면서도 생각과 전략이 필요하기 때문에 난 야구가 좋아. 지금까지 홈런을 다섯 개 쳤고, 내 포지션은 유격수야.

메모를 바탕으로 다음 문제에 답하시오.

Q 다음 중 화자에 대한 내용 중 사실인 것은?
  (a) 야구에 관련된 전략을 좋아한다.
  (b) 팀 스포츠만을 하기 좋아한다.
  (c) 자신의 팀에서 항상 최고의 선수이다.
  (d) 야구보다 축구 하는 것을 더 좋아한다.

■ 다시 듣고 빈칸을 채우시오.

Basic Drill Step 2

다음을 듣고 메모하시오.

W My name is Sally. I'm a big sports fan. I've been playing sports since I was a little kid. In the winter, I play hockey, which is my favorite sport of all. I'm a goalie. It's a tough position, but I'm good at it.

I also do martial arts in the winter. I study karate at a gym near my house. I like it because it keeps my body strong and improves my balance. I think it helps me when I play hockey.

When the weather warms up and I can't play hockey anymore, I switch to soccer. My position is forward, so I'm also a goal scorer. I love my soccer team. I have so many good friends on it.

I also play tennis in the summer. I take tennis lessons from my coach, who is awesome. I just started playing last summer, so I'm not great yet, but I really enjoy it.

▶ goalie 골키퍼 tough 힘든 be good at ~을 잘하다 martial art 무술 keep (어떤 상태에) 두다, 유지하다 balance 균형 switch 바꾸다 forward 포워드 scorer (경기의) 득점자

여 내 이름은 샐리야. 난 스포츠 광팬이야. 어렸을 때부터 스포츠를 해 왔거든. 겨울에는 아이스 하키를 하는데, 내가 제일 좋아하는 스포츠야. 난 골키퍼를 맡고 있어. 힘든 포지션이긴 하지만 잘하는 편이지.

또 겨울에 무술도 해. 집 근처 체육관에서 가라테를 배우거든. 몸을 강하게 유지시키고 균형 감각도 향상시켜줘서 좋아해. 아이스하키 할 때도 도움이 되는 것 같아.

날씨가 따뜻해져서 아이스 하키를 더 이상 할 수 없게 되면 축구로 바꿔. 포지션은 포워드야. 그래서 득점을 하기도 해. 난 우리 축구 팀이 맘에 들어. 팀에 좋은 친구들이 상당히 많아.

여름에는 테니스도 해. 코치한테 테니스 수업을 받는데, 정말 멋진 분이야. 작년 여름에 시작해서 아직 그렇게 잘하지는 않지만 테니스 치는 게 무척 좋아.

메모를 바탕으로 다음 문제에 답하시오.

1 샐리는 무엇에 관해 이야기하는가?
  (a) 제일 좋아하는 스포츠

  (b) 자기가 하는 스포츠
  (c) 여러 가지 스포츠에서의 자기 포지션
  (d) 잘하는 스포츠

2 맞으면 T, 틀리면 F를 쓰시오.
  (1) 샐리는 하키에서 포워드를 맡고 있다.
  (2) 샐리는 오랫동안 스포츠를 해 오고 있다.
  (3) 샐리는 겨울에 테니스를 한다.

다시 듣고 정답을 확인하시오.

Plus⁺ Question

1 샐리는 팀 스포츠를 ___개 하고, 개인 스포츠를 ___개 한다.
  (a) 0 / 4
  (b) 4 / 0
  (c) 1 / 3
  (d) 2 / 2

2 왜 그녀는 가라테를 하는가?
  (a) 재미있다.
  (b) 체력과 균형을 향상시킨다.
  (c) 많은 친구들도 역시 가라테를 한다.
  (d) 체육관이 집 근처에 있다.

EXERCISE Step 1

듣고 문제에 답하시오.

W When you think about sports, you usually think about baseball, basketball, soccer, and hockey, but if you're not good at these sports, don't worry. There are all kinds of lesser-known sports that you may be good at. For example, cheese rolling has been around for hundreds of years in England. In this sport, a large wheel of cheese is rolled down a steep hill, and the contestants chase it. The one who gets to the bottom first wins. He or she also gets the big piece of cheese!

▶ be good at ~을 잘하다 lesser-known 덜 알려진 roll down 굴려 떨어뜨리다 steep 가파른 contestant 경기자, 경쟁 상대 chase 뒤쫓다

여 스포츠를 생각할 때 보통 야구, 농구, 축구, 하키를 떠올립니다. 하지만 이 스포츠들을 잘 못한다고 해도 걱정하지 마세요. 여러분이 잘할 수도 있는, 온갖 종류의 덜 알려진 스포츠들이 있답니다. 예를 들어, 치즈 굴리기는 영국에서 수 백 년 동안 행해지고 있습니다. 이 스포츠에서는 커다란 치즈 바퀴가 가파른 언덕을 굴러 내려가고, 참가자들은 그 치즈를 쫓아갑니다. 언덕 아래에 제일 먼저 도착하는 사람이 우승입니다. 승자는 부상으로 큰 치즈 덩어리를 받지요!

1 치즈 굴리기 우승자는 무엇을 받는가?
  (a) (b) (c) (d)

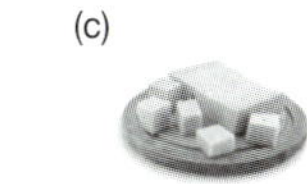

M What's your favorite sport, Susan?

W	Football.
M	I like football, too. The Super Bowl is coming up, huh?
W	Uh, no, I mean English football. I guess Americans call it soccer.
M	Oh, I get it. I wonder why Americans and British have different names for the same sport.
W	I think it goes back a long time. The British used the word "soccer" as the short form of the word "association." I guess it caught on with the Americans.
M	Cool, I didn't know that. It's still confusing because we have a totally different sport called football.
W	Yeah, I know.

▶ **Super Bowl** 슈퍼볼, 미국 프로 미식축구의 왕좌 결정전   **come up** 다가오다   **go back** 거슬러 올라가다, 회고하다   **catch on** 인기를 얻다, 유행하다   **confusing** 혼란시키는, 헷갈리는

남	수전, 제일 좋아하는 스포츠가 뭐야?
여	풋볼.
남	나도 풋볼 좋아해. 수퍼볼이 다가오고 있네?
여	어, 아니. 내가 말한 건 잉글리시 풋볼이야. 미국인들은 사커라고 부를 거야.
남	아, 알겠다. 미국인이랑 영국인들은 왜 똑같은 스포츠를 다르게 부르는지 궁금해.
여	그건 오래 전으로 거슬러 올라가는 것 같아. 영국인들은 "association"이라는 단어의 줄인 형태로 "soccer"라는 단어를 썼거든. 그 말이 미국인들한테 인기를 얻게 된 거겠지.
남	굉장한데. 그건 몰랐어. 그래도 완전히 다른 스포츠를 풋볼이라고 하니까 여전히 헷갈리기는 한다.
여	그래, 알아.

2 맞으면 T, 틀리면 F에 체크하시오.

(1) 미국인들에게는 풋볼이라고 하는 자기네 스포츠가 있다.
(2) "soccer"는 "football"의 줄인 표현이다.
(3) 미국인들과 영국인들은 몇 가지 다른 단어를 사용한다.
(4) 수전이 가장 좋아하는 스포츠는 축구다.

 **3-4**

M	Are you ready to go?
W	Yep. Just let me grab some extra mittens.
M	This'll be fun. I love going to hockey games.
W	Yeah, me too. Let's get some hot chocolate at the game.
M	For sure.
W	Are you wearing your Sabres coat?
M	Of course. I have to support my team.
W	Okay, let's go. I've got the tickets.

▶ **grab** 부여잡다, 잡아채다   **mitten** 벙어리 장갑   **For sure.** 물론 그래.   **support** 지지하다

남	갈 준비 됐어?
여	응. 벙어리 장갑 좀 여벌로 가져올게.
남	재미있을 거야. 난 아이스 하키 경기 보러 가는 게 정말 좋아.
여	응, 나도. 게임 보면서 핫초코 마시자.
남	물론이지.
여	세이버스 팀 코트 입었어?
남	그럼. 우리 팀 응원해야지.
여	좋았어. 가자. 티켓은 내가 가지고 있어.

64

3 화자들은 어디로 가고 있는가?
(a) 골프장
(b) 아이스 링크
(c) 경마장
(d) 미식축구 경기장

4 "Sabres"는 무엇인가?
(a) 코트의 일종
(b) 하키 선수
(c) 상표명
(d) 하키팀

Exercise   Step 2
듣고 문제에 답하시오.

1

W	Are you still watching that game?
M	Give me a break. It's the World Series!
W	Huh?
M	The championship game!
W	Okay. When will it be over? I want to watch my soap opera.
M	Well, it's the bottom of the ninth inning. There are 3 balls and 2 strikes, and the score is 5:5. It'll be over soon enough!
W	It had better be. It's the season finale of my show, too.

▶ **Give me a break.** 해 보게 해줘, 기회를 줘; 그만해, 이제 그만!   **soap opera** 연속 홈 드라마   **championship** 선수권 대회, 결승전   **bottom** (야구) 한 회의 말   **inning** (야구) 회   **finale** 대단원, 최후의 막

여	아직도 저 경기 보는 거야?
남	좀 봐줘. 월드 시리즈란 말이야!
여	뭐?
남	챔피언 결정전이라고!
여	좋아. 저거 언제 끝나? 나 드라마 보고 싶단 말이야.
남	음, 지금 9회 말이거든. 투 스트라이크에 볼 셋이고 5대 5 동점이야. 곧 끝날 거야!
여	빨리 끝나야 돼. 오늘 내가 볼 것도 시즌 마지막회라고.

1 점수는 어떻게 되는가?
(a) 5:5
(b) 2:3
(c) 9:2
(d) 3:5
(e) 9:5

 **2**

W	The Olympic Games are watched all over the world today, but they started in a little place in Greece called Olympia in the year 776 BC. The ancient Greeks celebrated their Olympic games every four years, and the games were considered a very important event. Only men were allowed to be in the Olympics, and they trained hard for the important festival. The winners were given an olive branch.

▶ ancient 고대의 celebrate (의식 등을) 거행하다 consider ~라고 생각하다
allow 허락하다 branch 가지

여 오늘날에는 올림픽 경기를 전세계에서 시청합니다. 하지만 이 올림픽은 기
원전 776년, 올림피아라는 그리스의 작은 장소에서 시작되었죠. 고대 그리
스인들은 4년마다 올림픽 경기를 거행했는데, 이 경기를 매우 중요한 행사
로 여겼습니다. 남자들만이 올림픽에 참가할 수 있었고요, 이 중요한 축제를
위해 열심히 훈련을 했습니다. 올림픽 경기에서 우승한 사람들은 올리브 가
지를 받았습니다.

2 다음 중 사실이 <u>아닌</u> 것은?
(a) 그리스의 올림피아는 올림픽의 발상지이다.
(b) 여성은 올림픽에 참여할 수 없었다.
(c) 올림픽 우승자들은 올리브 가지를 받았다.
(d) 올림픽 경기는 2년마다 거행되었다.
(e) 올림픽 경기는 대략 수천 년 동안 행해졌다.

3~5

M One sport that definitely isn't for everybody is
<u>competitive eating</u>. Competitive eaters <u>participate</u> in
eating contests to see who can eat the most of a <u>certain
type of</u> food. The interesting thing about this sport is
that you don't need to be a big person to win. Some of
the <u>toughest competitors</u> are very thin, small people.
You just need a stomach that <u>can stretch</u>. For example,
one of the best competitive eaters, Sonia Thomas, is only
44kg, but she can eat 5kg of cheesecake in 9 minutes!

▶ competitive 경쟁적인 participate in ~에 참가하다 tough 강인한; 불굴의;
질긴 stretch 늘어나다

남 절대 모든 사람이 다 할 수 있는 스포츠가 아닌 것이 바로 많이 먹기 대회입
니다. 특정 음식을 누가 가장 많이 먹나를 알아보기 위해 이 많이 먹기 대회
에 사람들이 참가하죠. 이 스포츠의 흥미로운 점은, 우승하는 데 꼭 몸집이
클 필요가 없다는 것입니다. 가장 억센 경쟁자들 가운데 몇 사람은 매우 마
르고 왜소한 사람들입니다. 필요한 건 늘어날 수 있는 위뿐이지요. 예를 들면,
많이 먹기 대회 최고의 선수 중 한 명으로 꼽히는 소냐 토마스는 겨우 44킬
로그램밖에 나가지 않지만 9분 동안 치즈 케이크를 5킬로그램이나 먹을 수
있답니다!

3 무엇에 관한 내용인가?
(a) 이상한 스포츠
(b) 몸집이 큰 사람들의 스포츠
(c) 많이 먹기 대회 선수인 소냐 토마스
(d) 많이 먹기 대회
(e) 다이어트 하기

4 많이 먹기 대회 참가자가 되려면 무엇이 필요한가?
(a) 늘어나는 위   (b) 좋은 식습관
(c) 큰 몸집   (d) 왜소한 몸집
(e) 집중력

5 내용을 가장 잘 요약한 것은 무엇인가?
(a) 많이 먹기 대회 참가자는 누가 가장 많이 먹을 수 있는지를 놓고
경쟁한다. 많이 먹기 대회의 가장 유력한 참가자 중 몇 명은 몸집
이 작은 사람들이다.
(b) 많이 먹기 대회 참가자들은 누가 가장 빨리 먹을 수 있는지를 놓고
경쟁한다. 몸집이 작은 사람들이 언제나 큰 사람들보다 더 잘한다.

PRACTICE TEST

들고 문제에 답하시오.

M Wow, she <u>performed</u> great.

W Yeah, that was beautiful. I bet she'll get a perfect score.

M You think? I'm <u>always</u> <u>surprised</u>.

W Here it comes… What? Only 8.2? But she was the best!
She didn't <u>fall down</u>, and her <u>footwork</u> was perfect!

M I think there's a lot about the <u>judging</u> we don't know,
Kelly.

W Well, that's not right.

M Of course not, but that's the way it works. Hopefully no
one will <u>beat her</u>. Keep your <u>fingers crossed</u>.

▶ score 점수 fall down 넘어지다 footwork 발놀림 judge 심사하다, 판정하다;
판단하다 hopefully 잘만 되면, 바라건대 beat 이기다 keep one's fingers
crossed 행운을 빌다

남 와, 저 선수 진짜 잘 했다.
여 응. 정말 멋졌어. 저 선수가 만점 받을 것 같아.
남 너도 그렇게 생각해? 항상 놀랍다니까.
여 점수 나온다. 뭐? 겨우 8.2점? 하지만 저 선수가 제일 잘했는데! 넘어지지도
않았고 풋워크도 완벽했다고!
남 켈리, 판정에 대해 우리가 모르는 것이 많은 것 같아.
여 글쎄, 이건 옳지 않아.
남 물론 그렇긴 하지만 그게 세상사 굴러가는 이치지. 바라건대 아무도 저 선수
를 이기지 못할 거야. 행운을 기원하자고.

1 화자들은 무엇을 보고 있는가?
(a) 골프   (b) 피겨 스케이팅
(c) 야구   (d) 배구
(e) 축구

2

W There is <u>no doubt</u> that the competition in the World
Cup gets tougher and tougher every year. With so much
stress on the soccer players to win for their country,
they're sure to <u>lose their tempers</u> and do bad things that
earn them red cards. As time goes on, more and more
players are getting red cards. In 1978, 3 players received
red cards. In 1986, 8 players were <u>sent off</u>. In 1994, 15
players were given red cards. 2002 saw 17 players sent
off the field. And, finally, in the most <u>recent games</u>, 25
players were given the <u>dreaded</u> red card.

▶ no doubt 확실히, 의심할 바 없이 competition 경쟁 sure to 꼭 ~하는 lose
one's temper 화내다, 참을성을 잃다 as time goes on 시간이 지남에 따라
receive 받다 send off 쫓아내다 dreaded 대단히 무서운

여 확실히 월드컵에서의 경쟁은 매년 더욱더 격렬해지고 있습니다. 조국을 위
해 이겨야겠다는 과중한 스트레스 때문에 축구 선수들은 성을 내고 레드 카
드를 받을 정도로 좋지 않은 행동을 하게 됩니다. 시간이 갈수록 점점 더 많
은 선수들이 레드 카드를 받고 있습니다. 1978년에는 선수 세 명이 레드
카드를 받았는데요, 1986년에는 여덟 명이 경기장 밖으로 쫓겨났습니다.
1994년에는 열다섯 명이 레드 카드를 받았고, 2002년에는 열일곱 명이 경
기장 밖으로 추방당했습니다. 그리고 마지막으로, 가장 최근에 개최된 월드
컵 경기에서는 스물다섯 명의 선수가 무시무시한 레드 카드를 받았습니다.

2 그래프를 완성하시오.

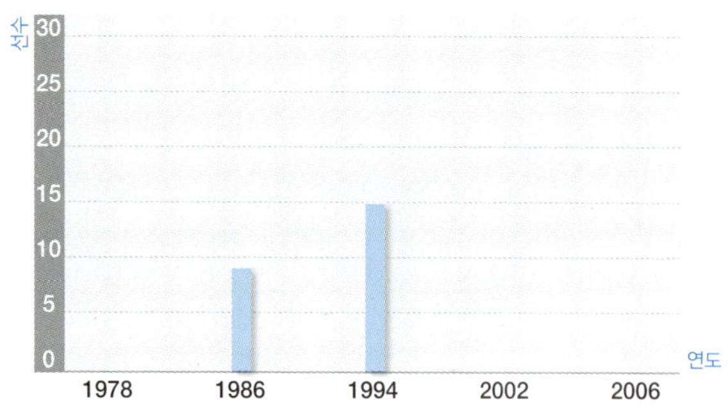

3-4

M Are you ready, Ada?

W Yeah.

M Okay, go out there and give it your best shot. Hit one out of the park for me and your mom.

W I will.

M And remember to keep your eye on the ball. Never take your eye off the ball. Got it?

W Yeah, yeah! I get it!

M Okay, go on. You're almost up to bat.

W Thanks.

M Break a leg!

▶ hit 치다 keep one's eye on the ball 방심하지 않다 up to ~을 할 수 있고, ~할 수 있을 정도로 뛰어나 bat 치다, 타자로 서다 Break a leg! 행운을 빌어!

남 에이다, 준비됐니?

여 네.

남 좋아. 저기 가서 멋지게 한 방 쳐봐. 나랑 네 엄마를 위해서 공원 밖으로 공을 넘겨버려.

여 그럴게요.

남 그리고 공에 집중해. 절대 공에서 눈을 떼면 안 되는 거야, 알았지?

여 예, 예! 알았어요!

남 좋아. 가라. 거의 한 방 날릴 것 같다.

여 고마워요.

남 행운을 빈다!

3 에이다와 남자의 관계는?

(a) 선수와 팬 (b) 학생과 교사
(c) 선수와 코치 (d) 딸과 아빠
(e) 여자친구와 남자친구

4 "break a leg"는 무슨 뜻인가?

(a) 다리 부러뜨리지 말아라. (b) 행운을 빈다.
(c) 서둘러. (d) 공을 쳐.
(e) 방망이를 부러뜨려.

5

W The first women's baseball league was founded in the U.S. in 1943. Many male baseball players were off fighting in World War II, so women were happy to keep the sport alive. But there were some "special" rules for women players. For example, they had to wear skirts, and they wore lots of makeup. They also played on a smaller field and threw the ball underhanded. Although this was a strange introduction for women into professional baseball, these first women players paved the way for women athletes today.

▶ found 설립하다, 창건하다 keep ~ alive 꺼지지 않게 하다, 명맥을 이어가다 throw 던지다 underhand(ed) (야구) 밑으로 던지는 introduction 도입, 창시 pave the way for ~의 길을 열다, 용이하게 하다 athlete 운동선수, 스포츠맨

여 최초의 여자 야구 리그는 1943년 미국에서 창설되었습니다. 많은 남자 야구 선수들이 제2차 세계대전에 참전하자 여성들은 기꺼이 야구의 명맥을 유지했습니다. 하지만 여자 선수들에게는 '특별한' 몇 가지 규칙이 있었습니다. 예를 들자면, 여자 선수들은 치마를 입어야 했고, 화장을 두껍게 했습니다. 또, 더 좁은 경기장에서 경기를 했고, 공은 언더스로로 던졌죠. 여성들이 프로 야구계에 발 담그게 된 이상한 신고식이었지만, 이 최초의 여자 야구 선수들이 오늘날 여성 스포츠인들을 위한 길을 열었습니다.

5 1940년대의 여자 야구선수들에게 해당하는 규칙이 아닌 것은?

(a) 화장을 해야 했다.
(b) 더 좁은 운동장에서 경기했다.
(c) 치마를 입었다.
(d) 특수한 공을 사용했다.
(e) 공을 아래로 던졌다.

6

M Have you ever wanted to play golf, but you didn't have any free time? Try speed golf! It's like regular golf, but you run from hole to hole while carrying your clubs. Your score is a combination of the time it takes you to complete a regular course plus your number of strokes. It's great for keeping fit, too! The Speed Golf Association meets on Saturday mornings at 7:00 a.m. at the Greenways Golf Course. Come and join us!

▶ club 골프채 combination 조합 complete 끝마치다 stroke 타격, 치기 keep fit 건강을 유지하다

남 골프를 하고 싶은 적은 있었지만 전혀 시간이 없으셨다고요? 스피드 골프를 해보세요! 일반 골프와 비슷하지만, 골프채를 들고 홀에서 홀까지 뛰어가야 합니다. 점수는 일반 코스를 마치는 데 걸린 시간에 타수를 더한 값입니다. 건강 유지에도 아주 그만입니다! 스피드 골프 협회는 토요일 아침마다 7시에 그린웨이즈 골프장에서 모입니다. 오셔서 함께 하시죠!

6 스피드 골프는 일반 골프와 어떻게 다른가?

(a) 팀을 이뤄서 한다.
(b) 아침 일찍 한다.
(c) 더 긴 골프 코스를 돈다.
(d) 시간 제한이 있다.
(e) 홀에서 홀로 뛰어다닌다.

7-8

W Are you trying out for the basketball team this year, Greg?

M Oh, I don't know.

W What do you mean?

M I think I'm going to pass this year.

W What? But you love playing basketball.

M I know, but all the guys are taller than me this year. I'm not the best anymore.

W Well, you can't be the best every year. And how do you know unless you try?

M Yeah, I guess so.

W Don't give up yet, Greg.

▶ try out (팀 선발 등에) 나가보다   unless 만약 ~이 아니면   give up 포기하다
cut the mustard (구어) 기대에 부응하다

여 금년에 농구팀 선발 경쟁에 참여할 거니, 그레그?
남 아, 모르겠어요.
여 무슨 말이 그래?
남 금년에는 그냥 지나가려고요.
여 뭐? 그렇지만 넌 농구하는 걸 무척 좋아하잖아.
남 알아요. 그렇지만 금년에는 애들이 다 나보다 키가 크던 걸요. 이제 디 이상 내가 최고가 아니라고요.
여 매년 네가 최고일 수는 없어. 그리고 해보지 않고 어떻게 알겠니?
남 음, 그런 것 같네요.
여 아직 포기하지 마, 그레그.

7 그레그는 농구팀 선발에 지원하는 것에 대해 어떻게 느끼는가?
(a) 희망적이다
(b) 낙관적이다
(c) 겁에 질려 있다
(d) 비관적이다
(e) 흥분된다

8 여자가 하는 조언을 가장 잘 표현한 것은 무엇인가?
(a) 포기하는 자는 절대 이길 수 없고, 이기는 자는 절대 포기하지 않는다.
(b) 연습이 완벽을 만든다.
(c) 피는 물보다 진하다.
(d) 그는 기대에 부응할 수 없다.
(e) 고수들은 생각하는 것도 비슷하다.

Developing Reading Skills

리딩 스킬을 향상시켜 주는 초급자용 독해 시리즈

- 초급자의 눈높이에 맞춘 다양한 학문 분야 주제의 지문 수록
- 리딩 스킬을 체계적으로 익힐 수 있는 activity 제공
- Comprehension, Summary, Vocabulary 등 다양한 문제와 활동 수록
- 주요 어휘 영영풀이와 관련 예문이 포함된 Word List 수록

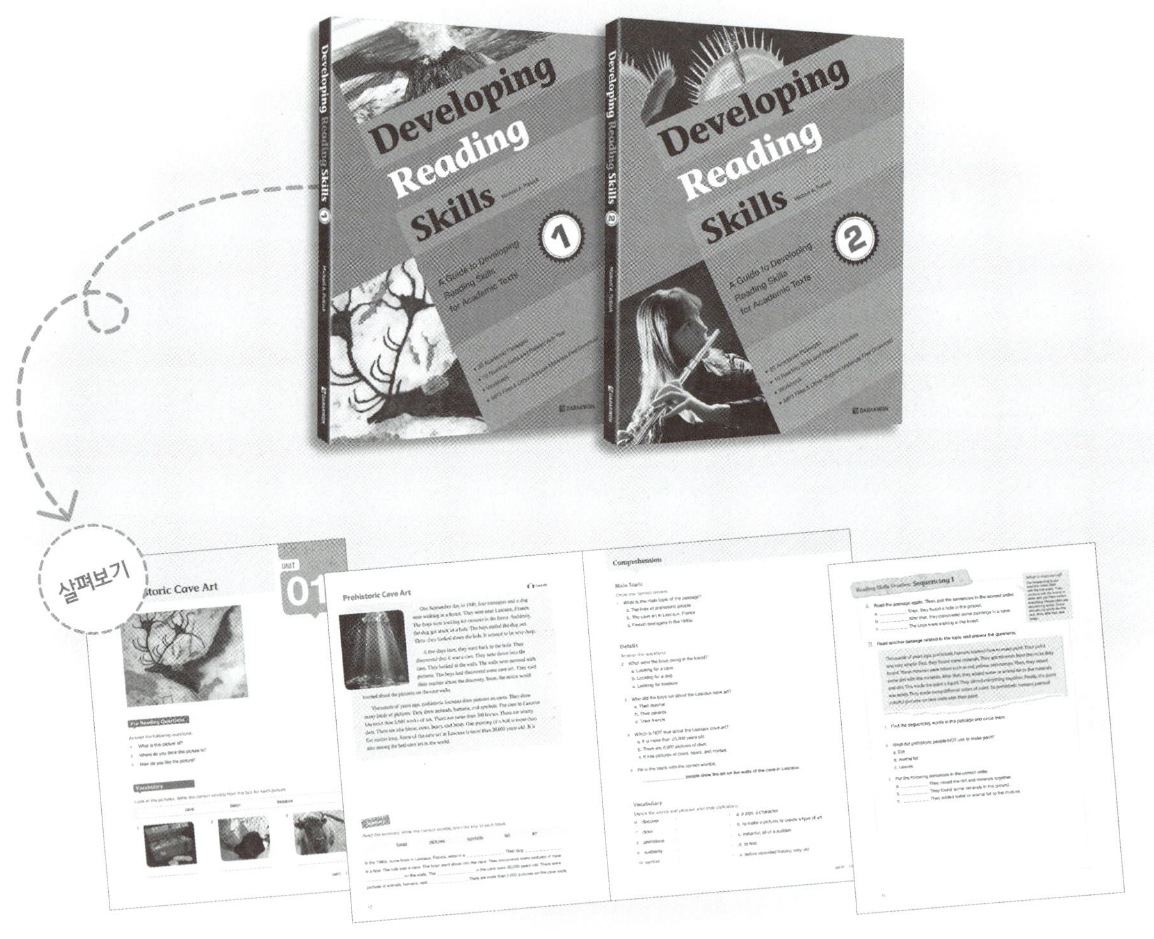

교재	구성	페이지	가격
Developing Reading Skills ①	교재 + 워크북 + MP3 파일	184 pages	11,000원
Developing Reading Skills ②	교재 + 워크북 + MP3 파일	184 pages	11,000원

Mastering Reading Skills

리딩 스킬을 향상시켜 주는 초 중급자용 독해 시리즈

- 초·중급자의 눈높이에 맞춘 다양한 학문 분야 주제의 지문 수록
- 리딩 스킬을 체계적으로 익힐 수 있는 activity 제공
- Comprehension, Summary, Vocabulary 등 다양한 문제와 활동 수록
- 주요 어휘 영영풀이와 관련 예문이 포함된 Word List 수록

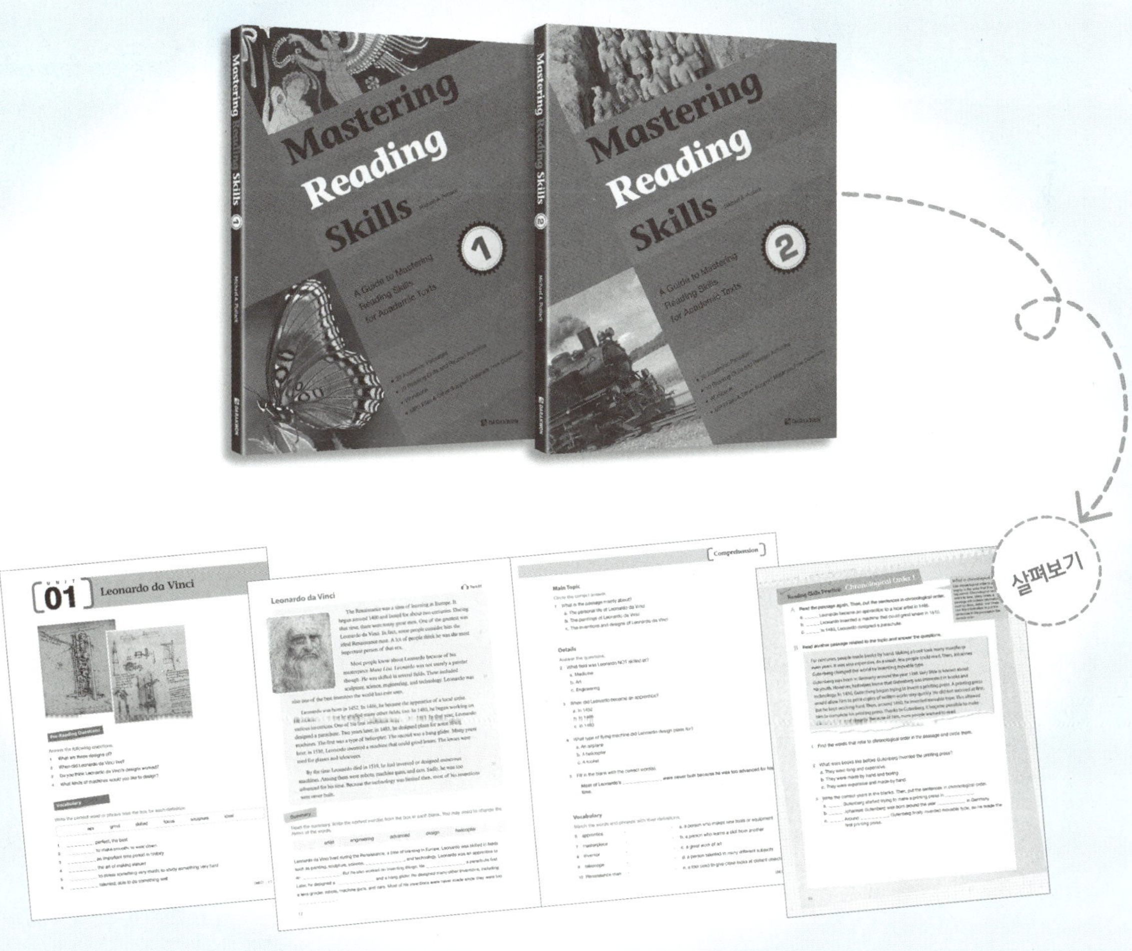

교재	구성	페이지	가격
Mastering Reading Skills ①	교재 + 워크북 + MP3 파일	184 pages	12,000원
Mastering Reading Skills ②	교재 + 워크북 + MP3 파일	184 pages	12,000원

Reading for Subject

교과목별 배경 지식을 쌓아 주는 독해 시리즈

- 역사, 과학, 사회, 수학, 미술 등 교과목별 다양한 주제의 지문 수록
- 단락&전체 요지, 세부 내용 파악, 추론, 서술형 등 다양한 독해 문제 수록
- 지문 구조 및 핵심 내용 파악을 위한 Graphic Organizer와 Summary 활동 수록
- 지문의 소재와 내신 수행평가 문제를 연계한 Writing 활동 수록

교재	구성	페이지	가격
Reading for Subject ①	교재 + 워크북 + MP3 파일	156 pages	14,000원
Reading for Subject ②	교재 + 워크북 + MP3 파일	156 pages	14,000원
Reading for Subject ③	교재 + 워크북 + MP3 파일	156 pages	14,000원
Reading for Subject ④	교재 + 워크북 + MP3 파일	156 pages	14,000원

Academic Reading Builder

다양한 학문 분야의 광범위한 배경지식과 어휘력 향상에 효과적인 읽기 프로그램

- 인문학, 예술, 사회과학, 자연과학, 생명과학에 속하는 다양한 학문 분야별 독해 지문 수록
- 토플에서 다뤄지는 주제를 반영한 광범위한 읽기 주제 포함
- 주요 학문 분야 소개와 진로 탐색 질문을 통한 학습자 동기 유발과 과목 이해도 향상
- 학술 지문 이해에 필요한 기본 어휘 학습과 어휘 확장 활동을 통한 어휘력 증강
- 특목고 대비, 토플 입문, 수능 대비에 적합한 교재

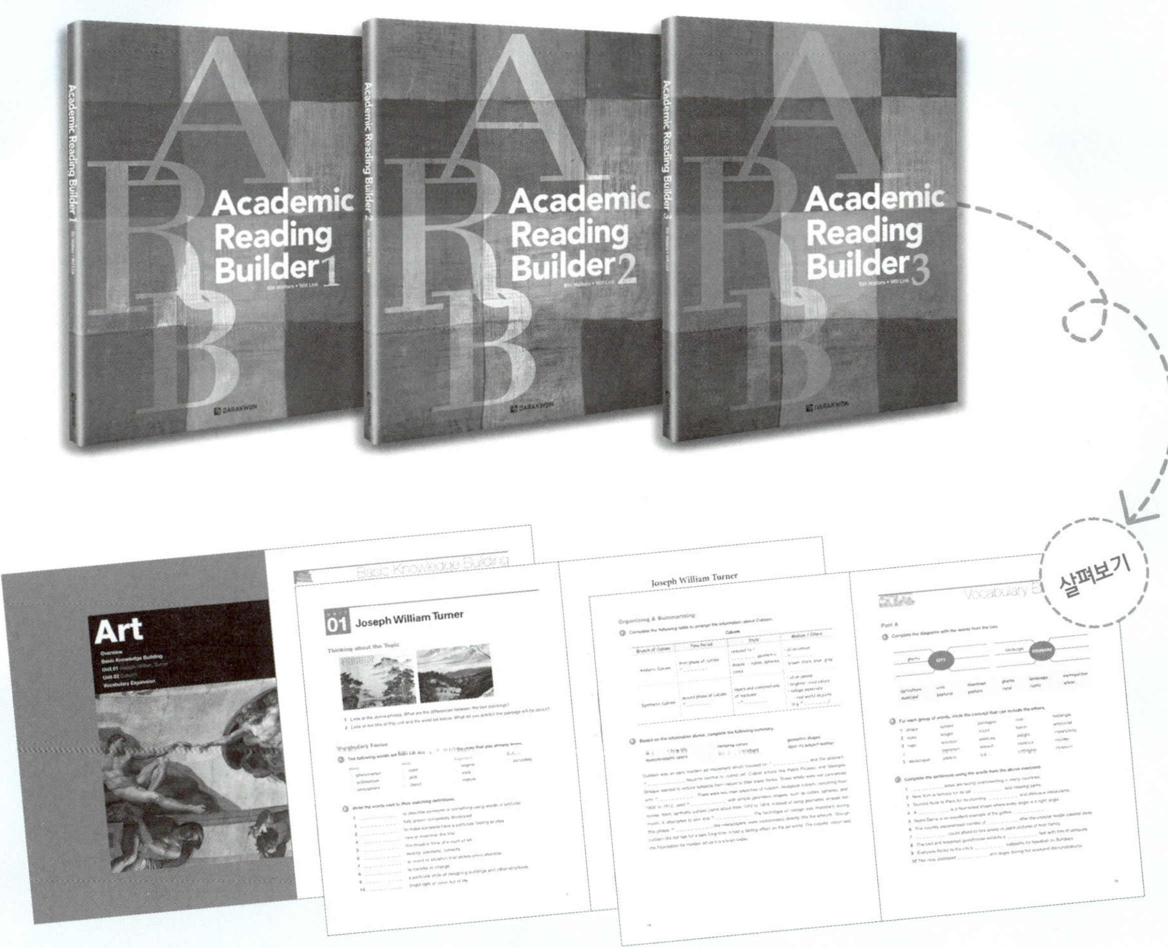

교재	구성	페이지	가격
Academic Reading Builder ①	교재＋MP3 CD 1개	216 pages	15,000원
Academic Reading Builder ②	교재＋MP3 CD 1개	216 pages	15,000원
Academic Reading Builder ③	교재＋MP3 CD 1개	216 pages	15,000원

Listening AVIATOR

RUN 1

Answer Book

Listening TOP

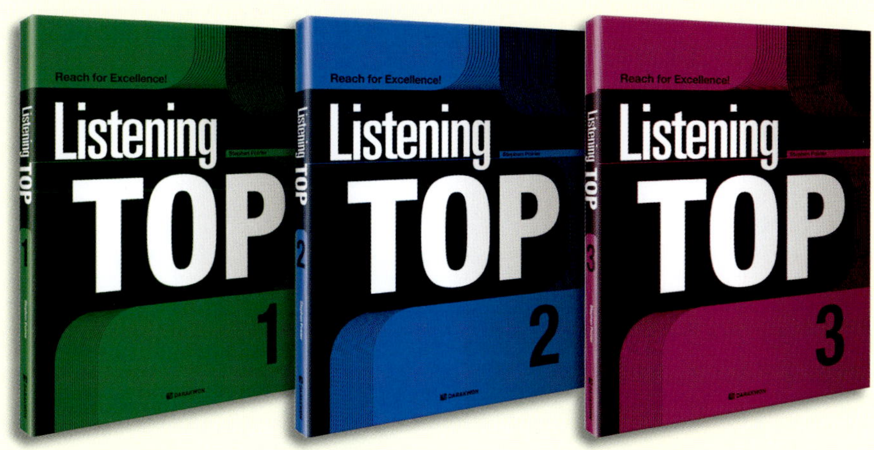

고난도 리스닝 실력 연마 및 각종 공인영어시험 대비에 최적인 리스닝 훈련서 시리즈

- 체계적, 단계적 청취 훈련을 거쳐 고난도 리스닝 실력 연마
- 여러 주제별로 재미있고 학술적이며 유용한 정보를 다양한 지문 형식으로 제시
- 노트테이킹, 오거나이저 작성 훈련, 각종 리스닝 시험의 주요 유형 문제 · 텝스형 문제 · 리스닝과 리딩 통합형 문제 · 장문의 강의 듣고 풀기 등 심도 깊은 문제 제공

교재	구성	페이지	가격
Listening TOP ①	교재 + 해설집 + MP3 CD 1개 + MP3·Vocabulary Quiz 다운로드	본책 176 pages + 해설집 128 pages	18,000원
Listening TOP ②	교재 + 해설집 + MP3 CD 1개 + MP3·Vocabulary Quiz 다운로드	본책 176 pages + 해설집 136 pages	18,000원
Listening TOP ③	교재 + 해설집 + MP3 CD 1개 + MP3·Vocabulary Quiz 다운로드	본책 176 pages + 해설집 144 pages	18,000원

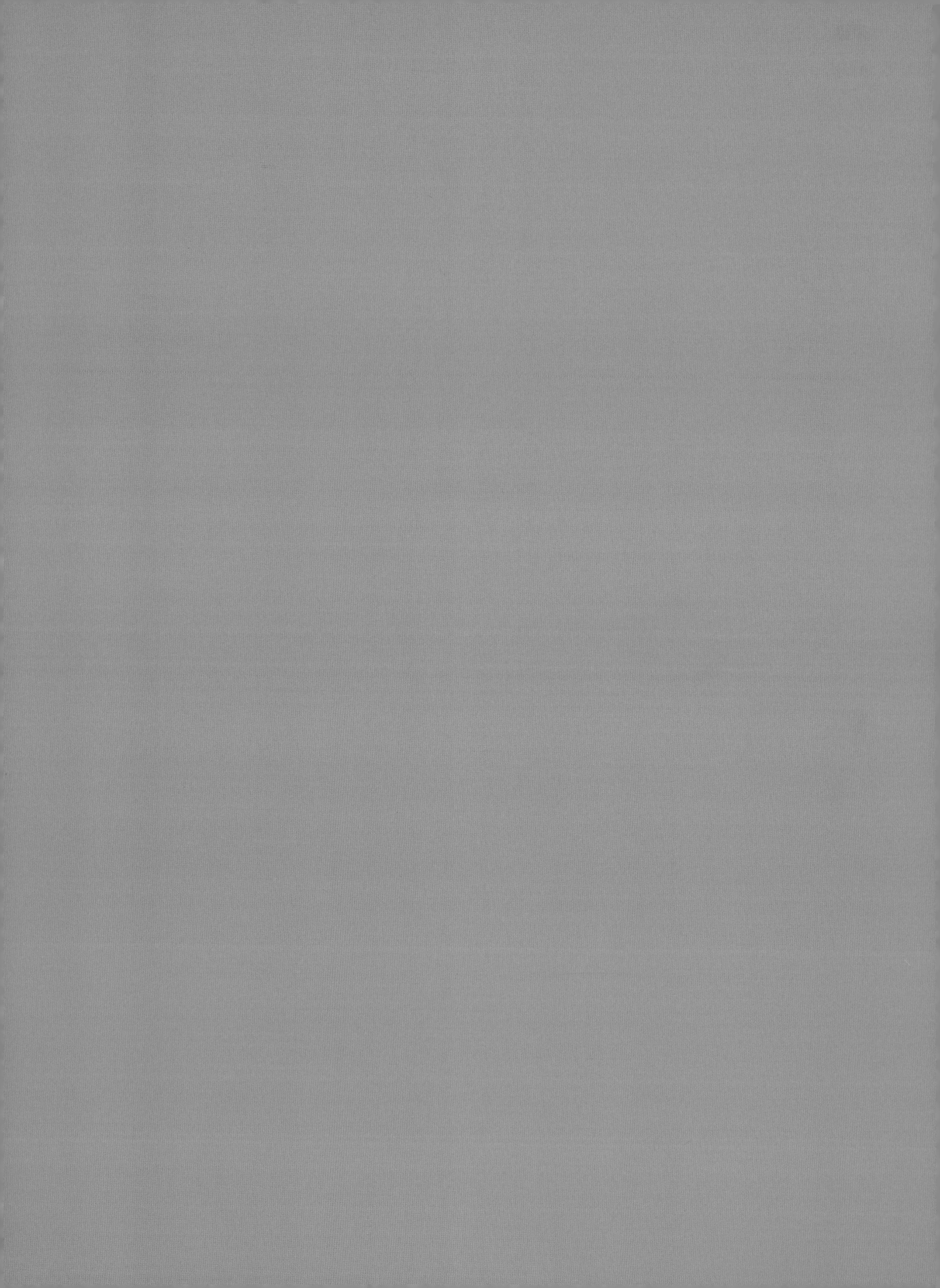